ADVANCED DIPLOMA IN PROCUREMENT AND SUPPLY

COURSE BOOK

Management in procurement and supply

© Profex Publishing Limited, 2012

Printed and distributed by:

The Chartered Institute of Purchasing & Supply, Easton House, Easton on the Hill, Stamford, Lincolnshire PE9 3NZ
Tel: +44 (0) 1780 756 777
Fax: +44 (0) 1780 751 610
Email: info@cips.org
Website: www.cips.org

First edition October 2012

While every effort has been made to ensure that references to websites are correct at time of going to press, the world wide web is a constantly changing environment and neither CIPS nor Profex Publishing Limited can accept responsibility for any changes to addresses.

We acknowledge product, service and company names referred to in this publication, many of which are trade names, service marks, trademarks or registered trademarks.

CIPS, The Chartered Institute of Purchasing & Supply, and its logo, are all trademarks of the Chartered Institute of Purchasing & Supply.

Contents

Page

Preface

Welcome to your new Study Pack. For each subject you have to study, your Study Pack consists of two elements.

- A **Course Book** (the current volume). This provides detailed coverage of all topics specified in the unit content.
- A small-format volume of **Revision Notes**. Use your Revision Notes in the weeks leading up to your exam.

For a full explanation of how to use your new Study Pack, turn now to page xi. And good luck in your exams!

A note on style

Throughout your Study Packs you will find that we use the masculine form of personal pronouns. This convention is adopted purely for the sake of stylistic convenience – we just don't like saying 'he/she' all the time. Please don't think this reflects any kind of bias or prejudice.

October 2012

The Unit Content

The unit content is reproduced below, together with reference to the chapter in this Course Book where each topic is covered.

Unit purpose and aims

On completion of this unit, candidates will understand different approaches to the management of individuals and groups or teams within organisations.

In order to develop expertise in developing and fulfilling organisational and functional objectives in procurement and supply, it is essential that candidates gain a wider appreciation of theories and techniques that relate to managing people involved with the procurement and supply function.

Learning outcomes, assessment criteria and indicative content

Chapter

1.0 Understand the development of management and organisational behaviour

1.1 Explain the main aspects of organisational behaviour

• The behaviour of people	1
• The process of management	1
• The organisational context in which the process of management takes place	1
• Organisational metaphors	1
• The psychological contract: individual and organisational expectations	1
• Interactions with the external environment	1

1.2 Evaluate the main influences that shape organisational behaviour

• The individual	1
• The group	1
• The organisation	1
• Societal influences and the wider environment	1
• The cultural environment and methodologies for assessing cultural types	1

1.3 Analyse the origins of management and organisational behaviour

• Classical approaches to organisational behaviour and management	2
• The development and application of scientific management	2
• Bureaucracy in organisational design and structure	2
• The human relations approach	2

1.4 Analyse the main contemporary approaches to management and organisational behaviour

• Organisations as a 'socio-technical' system	2
• The systems approach to organisational behaviour	2
• The contingency approach	2
• Postmodernism in organisations	2

How to Use Your Study Pack

Organising your study

'Organising' is the key word: unless you are a very exceptional student, you will find a haphazard approach is insufficient, particularly if you are having to combine study with the demands of a full-time job.

A good starting point is to timetable your studies, in broad terms, between now and the date of the examination. How many subjects are you attempting? How many chapters are there in the Course Book for each subject? Now do the sums: how many days/weeks do you have for each chapter to be studied?

Remember:

- Not every week can be regarded as a study week – you may be going on holiday, for example, or there may be weeks when the demands of your job are particularly heavy. If these can be foreseen, you should allow for them in your timetabling.
- You also need a period leading up to the exam in which you will revise and practise what you have learned.

Once you have done the calculations, make a week-by-week timetable for yourself for each paper, allowing for study and revision of the entire unit content between now and the date of the exams.

Getting started

Aim to find a quiet and undisturbed location for your study, and plan as far as possible to use the same period each day. Getting into a routine helps avoid wasting time. Make sure you have all the materials you need before you begin – keep interruptions to a minimum.

Using the Course Book

You should refer to the Course Book to the extent that you need it.

- If you are a newcomer to the subject, you will probably need to read through the Course Book quite thoroughly. This will be the case for most students.
- If some areas are already familiar to you – either through earlier studies or through your practical work experience – you may choose to skip sections of the Course Book.

The content of the Course Book

This Course Book has been designed to give detailed coverage of every topic in the unit content. As you will see from pages vii–ix, each topic mentioned in the unit content is dealt with in a chapter of the Course Book. For the most part the order of the Course Book follows the order of the unit content closely, though departures from this principle have occasionally been made in the interest of a logical learning order.

Each chapter begins with a reference to the assessment criteria and indicative content to be covered in the chapter. Each chapter is divided into sections, listed in the introduction to the chapter, and for the most part being actual captions from the unit content.

All of this enables you to monitor your progress through the unit content very easily and provides reassurance that you are tackling every subject that is examinable.

Each chapter contains the following features.

- Introduction, setting out the main topics to be covered
- Clear coverage of each topic in a concise and approachable format
- A chapter summary
- Self-test questions

The study phase

For each chapter you should begin by glancing at the main headings (listed at the start of the chapter). Then read fairly rapidly through the body of the text to absorb the main points. If it's there in the text, you can be sure it's there for a reason, so try not to skip unless the topic is one you are familiar with already.

Then return to the beginning of the chapter to start a more careful reading. You may want to take brief notes as you go along, but bear in mind that you already have your Revision Notes – there is no point in duplicating what you can find there.

Test your recall and understanding of the material by attempting the self-test questions. These are accompanied by cross-references to paragraphs where you can check your answers and refresh your memory.

The revision phase

Your approach to revision should be methodical and you should aim to tackle each main area of the unit content in turn. Read carefully through your Revision Notes. Check back to your Course Book if there are areas where you cannot recall the subject matter clearly. Then do some question practice. The CIPS website contains many past exam questions. You should aim to identify those that are suitable for the unit you are studying.

Additional reading

Your Study Pack provides you with the key information needed for each module but CIPS strongly advocates reading as widely as possible to augment and reinforce your understanding. CIPS produces an official reading list of books, which can be downloaded from the bookshop area of the CIPS website.

To help you, we have identified one essential textbook for each subject. We recommend that you read this for additional information.

The essential textbook for this unit is Laurie Mullins, *Management and Organisational Behaviour*.

CHAPTER 1

Introduction to Organisational Behaviour

Assessment criteria and indicative content

1.1 Explain the main aspects of organisational behaviour

- The behaviour of people
- The process of management
- The organisational context in which the process of management takes place
- Organisational metaphors
- The psychological contract: individual and organisational expectations
- Interactions with the external environment

1.2 Evaluate the main influences that shape organisational behaviour

- The individual
- The group
- The organisation
- Societal influences and the wider environment
- The cultural environment and methodologies for assessing cultural types

Section headings

1. What is organisational behaviour?
2. The psychological contract
3. The process of management
4. The organisational context
5. The external environment
6. The influence of culture

Introduction

It is important for a manager to understand what is going on at a given time in his or her organisation or team — and why; and to use that understanding to seek to predict and control events, in pursuit of organisational goals.

In this chapter we give a brief overview of the discipline of organisational behaviour: the sense in which organisations 'behave'; the dimensions or elements that make up organisational 'behaviours'; and what influences those 'behaviours'.

1   What is organisational behaviour?

1.1   An organisation has been defined *(Andrzej Huczyinsi & David Buchanan, Organisational Behaviour)* as 'a social arrangement for the controlled performance of collective goals.'

1.2   As we noted in our introduction, it is important in any kind of organisation for a manager to understand what is going on, and why, in order to be able to 'manage' – explain, predict, direct, facilitate or control – those behaviours and events. A business organisation, in particular, has to account to its shareholders, investors and regulatory bodies (among other stakeholders) for its activities and use of resources. It has certain objectives and responsibilities. In order to fulfil either or both, it must exercise direction and control over the diverse individuals, groups and activities that make up 'the organisation' and its 'behaviour'.

1.3   Organisations cannot be said to 'behave' in the sense that a human being or an animal does. However, they consist of:

- *Systems* which 'function' in observable ways, adapting to the internal and external environment and
- *People,* who do 'behave' – acting, reacting and interacting in the pursuit of their individual and/or shared goals.

1.4   'Organisational behaviour' is a shorthand expression for all those functions, embracing:

- The human element and behaviours of people (individuals and groups) at work; *directed and controlled by*
- The processes of management and leadership, as an integrating and co-ordinating activity; *within*
- The structure, strategies, processes, systems and functions of the organisation by which work is executed; *interacting with*
- Factors in the 'outside' environment which shape and influence all of the above.

1.5   The term 'organisational behaviour' has been given to 'the study of the structure, functioning and performance of organisations, and the behaviour of groups and individuals within it' (Huczynski & Buchanan). Laurie Mullins *(Management & Organisational Behaviour)* defines it as: 'the study and understanding of individual and group behaviour and patterns of structure in order to help improve organisational performance and effectiveness.' Mullins summarises this as follows: Figure 1.1

Figure 1.1 *Mullins's framework for analysing organisational behaviour*

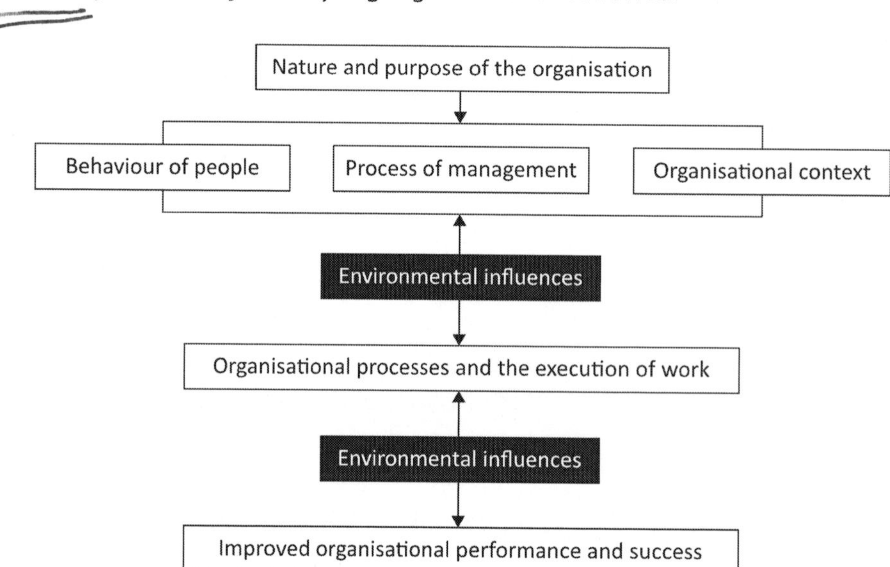

1.6 Organisational behaviour concepts thus include society-level concepts (such as politics, culture, ethics, corporate social responsibility and sustainability); organisation-level concepts (such as systems, structure and organisational culture); group-level concepts (such as the dynamics of team development and decision-making, leadership, conflict and co-operation); and individual-level concepts (such as personality, learning and motivation).

1.7 It is a multi-disciplinary study, encompassing research and concepts from psychology, sociology, anthropology, economics and political science. This reflects the wide impact which organisations of different types have on societies and individual lives, and also the many levels on which individuals are engaged in relationships with – and within – organisations.

1.8 The study of organisational behaviour faces certain difficulties of methodology and application. People can't be studied scientifically in the way that other natural phenomena can – and it is almost impossible to exclude subjectivity from research and its interpretation. Different disciplines (and approaches or 'schools' within disciplines) come up with different explanations of the same behaviours. And even relatively stable behavioural concepts (such as motivation and personality) don't allow us reliably to predict or control behaviour. There are too many variables, not all of them within managerial control.

1.9 Nevertheless, organisational behaviour concepts and models offer workable theories to explain how different organisational and environmental variables affect each other, and how some variables can be controlled to get desired results. The importance of the *human* variable, in particular, is the main reason why managers need to understand the behavioural implications of their plans, decisions and managerial approaches.

The behaviour of people

1.10 Organisations are made up of people, both individuals and groups.

- Mullins notes that: 'where the needs of the individual and the demands of the organisation are incompatible, this can result in frustration and conflict. It is the role of management to integrate the individual and the organisation to provide a working environment that permits the satisfaction of individual needs as well as the attainment of organisational goals'.
- People in groups influence each other, and group functioning and maintenance creates its own behavioural norms and distinctive dynamics. Groups 'behave' differently from individuals acting, or making decisions, on their own. We will explore this idea in detail in Chapters 6 and 7 on the nature of groups and team working.

The process of management

1.11 Management is such a universal feature of the business and employment landscape, that you may not have thought much about what 'management' means – or might mean. For hundreds of years, people have been 'doing management' in organisations. Yet every year there is new research and new ideas about why management is necessary; what managers actually do; and how they can do it better.

1.12 There are many definitions of management – and some of them have been adjusted in the light of the emerging focus on 'leadership'. Here are a few to be starting with.

- Management is the process of getting results by making the best use of available human, financial and material resources. 'The most important part of management will be... getting things done through people, but managers will be concerned directly or indirectly with all other resources, including their own [experience, know-how, skill, competencies and time].' (*Armstrong*)
- The key purpose of management (and leadership) is to 'provide direction, facilitate change and achieve results through the efficient, creative and responsible use of resources'. (*Management Standards Centre*)

- Management is 'a social process entailing responsibility for the effective and economical planning and regulation of the operations of an enterprise, in fulfilment of given purposes or tasks, such responsibility entailing: (a) judgement and decision in determining plans and in using data to control performance and progress against plans; and (b) the guidance, integration, motivation and supervision of the personnel composing the enterprise and carrying out its operations.' (*EFL Brech*)

The organisational context

1.13   The need for 'controlled performance of collective goals' creates key contextual features of organisations such as: a deliberately ordered environment; the allocation of tasks (division of labour); the setting of standards and targets (planning); and the measurement of results against them (control). This implies a structure of power and responsibility relationships (whereby some individuals determine and/or oversee the work of others) and a structure of communication channels (through which instructions, reports and feedback information flow).

1.14   All these elements are features of formal organisation structure. 'It is through the formal structure that people carry out their organisational activities to achieve aims and objectives. Behaviour is influenced by patterns of structure, technology, styles of leadership and systems of management through which organisational processes are planned, directed and monitored' (Mullins).

1.15   Alongside the formal organisation structure, however, organisations also develop informal groupings (eg cliques), patterns of influence (eg informal leaders), communication channels (eg 'the grapevine') and ways of doing things (eg short-cuts and informal norms of behaviour) – which may diverge from the formal design and processes. This is often identified with the concept of organisational style or 'culture'.

1.16   It is possible to look at organisations in many different ways, because organisations mean different things to different people, depending on their perspective. People may conceptualise and experience organisations differently, depending on:

- Their relationship with them: as employees, as managers, as owners, as competitors, as suppliers. All these groups have a different interest or 'stake' in the organisation. We discuss organisational *stakeholders* in Chapter 7.
- Their beliefs and perceptions: ideologies about capitalism, say (or power and control, or the meaning of work, or the value of technology) may influence how organisations are regarded. Over time, organisational theory has substantially changed its focus and emphasis, from scientific efficiency to human motivation to the importance of flexibility. We discuss these different approaches, and their view of organisation, in Chapter 2.

1.17   For now, however, let's hold on to some very basic characteristics, which all organisations share.

- *Structure* (controlled performance): a formal network of authority and responsibility relationships, division of labour and communication channels.
- *Objectives* (collective goals): stated quantitative and/or qualitative aims towards which activity will be directed, and against which performance will be measured.
- *People* (social arrangements): organisations are 'made up' of people, in a complex network of formal and informal roles and relationships, individual and collective effort, decision-making and communication.

The external environment

1.18   All organisations function as part of the broader society and external environment of which they are a part. Organisations are seen as 'open systems': influencing, and influenced by, factors in their external environment.

- Organisations take in resources or inputs from the external environment – including labour, finance, information and raw materials.

- They release outputs (products and by-products of their operations) to the external environment – including information, products, finance and environmental and social impacts.
- Their strategies are shaped by opportunities and threats in the external environment, including the influence and activities of key stakeholders such as suppliers, customers and competitors.
- They are subject to change – these days, often a high degree of uncertainty and turbulence – in the external environment: change in worker expectations and consumer demands, change in technology and legislation, and so on.

1.19 Essentially, the study of organisational behaviour seeks to understand how organisations are shaped by, and attempt to respond and adapt to, changing external demands and influences.

2 The psychological contract

2.1 We will be looking at individual and group behaviour in detail in Chapters 3–7 of this Course Book, focusing on some of the key aspects for management: personality and individual difference; learning; motivation and job satisfaction; teamworking; and the management of roles, conflict and co-operation.

2.2 One underpinning concept, however, that links individual and group behaviour to the process of management and the organisational context is the **psychological contract of employment.**

2.3 The 'psychological contract' is the unwritten set of values which describes what an organisation expects of its employees, and what they expect of it, within the employment relationship. It reflects both parties' beliefs, perceptions and understanding of their mutual obligations and rights within the relationship – regardless of what may be formally written down in a legal contract of employment.

2.4 These unwritten 'terms and conditions' underpin the employment relationship, and the way that people behave at work. The Chartered Institute of Personnel & Development (CIPD) argues that they have implications for the human resource management strategies of organisations in areas such as: developing process equity (eg consideration and consultation in decision-making); employee relations and communication; managing employee expectations (especially during recruitment and induction); monitoring employee attitudes (as an important element in performance); and management style (eg harnessing employee commitment, knowledge and aspirations).

2.5 Employing organisations typically expect individuals to fulfil certain obligations in return for the rewards and benefits it offers. For example, employees may be expected to act as follows.

- Working diligently, as instructed (or in pursuit of organisational objectives)
- Complying with the policies, procedures and rules of the organisation
- Respecting the reasonable authority of managers
- Upholding the values, reputation and corporate image of the organisation
- Behaving ethically, and not betraying positions of trust (eg in regard to the protection of confidential data and the proper use of funds and resources)

2.6 Similarly, individuals expect to derive certain benefits from the organisation in return for their labour, contribution and commitment. For example, employers may be expected to act as follows.

- Fairly rewarding work, contribution and/or performance
- Implementing equitable (and if possible, considerate) HR policies and systems, beyond the minimum standards required by law (eg for equal opportunity)
- Providing safe and hygienic working conditions
- Respecting the role of employee representatives, and employees' desire for consultation and involvement in decisions that affect them
- Attempting, as far as possible, to protect job security and facilitate personal and career development
- Attempting, as far as possible, to offer job satisfaction and to alleviate alienating, stressful and monotonous aspects of work

2.7 The nature and level of workers' expectations will vary – as will the willingness and ability of employing organisations to meet those expectations. The two sets of expectations may diverge or conflict, and disappointed expectations (eg in areas such as job security or rewards) will influence the employee relations climate of the organisation.

2.8 Jeff Cartwright *(Cultural Transformation)* emphasises that **mutuality** (the dovetailing of individual self-interest with the interests of the organisation, in order to create a 'win-win' outcome from co-operation) is the basis of a positive psychological contract. This is one of the reasons why – as we will see throughout this Course Book – positive human resource management practices, and attention to 'people' aspects of management, are regarded as essential to committed and constructive employee behaviour.

What do individuals want from work?

2.9 For economic reasons, work is for many people a major part of their lives. However, the extent to which work will be a core interest for an individual will depend on a number of factors, including the relative strengths of his various needs and goals, and the choices he makes about how to achieve them: in other words, his *orientation* to work.

2.10 Goldthorpe, Lockwood, Bechofer and Platt (*The Affluent Worker: Industrial Attitudes and Behaviour*) identified three possible orientations to work (within a UK culture).

- *Bureaucratic orientation:* work as a central life issue, with a sense of identification with the work of the organisation and its career structure. Work can be an important part of an individual's self-identity, and the main opportunity for challenge, self-development and learning.
- *Instrumental orientation:* work as a means to an end, through the earning of income to support valued non-work activities and rewards. This is an important orientation for the concept of 'work-life balance', which is discussed further later in this chapter.
- *Solidaristic orientation:* work as an opportunity to engage in social relationships and group activities, with a core sense of solidarity with the work group or team.

2.11 We will explore these ideas in more detail in Chapter 5.

A changing psychological contract

2.12 It is widely recognised that the changing business environment has placed an increased *importance* on the psychological contract (and the human resource management practices which underpin it). People-based factors such as service, knowledge, innovation, flexibility and commitment have been recognised as key sources of competitive advantage and business success. We will discuss these aspects in Chapter 8.

2.13 Meanwhile, economic recession, increased competition, the application of technology and other environmental factors have led to a shift in the psychological contract itself in recent decades.

- It has become acknowledged as less possible for organisations to offer employees long-term job security, career development or even reliable pay increases. Organisations have had to make explicit a new set of expectations and rewards. 'New' rewards (such as recognition, personal development, opportunities for teamworking and involvement, and more inspiring styles of leadership) are increasingly being offered as an incentive to loyalty and committed performance.
- The recognition of the added value of employee 'commitment' (voluntary pursuit of organisational goals) over mere 'compliance' (obedience to organisational directives) has contributed to a shift from transactional or *calculative contracts* (based on an exchange of effort and contribution for equitable rewards) to *relational or co-operative contracts* (where managers attempt to integrate employees' interests with those of the organisation).

3 The process of management

3.1 Mullins argues that: 'It is through the process of management that the efforts of members of the organisation are co-ordinated, directed and guided towards the achievement of its goals. Management is the cornerstone of organisational effectiveness… It is essentially an **integrating activity** that permeates every facet of the organisation's operations and should serve to reconcile the needs of people at work with the requirements of the organisation. Management should endeavour to create the right balance between the interrelated elements that make up the total organisation and to weld these into coherent patterns of activity best suited to the external environment in which the organisation is operating.'

3.2 In other words, effective management involves:

- Satisfying the needs of people at work (in order to maintain a positive psychological contract and employee relations)
- Creating a positive organisational ecology, environment or 'climate' which enables people to work willingly and effectively
- Achieving the strategic objectives and activities of the organisation.

The functions of management

3.3 Classical management theory, formulated by early writers such as Henri Fayol and EFL Brech, suggested that management involved certain basic functions, designed to bring system, order, rationality and consistency to the organisational environment.

3.4 Fayol (*General & Industrial Management*) suggested the following five functions of management.

- Planning: defining objectives or desired results, and formulating courses of action (strategies, policies, procedures and so on) to achieve them
- Organising: establishing a structure of tasks which must be performed to achieve the objective, and allocating them to appropriate individuals and units
- Commanding: instructing and influencing people towards the accomplishment of tasks and goals
- Co-ordinating: integrating the goals and activities of individuals and groups within the organisation, through communication
- Controlling: measuring and monitoring the process of work in relation to the plan, and taking corrective action where necessary.

3.5 Brech (*Organisation: the Framework of Management*) identifies four main functions.

- Planning: determining strategies and methods of carrying them out, and setting performance standards
- Control: checking progress and performance against standards as a basis for correction and further planning
- Co-ordination: balancing and maintaining the team by dividing work suitably [organising] and harmonising the work of different units towards shared goals
- Motivation: inspiring, supervising and fostering morale, with the aim of getting team members to work effectively and to be committed and loyal to the group and the task.

3.6 Peter Drucker (an American business consultant and prolific writer on management) argued that the manager of a business has one basic function: to secure economic results. Within this basic function, he categorised basic managerial operations as follows.

- Objective setting: determining objectives, goals and targets
- Organising: classifying and dividing tasks, creating organisation structure, selecting staff
- Motivating and communicating: creating effective and committed teams
- Measuring: establishing targets and standards for individuals, units and the organisation as a whole, for the purposes of control

- Developing people: directing, supporting, challenging, training and empowering team members.

3.7 You may be able to see, in the development of management theory from Fayol to Brech to Drucker, a growing focus on the people resource – including managers themselves. Drucker also argued that the role of the manager was to provide *leadership*. 'The manager is the dynamic, life-giving element in every business. In a competitive economy, above all the quality and performance of the managers determine the success of a business, indeed they determine its survival.'

3.8 Mullins notes that 'Many problems in the people-organisation relationship arise not so much from the decisions and actions of management as from the manner in which such decisions and actions are carried out. Often, it is not so much the intent as the manner of implementation that is the root cause of staff unrest and dissatisfaction. For example, staff may agree on the need to introduce new technology to retain... competitive efficiency... but feel resentment about the lack of pre-planning, consultation, retraining programmes, participation in agreeing new working practices... and similar considerations arising from the manner of its introduction.'

Managerial roles

3.9 The classical approach to categorising management functions is simple and useful for management education, but it has been argued that it does not do justice to the complexity of the manager's 'job' in the real world. A rather different approach to defining management was taken by Henry Mintzberg *(The Nature of Managerial Work)*, who studied what managers actually 'do'.

3.10 Mintzberg's research suggested that managers are not separate from, or 'above', the demands of everyday work. Their work is sometimes routine and often disjointed and discontinuous: they are not always able to be reflective, systematic thinkers. Despite the development of formal management information systems, managers generally prefer verbal and informal information.

3.11 Mintzberg suggested that in their daily working lives, managers fulfil a range of managerial roles: Table 1.1.

Table 1.1 *Mintzberg's managerial roles*

NATURE OF ROLE	ROLE DEFINITION
Interpersonal Arising from a manager's formal authority or position in the organisation and unit	• **Figurehead**: a ceremonial role, representing the organisation in public • **Leader**: hiring, supervising, developing, motivating, team building and so on • **Liaison**: networking and co-ordinating with peers in other units or functions
Informational Arising from a manager's access to internal and external contacts	• **Monitor**: gathering information • **Spokesperson**: giving information on behalf of the unit or organisation • **Disseminator**: sharing information with relevant stakeholders or interested parties
Decisional Arising from a manager's formal authority and access to information, which places him in the best position to solve problems relating to the unit or department as a whole	• **Entrepreneur**: initiating action to exploit opportunities • **Disturbance handler**: responding to threats and pressures, taking corrective action • **Resource allocator**: distributing limited resources where they will be most effective • **Negotiator**: resolving conflicts and securing favourable outcomes in matters involving others

3.12 In terms of roles (the 'hats' they wear as tasks are performed), therefore, purchasing managers may be: figureheads (at a CIPS conference, say); leaders (directing the Purchasing and Supply department); liaisons (at cross-functional management or quality meetings); information handlers (analysing supply market risks and costs, and managing purchasing information systems); entrepreneurs (initiating new quality initiatives, perhaps); disturbance handlers (responding to unforeseen supply problems or team conflicts); resource allocators (selecting suppliers); and negotiators (not just on price, but to get purchasing policy approved by senior management, say).

Management and leadership

3.13   The terms 'manager' and 'leader' are often used interchangeably – although 'leader' is now the more fashionable term.

3.14   *John P Kotter* ('What leaders really do': *Harvard Business Review)* has made a detailed and helpful distinction between leadership and management. He suggests that management is about coping with **complexity**: managerial functions are to do with logic, structure, analysis and control. Management can be exercised over processes, projects, resources, time and so on. Leadership, on the other hand, is about coping with **change**. It can, essentially, only be exercised over people, and requires a completely different set of activities.

- Creating a sense of direction: finding a vision for something new out of the challenge of dissatisfaction with the *status quo*.
- Communicating the vision: meeting the needs of other people, giving the vision credibility.
- Energising, inspiring and motivating: stimulating others to translate the vision into achievement.

3.15   Other influential attempts to distinguish between the two concepts have been as follows.

- Gary Yukl *(Leadership in Organisations)* suggests that while management is defined by a formal role and position in the organisation hierarchy, leaders are given their roles by the perceptions and choice of others. Managers have subordinates: leaders have followers.
- Abraham Zaleznik ('Managers and leaders: are they different': *Harvard Business Review)* suggests that while managers are primarily concerned with order and maintaining the *status quo*, focusing on diplomacy and decision-making processes in the organisation, leaders are more concerned with introducing new ideas and approaches, focusing on excitement, vision and empathy for people.
- D Katz and RL Kahn *(The Social Psychology of Organisations)* suggest that while managers aim to secure compliance with routine organisational objectives, leaders aim to secure willingness, enthusiasm and commitment.
- Pedler, Burgoyne & Boydell *(A Manager's Guide to Leadership)* suggest that 'leading is more concerned with finding direction and purpose in the face of critical challenges, whereas managing is about organising to achieve desired purposes – efficiently, effectively and creatively.'

3.16   David A Whetten and Kim S Cameron *(Developing Management Skills)* argue that the distinction between managers and leaders is no longer very useful. 'Managers cannot be successful without being good leaders, and leaders cannot be successful without being good managers.' It may be important for managers to become (or be developed) as leaders in today's business environment because:

- Leaders energise and support change, which is essential for survival in highly competitive and fast-changing business environments.
- Leaders secure commitment, mobilising the ideas, experience and motivation of employees – which contributes to innovation and improved quality and customer service.
- Leaders set direction, helping teams and organisations to understand their purpose and goals. This facilitates teamworking and empowerment without loss of co-ordination.
- Leaders support, challenge and develop people, maximising their contribution to the organisation.
- Leaders use a facilitate-empower style (rather than a command-control style), which is better suited to the expectations of empowered teams and the need for information-sharing.

3.17   As we will see in Chapter 6, with the emphasis on empowered teamworking, the manager's role has changed. Many of the managerial functions of planning, organising and controlling work have been taken over by team decision-making processes. This has shifted the team leader's role:

- from planner to vision-creator
- from instructor to coach and facilitator
- from controller to co-ordinator
- from commander to persuader, motivator and inspirer.

Management styles

3.18   Not all managers operate in the same manner. It is possible to identify a wide variety of behaviours which different managers use as their 'preferred' approach or 'style'. Many attempts have been made both to classify styles and to identify which is the most effective style for a manager to adopt.

3.19   We will discuss management styles as an aspect of motivation in Chapter 5.

4   The organisational context

Reasons for organisations

4.1   Organisations exist – at the most basic level – because they can achieve things which an individual could not achieve alone. Individuals are subject to a number of limitations, which have been described (in a classic illustration by Chester Barnard) in the context of a person trying to roll a large stone uphill.

- Environmental limitations: the stone is too big for one person to move alone.
- Personal and biological limitations: the person is too 'small' to move the stone.

By banding together with another person, and applying combined effort, it is possible to overcome both limitations: two people can move the stone.

4.2   In greater detail, the reasons why people form organisations may be as follows.

- For *social reasons*. Organisations meet human beings' psychological needs for relationship, belonging and identifying with something 'bigger' than themselves. (This is actively encouraged by organisations, to promote employee commitment to organisational objectives.)
- To *enlarge abilities* or increase productive capacity. This is done not only by 'pooling' energies and resources, but by facilitating specialisation. When labour is divided among a group of people, each person can stick to what he is best at: the group fulfils the full range of tasks and skills required. This provides maximum efficiency: the principle of specialisation has (until quite recently) held sway in approaches to organisation and management.
- To *accumulate information and knowledge.* Because organisations are continuous, they build up a knowledge base through the combined learning and information-gathering of members over time. The social nature of organisations also fulfils the individual need for networking: creating multiple sources of information for personal and career development.
- To *facilitate efficiency*. Organisations make it possible for objectives to be achieved with less expense of time and resources than individuals can manage working on their own. Combined effort, efficient specialisation, information-sharing and economies of scale create a synergistic effect whereby the whole is greater than the sum of its parts: 2 + 2 = 5.

4.3   In addition, of course, different types of organisation will be formed for more specific purposes: to fulfil a need or niche in a given market; to make money; to raise funds or awareness for a good cause; and so on. The fact remains, however, that these aims could be pursued by individuals acting alone: people form organisations to pursue them because of the reasons outlined above.

Organisational metaphors

4.4 A metaphor is a way of describing something as something else, to draw out its essential features by analogy.

4.5 Gareth Morgan (*Creative Organisation Theory*) describes eight organisational metaphors, each of which presents one perspective on the organisation.

- **The organisation as machine.** A machine consists of many moving parts, all acting in an orderly, prescribed manner in relation to each other. The action of each part affects another in a predictable way. The idea of 'mechanistic' organisation (discussed above) sees organisations in the same way: different parts (people, processes) interact in defined, routine and expected ways. Altering one variable has a predictable effect on the others. This analogy leads to bureaucratic organisation, with its benefits for stability and efficiency – and its rigidity in the face of change.
- **The organisation as biological organism.** A living organism grows, matures, learns and adapts to its environment. It takes in nutrients (and other influences) from its environment and processes them (as energy, excretion and so on). An organism is (by another analogy) a living, open system (discussed in Chapter 2). The idea of 'organismic' organisation sees organisations in the same way: the organisation matures (over its 'lifecycle'), learns and adapts to its environment, by absorbing and processing resources and influences (information, skills, technology) so that it can meet changing demands over its lifespan.
- **The organisation as brain.** Human minds are rational, inventive and purposive. They use logical problem-solving and generate new ideas in pursuit of goals. They monitor, gather and process information, making new associations and connections which enable learning. Minds are continuously developing and changing as they absorb sensory experiences. Seeing an organisation in this light focuses on its ability to set goals; to use systematic, rational problem-solving processes; to scan, gather and process information; to accumulate and manage knowledge for learning; to create genuine innovation and change; to attribute 'meaning' to events (as in the formation of organisation culture).
- **The organisation as culture.** Cultures may be defined (Geert Hofstede) as 'a collective programming of the mind which distinguishes the members of one category of people from another'. Culture includes patterns of beliefs and values, rituals and behaviours which are shared by a nation, region, or organisation. (Organisations in fact are cultures; this is not just an analogy.) Seeing an organisation in terms of its behavioural norms, rituals, artefacts and values (in effect, 'the way we do things round here') is a helpful way of talking about the distinctive 'style' that each organisation has. It also describes how underlying values and beliefs colour the behaviour of the organisation.
- **The organisation as political system.** Political systems are about exercising power and influence over others in order to establish control in the interests of shared goals (the common good). They are also about political 'games': building power bases, networks and alliances; competing for limited power and resources; and lobbying or negotiating on behalf of individual or group interests. Seeing the organisation in this light highlights organisational politics, interpersonal relationships and influence. Mintzberg, among others, has described organisations as intensely political systems.
- **Psychic prisons.** Organisations are in part psychic phenomena (according to Jungian psychology), shaped by unconscious mental processes. They create a shared mythology, project an outward image (or 'persona') to the outside world, and try to repress their 'shadow' or dark side. They can become trapped (or 'imprisoned') by these constructions of reality. Viewing organisations in this way reminds managers that perception, image and illusion are as important in organisational behaviour as rational decision-making.
- **Flux and transformation** – also called 'chaos' or 'turbulence' (after related scientific theories). 'Flux' means continuous change or instability; it is a basic condition of the cosmos. Seeing organisations as subject to continuous pressures for, and processes of, change helps to understand the dynamics of organisational learning, resistance to change and change management.
- **Instruments of domination.** Social domination is a process whereby powerful groups seek to

control and impose their will on others. Organisations inevitably feature inequalities of influence and authority. Pluralist ideology suggests that this is a normal mechanism for securing disciplined cooperation in pursuit of shared goals. Marxist ideology suggests that it is aimed at the enrichment of the bourgeoisie at the expense of the workers. Understanding organisations as systems of control highlights issues such as the balance of control and trust; the need to apply controls without manipulation or coercion; and sources of inequity in organisational systems and relationships.

Organisation structure

4.6 Mintzberg *(Structures in Fives: Designing Effective Organisations)* defines an organisation's formal structure as: 'the sum total of the ways in which it divides its labour into distinct tasks and then achieves co-ordination among them'. Mullins defines it as 'the pattern of relationships among positions in the organisation and among members of the organisation. Structure makes possible the application of the process of management and creates a framework of order and command through which the activities of the organisation can be planned, organised, directed and controlled'.

4.7 Formal organisation structure or design consists of a framework designed to:

- *Define work roles and relationships*, so that areas and flows of authority and responsibility are clearly established. In classical organisations, this creates the scalar chain of command, whereby authority flows downwards from senior management to each level of the organisation, with accountability (reporting responsibilities) flowing back up.
- *Define work tasks and responsibilities*, grouping and allocating them to suitable individuals and groups. The basis on which this is done (function, geographical area or product type, say) creates distinct organisational forms.
- *Channel information flows* efficiently through the organisation.
- *Coordinate goals and activities* of different units, so that organisational goals can be efficiently achieved (ie without duplication of effort).
- *Control the flow of work, information and resources*, through planning, monitoring and other systems.
- *Support flexible working* and adaptability to changing internal and external demands. Structures themselves may be kept flexible (eg temporary teams, loosely defined job descriptions). They can also actively support organisational flexibility, (eg by encouraging information flow, cross-functional working, empowerment and so on).
- *Facilitate organisational learning*, via the gathering and transfer of knowledge throughout the organisation.
- Encourage and support the *commitment, involvement and satisfaction* of the people who work for the organisation, by offering opportunities for participation, challenge, interest, responsibility, teamworking and so on.
- Support and improve the *efficiency and effectiveness* of the organisation's performance through all of the above

4.8 Peter Drucker has argued that: 'Good organisation structure does not by itself produce good performance. But a poor organisation structure makes good performance impossible, no matter how good the individual managers may be. To improve organisation structure ... will therefore always improve performance.'

4.9 Note, however, that an effective organisation structure is one that both facilitates organisational effectiveness and efficiency in the long term (taking into account the need for change) *and* meets the needs of the people working within it. Some researchers have shown (as we will see in Chapter 2) that highly formalised structures can restrict employees' growth and fulfilment, discourage creativity and initiative, and be dysfunctional in the face of change. Organisational design influences the behaviour, performance and satisfaction of individuals and groups within it.

4.10 Signs that a structure may be **ineffective** include problems such as the following.

- Slow decision and response times, due to the need to refer decisions via overly lengthy formal communication channels
- Inter-departmental conflicts, due to ambiguities or overlaps of responsibility
- Excessive layers of management (often middle management), which slows communication, increases overheads and often requires work creation to justify the positions
- Lack of co-ordination between units, seen in customer complaints, production bottlenecks, inconsistent communications, and the creation of special co-ordinating mechanisms (liaison officers, committees etc)
- High labour turnover among skilled junior staff, suggesting lack of development opportunities
- Lack of identifiable accountabilities for key tasks

4.11 There are many **influences on organisation structure**. There are certain internal principles and dynamics of organisation: how far power and authority are held at the top (centralised) or given to lower levels (decentralised); the span of control (the number of subordinates that can be supervised by any one superior); the division of labour; the grouping of people into working units; the need for communication channels, and so on. These determine some elements of structure, to an extent, according to internal logic.

4.12 According to contingency theory, however, there are still managerial choices to be made in order to optimise the structure. A number of contingent variables may influence structural choices and organisational development.

- The **strategic objectives** or **mission** of the organisation, and how these are broken down to define and guide the work of sub-units. Diversified organisations, for example, may require more decentralised structures.
- The **task** or 'business' of the organisation, which will determine which line or task functions are required (development, production, marketing, finance) and which support or staff functions (HR, planning, quality control, maintenance).
- The **technology** of the task may necessitate certain forms of organisation to maximise its efficiency and the needs of people.
- The **size** of the organisation. As it gets larger, its structure will get more complex: specialisation, subdivision and formalisation are required in order to control and coordinate performance (typically leading to the bureaucratisation of large organisations).
- **Geographical dispersion** may require federalised structures to take into account relevant factors at local, regional, national, international or global levels of operation.
- The **environment** of the organisation. Factors (and especially changes) in the legal, commercial, technical and social environment represent demands and constraints on organisational activity, and opportunities and threats to which organisation structure must adapt. As one example, information and communication technology (ICT) has enabled organisations to adopt looser, more network-style units or 'virtual teams'.
- The **culture and management** style of the organisation: eg the willingness of management to delegate authority and adopt more fluid facilitate-and-empower roles; organisational values about teamworking, formality, flexibility and so on.

Elements of organisation structure

4.13 Henry Mintzberg (*The Structure of Organisations*) provided a framework and language for discussing organisation structure, by categorising the building blocks of organisations and showing that organisations operate as a hierarchy, building from a large operating core to a small strategic apex. He suggested that there are five basic component parts in any organisation: Figure 1.2.

Figure 1.2 *Components of organisation structure*

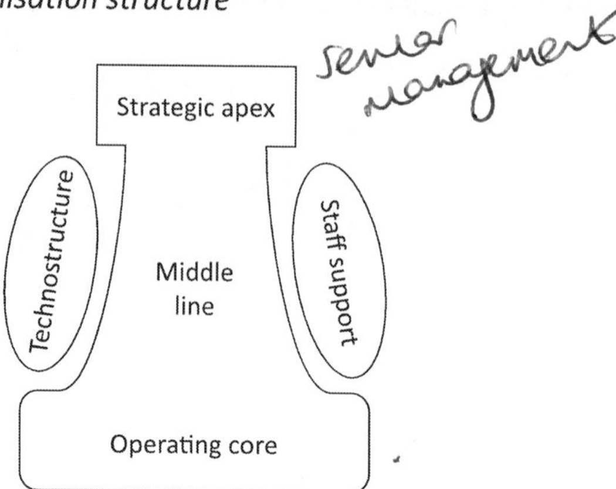

4.14 Working through the sections of the model:

- The *strategic apex* (senior management) ensures that the organisation pursues its objectives and serves the needs of its owners and stakeholders. Its tasks include strategic planning, resource allocation and boundary management (acting as ambassadors between the organisation and the outside world).
- The *operating core* contains those people directly involved in production: securing inputs and processing and distributing them as outputs (goods and services).
- The *middle line* (managers and supervisors) form the chain of command that runs between the strategic apex and the operating core. Its task is the organisation, planning and control of work, acting as the interface between senior management and operational employees and between the organisation and external contacts (eg the supply chain).
- The *technostructure* (specialist advisers and analysts) offers technical support to the rest of the structure. Its main task is the design and maintenance of systems to standardise work throughout the organisation. Examples include strategic planning, quality control, systems analysis and design, financial control, production scheduling and HR planning.
- *Staff support* offers administrative and ancillary services to the rest of the structure. Examples include personnel management, legal advice, public relations, research and development, and services such as maintenance, mail, security, reception and catering.

4.15 In his book *Structures in Fives: Effective Organisations*, Mintzberg demonstrates how different configurations of these elements create organisations of five general types.

- **Simple (or entrepreneurial) structure**: a small, hierarchical organisation based on centralised control by a single leader – eg a salon owner and a team of hairdressers. Because of their small size and strong hands-on leadership, they are characterised by coherent direction, informal relationships and flexibility. This is suited to small, entrepreneurial owner-managed firms consisting mainly of the strategic apex and operating core.
- **Machine structure**: mechanistic, hierarchical, bureaucratic organisations (as already discussed). Suited to stable environments and tasks requiring strict standardisation and compliance. Tend to have many layers of middle line, and an enlarged technostructure (to standardise work procedures) and staff support.
- **Professional structure**: hierarchical, but recognising the power of professional expertise, this structure tends to be flatter and more participative than machine structures. Suited to the expectations and abilities of professional staff (doctors, lawyers, accountants). Tend to have little middle line or technostructure (since the operating core are experts), but a substantial staff support element for administrative and clerical support.
- **Divisional (independent) structure**: a number of more or less autonomous divisions, coordinated by centralised strategic and support functions. Suitable for devolved structures (such as regionally or

internationally dispersed divisions) where central direction is required for brand identity, investment strategy and so on. Effectively duplicate the whole middle-line/operating-core structure within each division, reporting to the central strategic apex; the centralised technostructure and support structures appear relatively small.

- *Ad hoc* **(flexible) structure**: an organic, decentralised structure of temporary, flexible project teams and networks. Suitable for new technology businesses (IT, R&D), consultancies, small media companies and other organisations focused on creativity and innovation. Tend to be made up of technostructure and support staff, flexibly banding together and acting as operating core where required.

Organisational flexibility

4.16   Modern trends in flexible organisation include the following.

- The **flattening of organisation hierarchies**. The trend is towards 'delayering', or reducing the middle line of organisations. Flatter structures are more adaptive and responsive, because there is a shorter distance between the strategic apex and the customer-facing operational core.
- **Project management structures**. Structures focus on the customer and outputs or results, rather than on internal processes and functions for their own sake. A project management orientation is being applied to the supply or services within the organisation (ie to internal customers) as well as to the external market. 'Full-service' project management can be offered by multi-functional project teams, so that the customer does not experience any vertical barriers.
- **Horizontal structures**. Tom Peters *(Thriving on Chaos)* gives this term to structures which allow work and information to flow freely across functional boundaries, without the 'vertical barriers' created by specialisation, departmental job demarcations and formal communication channels. Peters suggests that customers' experience of the organisation is horizontal: they need to speak to different functions (sales, delivery, accounts, after-sales service) as they proceed through the purchase process. Product development and innovation, partnering, networking and learning are all horizontal activities, requiring the free exchange of information across functional boundaries.
- **Boundaryless structures** (George T Milkovich and John W Boudreau, *Human Resource Management*) are structures in which all barriers are eliminated or softened, in order to align processes for the achievement of objectives. This includes vertical or functional barriers, but also status barriers (between managers and workers), and even organisational boundaries (eg between divisions, domestic and foreign units, and supply chain partners).
- **Functional flexibility** or versatility. This may be achieved by methods such as multidisciplinary teamworking (eg multifunctional project or procurement strategy teams, bringing together individuals with different skills and specialisms, across functional boundaries, so that their competencies and resources can be pooled or exchanged) and multi-skilling (where each individual within a team is functionally versatile, and able to perform a number of different tasks as required).
- **Numerical flexibility**: the ability to shrink or enlarge the labour force in response to fluctuations in demand. This may be done by: using non-standard-contract and subcontracted labour (temporary, short-contract or freelance workers); outsourcing functions to other organisations; or introducing flexible working hours schemes. In practice, an organisation may adopt a 'core-periphery' model. Handy *(Understanding Organisations)* proposes a 'shamrock' configuration, with various 'leaves':
  — a small, stable core of full-time permanent labour
  — a periphery of part-time and temporary labour which can be deployed flexibly according to workflow peaks and troughs
  — the option of contracting out areas of work to other service organisations
  — a possible fourth 'leaf' where work can be devolved to customers (eg through self-service, online information search and ordering, and so on).

Inter-organisational and network structures

4.17 Inter-organisational structures are structured relationships between two or more organisations. Huczynski and Buchanan contrast organisational relationships that exist in:

- **Markets:** separate firms act independently of each other, forming temporary relationships based on competition or transactions and exchanges.
- **Hierarchies:** an organisation forms a single, structured entity, within which all relationships are formally defined and all activities integrated, as in a bureaucracy.

4.18 In between these extremes there are inter-organisational relationships: non-market, non-bureaucratic relationships 'in which two or more organisations share resources and activities to pursue a common strategy'.

4.19 At the 'hierarchy' end of the scale, organisations may enter into mergers or acquisitions, whereby the assets (including the human resources) of two organisations are integrated and jointly managed. However, such arrangements lack the flexibility of markets and contractual relationships.

4.20 The alternative is non-market, non-bureaucratic relationships, based on various forms of controlled co-operation. Inter-organisational relationships are a significant feature of the business environment because of the realisation that a single organisation's opportunities will be enhanced if alliances with other parties are entered into, in terms of:

- Access to overseas distribution channels, customers, expertise and technology, provided the other party has an established presence in the area
- Reduction in the effects of competition. As the two allies are no longer competing with each other, they can defend against existing competition better together, they can join forces against new entrants, and they can plan on the basis of known, long-term markets.
- Benefiting from economies of scale in joint production and sales
- Sharing and thereby reducing the financial and operational risk of new ventures and new products and markets
- Access to funds for expansion
- Aiding economic recovery in a region (often supported by government policy and incentives).

4.21 There are a number of popular inter-organisational forms, including: joint ventures, strategic alliances, outsourcing and franchising.

4.22 The term 'network organisation' refers to a looser, dynamic, more informal affiliation of autonomous and broadly equal organisations, who exchange information and pursue ongoing (typically long-term) relationships for mutual benefit.

4.23 There are no direct contractual or financial obligations (eg investment by one company in another) shaping these relationships: they are purely based on collaboration, communication, trust and mutual advantage. Huzcynski and Buchanan note that: 'the formation of a network involves companies whose domains overlap in terms of products, markets, operating modes or territories, contacting one another and recognising the benefits of co-operation.' In a sense, therefore, any attempt at long-term supply chain or customer relationship management is a network.

4.24 A special form of the network concept is the **virtual organisation**, where companies (or units of a single company) collaborate, coordinate their activities and share data, using information communications technology (ICT) as their main – or only – point of contact.

4.25 Operations can be geographically dispersed, global expertise drawn on, functions outsourced and 24/7 communication maintained – while operating (to all intents and purposes) as a single organisational entity. Tasks are typically fragmented, performed by widely dispersed individuals, but integrated by web-based communication and data-sharing tools.

4.26 The virtual organisation model is gaining popularity as an organisational structure for several reasons. Virtual organisations:

- Are supported by ongoing developments in ICT which allow data-sharing and synchronisation, interactive communication and virtual meetings (eg by webcast), across barriers of time and geographical distance
- Allow a high degree of flexibility (numerical, temporal and functional). Membership is diverse and structurally fluid enough to respond flexibly to equally diverse and changing customer and client requirements.
- Enable information and other resources to be mobilised efficiently in widely dispersed regions and specialist sectors, while allowing central control, pooled information and consistency of service and image where required
- Offer cost savings in areas such as employment (no redundancy obligations, benefits), overheads and logistics, due to the physical dispersal of (and loose contractual relationship with) members
- Exploit an increasingly knowledge-based economy, where the prime commodities are knowledge, information and expertise
- Exploit international markets, as they enable members to take advantage of local knowledge, indigenous language speakers, indigenous trading partnerships, etc.

Organisational culture

4.27 Organisational culture is, in simple terms, the way in which a particular organisation does things: its distinctive 'climate' and 'style'. Structure and culture are often discussed together, as ways of describing an organisation and how it 'works': the formal arrangements are overlaid by a kind of collective 'personality'. This topic effectively underpins the entire practice of management: a manager's approach to team leadership, motivation, decision-making, delegation, risk management and so on will depend to a large extent on the cultural values and norms of the organisation.

4.28 An influential writer on culture, Geert Hofstede *(Cultures & Organisations)*, summed up culture as 'the collective programming of the mind which distinguishes the members of one category of people from another'. In other words, culture is the shared ways of behaving and understanding that are distinctive to a particular group of people. This 'group' or category may be a nation or ethnic group, a social class, a profession or occupation, a gender, or an organisation: each may have its distinctive way of thinking and doing things. These are sometimes called 'spheres' of culture. We will discuss national and organisational culture separately in Section 6 of this Chapter.

5 The external environment

5.1 The environment of a given organisation (or purchasing and supply function) can be seen as a series of concentric circles.

- The internal environment of the organisation consists of its formal organisation structure; its style, climate or 'culture'; its systems and technology; its strategic objectives and plans; policies, procedures, rules and informal practices; and so on.
- The immediate operating or micro environment of the organisation includes the customers, suppliers and competitors who directly impact on its operations.
- The general or macro environment incorporates wider factors in the market and society in which the organisation operates: industry structure, the national and international economy, law, politics, culture, technological development and natural resources – and so on.

5.2 Mullins emphasises that: 'In order to be effective and maintain survival and growth, the organisation must respond to the opportunities and challenges, and the risks and limitations, presented by the external environment of which it is a part. Changes in the environment will affect inputs, and changes in inputs will affect the transformation or conversion process and hence the outputs.'

5.3 The **open systems** model of organisations emphasises the importance of taking the environment into account. Firstly, because an organisation *depends* on its environment as the source of its inputs (including labour); the market for its outputs; and a key source of feedback information to measure and adjust its performance. And secondly, because an organisation also *impacts* on its environment, in the process of taking in inputs and creating outputs (both products, such as goods and services, and 'by products' such as waste, pollution, supplier development or local employment).

5.4 The external environment exerts an important influence on the organisation (and its supply chain), in three basic ways.

- It presents *threats* (such as restrictive legislation, competitor initiatives, technology obsolescence or labour shortages, say) and *opportunities* (such as changing consumer demand or technological improvements). These affect the organisation's ability to compete and fulfil its objectives. Environmental threats and opportunities are key factors in the formation of organisational strategies and plans.
- It is the source of *resources* needed by the organisation (labour, materials, supplies and services, energy, finance, information and so on). Environmental factors determine to what extent these resources are, or are not, available in the right quantity, at the right time and at the right price – and what sort of supply chain and human resource management strategies, policies and practices will help to secure supply.
- It contains *stakeholders* who may seek, or have the right, to influence the activities of the organisation. These include suppliers and their supply chains – and also law makers, regulatory bodies, industry associations and other parties with an interest or 'stake' in supply chain ethics, management and performance.

STEEPLE factors

5.5 A popular tool for analysing external macro environment or supply market factors is described by the acronym PEST (and more comprehensive variants such as PESTLE). The most comprehensive version of this model is STEEPLE: Table 1.2. We have chosen some illustrative examples of STEEPLE factors which impact most clearly on organisations, management and the employment relationship.

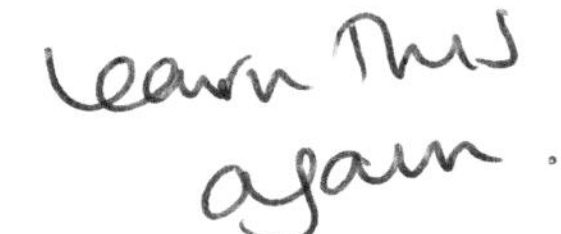

Table 1.2 *The STEEPLE framework*

FACTORS	EXAMPLES
Socio-cultural	• Demographics (age, gender, ethnicity, population movements and so on) affecting demand for goods and services, and the availability of skills • Consumerism and consumer power • Education and skilling infrastructure (affecting the availability and price of skills) • Values (eg re corporate social responsibility and diversity, and shaping the psychological contract) • Attitudes to work, employment equity and employee relations • Cultural differences (impacting on cross-cultural and multi-cultural management) • Gender roles (affecting expectations of equal opportunity)
Technological	• Information and communications technology (ICT) developments changing products, business processes (eg e-commerce) • Automation and ICT facilitating workforce rationalisation or downsizing; 'virtual' organisation; outsourcing (through improved communication, integration and control) • Automation and ICT changing job roles and organisation; skill requirements
Economic	• The economic strength and stability of the industry or market (eg affecting employment, investment in HR, priority for business survival, sources of competitive advantage) • Rates of inflation, interest and taxation (impacting on disposable incomes, the costs of business finance, pay rates and expectations) • In international supply markets: exchange rates, comparative wages and taxes, freedom of labour and capital movements, trade agreements and so on.
Environmental (or 'ecological')	• Consumer demand and public pressure for eco-friendly products and processes • Law and regulation (and related compliance risks) on environmental issues such as pollution, carbon emissions and waste management • Emerging or local priorities re green 'issues': eg water management, de-forestation, climate change and greenhouse gas emissions • The availability, scarcity and price of natural resources and commodities
Political	• Government policies (eg on international trade, support for business and innovation, public sector spending cuts, or HR policies eg work-life balance, life-long learning and skilling) • Grants and subsidies available eg for employee, supplier or regional development Political risk (eg political or civil unrest or war) in operational regions or supply and labour markets
Legal	• A wide range of law and regulation on issues such as: employment rights and obligations; workplace health and safety; equal opportunity; working hours; minimum wage; environmental protection; consumer rights and contracts; data protection; and public sector procurement procedures.
Ethical	• Consumer demand for ethically sourced and produced goods and services (eg fair pricing, supply chain labour standards, avoidance of animal testing, sustainable sourcing of non-renewable resources) • Ethical codes and standards published by buyers and suppliers, professional bodies (such as CIPS), trade unions and pressure groups • Ethical and reputational risk arising from exposure of, or association with, unethical practices in the supply chain • The 'employer brand' of the organisation (the labour market's perception of the organisation as an ethical employer, affecting its ability to attract and retain quality labour).

5.6 It is well worth remembering these categories: if you are asked in the exam to comment on the external environment or supply market of an organisation, they provide a good 'checklist' around which to build a systematic and well-structured answer.

Societal influences

5.7 **Ethics** are a set of moral principles or values about what constitutes 'right' and 'wrong' behaviour. For individuals and groups, these often reflect the assumptions and beliefs of the families, national cultures and educational environment in which their ideas developed. Ethics are also shaped more deliberately by public and professional bodies, in the form of agreed principles and guidelines which are designed to protect society's best interests.

5.8   Ethical issues may affect businesses (and public sector organisations) at three levels.

- At the *macro* level, there are the issues of the role of business and capitalism in society: the debate about globalisation, the exploitation of labour, the impacts of industrialisation on the environment and so on. This is the sphere addressed by the Ethical Trading Initiative, for example.
- At the *corporate* level, there are the issues which face an individual organisation as it formulates strategies and policies about how it interacts with its various stakeholders. Some of these matters will be covered by legislative and regulatory requirements, and an organisation may have a 'compliance based' approach to ethics which strives merely to uphold these minimal requirements. The sphere generally referred to as corporate social responsibility covers policies which the organisation adopts for the good and wellbeing of stakeholders, taking a more proactive 'integrity based' approach.
- At the *individual* level, there are the issues which face individuals as they act and interact within the organisation and supply chain: whether to accept gifts or hospitality which might be perceived as an attempt to influence supplier selection, say. This is the sphere which is often covered in Codes of Ethics.

5.9   The term **corporate social responsibility (CSR)** is used to describe a wide range of obligations that an organisation may feel it has towards the society in which it operates: its 'secondary' stakeholders (ie those not directly connected with the organisation, but affected by its operations). This is sometimes expressed in terms of 'externalities': the costs of business activities which are not absorbed in a product or service or paid for by consumers, but which are borne by the wider community – such as the costs of pollution, including associated costs of illness, environmental degradation and so on.

5.10   One CIPS examiner has summed up CSR as follows.

'CSR means the commitment to systematic consideration of the environmental, social and cultural aspects of an organisation's operations. This includes the key issues of sustainability, human rights, labour and community relations, and supplier and customer relations beyond legal obligations. The objective [is] to create long-term business value and contribute to improving the social conditions of the people affected by our operations.'

5.11   Any or all of the following considerations may be relevant in assessing an organisation's CSR obligations.

- **Sustainability** issues: the conservation and perpetuation of the world's limited natural resources (eg by limiting greenhouse gas emissions or logging)
- **Environmental** issues: the reduction of environment pollution, waste management, the avoidance of environmental disfigurement, land reclamation, promoting recycling, energy conservation and so on
- **Ethical trading**, business relationships and development: consumer protection; the upholding of principles of good corporate governance; improvement of working (and social) conditions for employees, suppliers and subcontractors (particularly in developing nations); avoidance of exploitation and debt minimisation; upholding ethical employment practices (such as equal opportunities and employment protection); adherence to ethical codes for fair trading and so on.

5.12   There are many ways in which a purchasing function can contribute to CSR objectives. For example, it can draw up and enforce codes of ethical practice in sourcing or adhere to the rules laid down in the CIPS ethical code and the Ethical Trading Initiative; it can encourage (or even insist on) ethical employment and/ or environmental practices in its suppliers; it can adhere to health and safety, equal opportunities and other ethical practices in its own workplace and so on.

5.13   Various arguments have been put forward for ethical behaviour.

- It is a moral duty. (This is sometimes called a deontological position, from the Greek root word for 'obligation'.)
- It is functional or practical. (This is sometimes called a utilitarian position, from the Latin root word for 'useful'.)

- It supports organisational goals. (This is sometimes called a teleological position, from the Greek root word for 'purpose'.)

5.14 Economist Milton Friedman took the view that 'the social responsibility of business is profit maximisation': to give a return on shareholders' investment. Spending funds on objectives *not* related to shareholder expectations is irresponsible: regard for shareholder wealth is a healthy discipline for management, providing accountability for decisions. The public interest is already served by profit maximisation, because the State levies taxes.

5.15 'Consequently,' argued Friedman, 'the only justification for social responsibility is *enlightened self interest*' on the part of a business organisation. So how does CSR serve the interest of the firm?

- Law, regulation and Codes of Practice impose certain social responsibilities on organisations (eg in relation to health and safety, employment protection, consumer rights and environmental care). There are financial and operational penalties for failure to comply (eg 'polluter pays' taxes).
- Voluntary measures (which may in any case only pre-empt legal and regulatory requirements) may enhance corporate image and build a positive brand. A commonly quoted example is the environmental and sustainability strategy adopted by The Body Shop.
- Above-statutory provisions for employees and suppliers may be necessary to attract, retain and motivate them to provide quality service and commitment – particularly in competition with other employers and purchasers.
- Increasing consumer awareness of social responsibility issues creates a market demand for CSR (and the threat of boycott for irresponsible firms)

5.16 *Mintzberg* notes that a business's relationship with society is not purely economic: a business is an open social system which makes a variety of non-economic exchanges with the society in which it operates (people, information, image), and creates a variety of non-economic impacts. Social responsibility helps to create a social climate and infrastructure in which the business can prosper in the long term.

5.17 In the same way, ethical sourcing helps to create a climate in which mutually beneficial long-term trading relationships can be preserved. Exploitation, abuse and disappointed expectations will inevitably lead to broken relationships or reciprocal 'corner cutting' by suppliers. The modern focus on partnership in supply chains therefore puts the spotlight firmly on ethical sourcing practices.

6 The influence of culture

Levels of culture

6.1 Culture has been defined as 'the collective programming of the mind which distinguishes the members of one category of people from another' (Hofstede).

6.2 Another influential writer on culture, Fons Trompenaars *(Riding the Waves of Culture)*, suggested that culture operates on three levels: Figure 1.3

Figure 1.3 *Elements of culture*

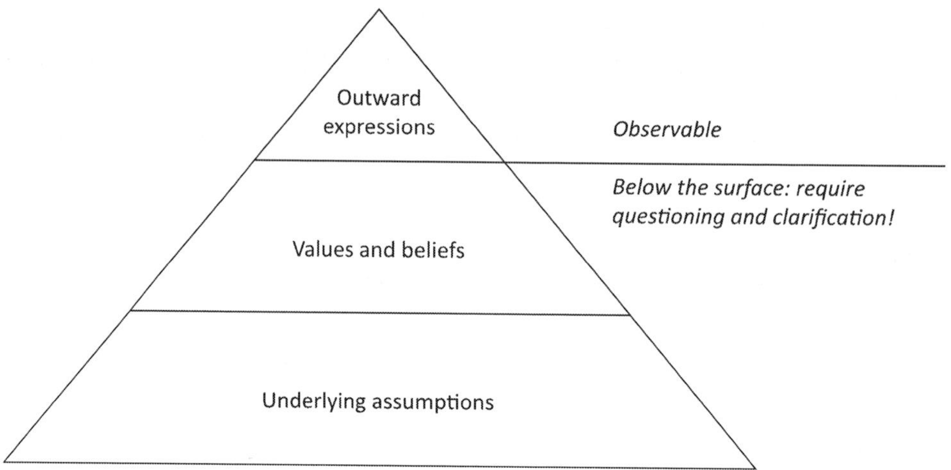

6.3 The most easily recognisable elements of culture, because they are directly observable, are its outward expressions.

- *Behaviour:* norms of personal and interpersonal conduct; customs and rules about the kinds of behaviour that are acceptable or unacceptable within the group
- *Artefacts:* products of the culture such as its music, writing and art; its myths, heroes and symbols
- *Rituals:* patterns of behaviour which have symbolic or traditional value, such as social formalities, ceremonies and rites of passage.

6.4 Beneath these outward expressions are the values and beliefs which give them their special meaning and significance within the culture. They may be explicit in sayings or mottos but often they are not directly expressed so much as reflected in behaviour, artefacts and rituals. So, for example, a society that believes that age deserves respect will develop behaviours honouring older people, will reward seniority in organisations, will create myths about wise elders and so on.

6.5 Beneath values and beliefs lie assumptions: ideas which shape the culture's ways of thinking and behaving – but which have become so ingrained that they are no longer consciously recognised or questioned. The rights of the individual, or the legitimacy of authority, may come into this category.

6.6 The 'underlying' elements of culture – like the part of the iceberg that lies under the water – are the ones that cause problems. They are difficult to manage, whether in societies or in organisations, because of the potential for misunderstanding (and, from there, conflict). An important skill of cross-cultural management, as we will see, is being aware that, when dealing with other cultures, we don't always know what it is that we don't know!

6.7 Different countries (or world regions) have different cultural norms, values and assumptions which influence how they do business and manage people. It is increasingly important to understand this, since managers are increasingly likely to work in organisations that have multinational or multi-ethnic elements, or in another culture.

6.8 Distinctive national features may be a source of competitive advantage in domestic and international markets (because of 'fashions' for the products or management techniques of particular cultures, and because of the synergy that may arise from diverse viewpoints and skills). However, they may also be a source of difficulties in cross-cultural business relationships and marketing (because of failure to understand underlying needs and expectations).

The Hofstede model

6.9 Geert Hofstede *(Cultures & Organisations)* carried out major cross-cultural research at IBM in the 1980s, and formulated one of the most influential models of work-related cultural differences. The Hofstede Model describes five key dimensions of difference between national cultures, which influence all aspects of organisation and management: HR policies, communication and conflict, leadership styles, teamworking and so on. The five key dimensions are set out in Table 1.3.

Table 1.3 *Hofstede's dimensions of culture*

DIMENSION	LOW ⟶	HIGH
Power distance The extent to which unequal distribution of power is accepted.	• Less centralisation, flatter organisation structures • Subordinates expect involvement and participation in decision-making *Eg: Germanic, Anglo, Nordic*	• Greater centralisation, top-down chain of command, closer supervision • Subordinates have little expectation of influencing decisions *Eg Latin, less developed Asian*
Uncertainty avoidance The extent to which security, order and control are preferred to ambiguity, uncertainty and change	• Value flexibility, creativity; generalists; variability • Less task structure, written rules • Tolerance of risk, dissent, conflict, deviation from norm *Eg Anglo, Nordic*	• Value control, certainty and ritual; specialists and experts; standardisation • Value task structure, rules and regulations • Need for consensus; low tolerance of deviance, dissent *Eg Latin, Germanic, Japanese*
Individualism The extent to which people prefer to live and work in individualistic ('I') rather than collectivist ('We') ways.	• Collectivist: emphasise inter-dependence, reciprocal obligation, social acceptability • Organisation seen as 'family': relationship more important than task achievement • Management of teams *Eg less developed Asian/Latin*	• Individualist: emphasise autonomy, individual choice and responsibility, initiative • Organisation impersonal: task achievement more important than relationship • Management of individuals *Eg Anglo, Nordic, more developed Latin*
Masculinity The extent to which social gender roles are distinct.	• Feminine: minimise gender role differences • Feminine values dominant (modesty, consensus, relationship, quality of life) *Eg Nordic*	• Masculine: clearly differentiated gender roles • Masculine values dominant (assertiveness, competition, decisiveness, material success) *Eg Japanese, Germanic, Anglo*
Long-term orientation The extent to which society embraces long-term devotion to traditional, forward thinking values.	• Immediate value for fulfilling social obligations, protecting 'face' • Change can occur rapidly *Eg Anglo, Germanic*	• 'Confucian' (Chinese) work dynamism and values • Long time frames: respect for tradition; thrift; perseverance • Change may be slow *Eg Japanese, Chinese*

6.10 This model has been extremely influential, and it is easy to see how the basic concepts can be applied to management in international and cross-cultural settings: anticipating, for example, the differences arising from individual and collective orientations in cross-cultural teamworking, motivation or negotiation; or anticipating the differences arising from power distance in managerial style and organisational hierarchies.

6.11 However, there have been a number of criticisms of the model. While Hofstede was confident that the cultural differences he identified were relatively stable and enduring, critics have pointed out that:

- The model may be outdated, as social values and cultural constructs are subject to accelerating change and convergence, due to increased travel, and globalised communication and media
- The model does not take into account regional differences within certain countries (such as Spain)
- Intermediate classifications (between the two extremes) are hard to operationalise.

The Trompenaars model

6.12   Fons Trompenaars and Charles Hampden-Turner *(Riding the Waves of Culture)* similarly researched cultural differences. Their findings suggested that certain cultures emphasise some values more than others, on seven key dimensions. Cultures do not embody one value *or* another in each dimension, but are different in the amount of emphasis placed on each.

6.13   In relation to how individuals relate to other people, a society may emphasise any of the following five aspects.

- **Universalism** (behaviour in a relationship is governed by the standards, rules and norms of the society or group: eg North America, Scandinavia) or **particularism** (behaviour is governed by one's relationship with the individual concerned: eg China, Indonesia, Korea)
- **Individualism** (emphasis on the individual, individual contribution and independence: eg US, Eastern Europe, Denmark) or **collectivism** (emphasis on the group, team contribution and interdependence: eg Japan, India).
- **Affective** (issues are dealt with emotionally and emotions are openly expressed and displayed: eg Middle East, Southern Europe) or **neutral** (issues are dealt with rationally and unemotionally, with a focus on goal-directed behaviour: eg UK, Germany, Japan, China)
- **Specific** (work and non-work roles and relationships are kept separate, to preserve privacy and personal autonomy: eg US, UK, Sweden) or **diffuse** (work and non-work roles and relationships are integrated and merged: eg China, Korea)
- **Achievement** (status is based on personal attainments and abilities: eg North America, Austria) or **ascription** (status is based on attributes such as age, gender or background: eg Egypt, South America, Spain, Korea).

6.14   In relation to time and the environment, societies may emphasise any of the following two aspects

- **Past/present** (the future is seen as growing from the past, history and tradition: eg France, Japan, UK) or **future** (the future is seen as disconnected from the past, created from a 'zero base': eg US)
- **Internal control** (individuals are presumed to be in control of their own lives, shaping events and creating new things: eg North America, UK, Israel) or **external control** (nature, society and other external forces are presumed to control much of life: individuals adapt to events and refine existing things: eg Japan, China).

Hall's communication (high- and low-context) model

6.15   Edward Hall *(Beyond Culture)* suggested that another dimension of cultural difference is the extent to which the content and understanding of communication is influenced by its context: non-verbal aspects, underlying implications, interpersonal factors and so on.

- **High-context** cultures (eg Japanese, Asian, African, Latin American, Middle-Eastern, Southern European) interpret and exchange more complex messages. A high proportion of information is internalised. Informal face-to-face and oral communication is preferred: less information tends to be divulged via official and written forms. Non-verbal cues and unspoken implications (indirect communication styles) have a high value, compared to direct words. These cultures are good at developing networks and shared group understandings, often based on the past and tradition. Trust and personal relationships are important in business (a 'diffuse' culture in Trompenaars' terms).
- **Low-context** cultures (eg Germanic, Scandinavian, North American) tend to take the content of communication at face value: words say what they mean. A high proportion of communication is directly expressed, with a preference for clear, written, explicit communication. Past exchanges and context are less important in understanding present meanings. Rules and contracts are more important in business relationships than personal relationships (a 'specific' culture in Trompenaars' terms.)

6.16 Mullins uses the example of American managers visiting China. '[They] may find that a business transaction in that country will take more time than at home. They may find it difficult to interpret the true feelings of their Chinese host and may need to decode non-verbal communication and other signals. They may seek to negotiate a rules-based contract whereas their Chinese counterpart may lay greater stress upon building a mutually beneficial reciprocal relationship. There is scope for potential miscommunication between the two cultures...'

Cross-cultural management

6.17 There has been increasing demand for managerial competence in working with (or within) different cultures in recent decades. Domestic skill shortages have encouraged international recruitment, supported by freedom of labour movement in blocs such as the European Economic Area. Meanwhile communications technology and e-commerce have facilitated the globalisation of markets, and there has been an increase in internal mergers, acquisitions and joint ventures as organisations have sought to operate effectively across national boundaries.

6.18 Such factors have arguably contributed to the 'convergence' of international cultures (with a narrowing of cultural differences, especially in the sphere of business and marketing). However, they have also contributed to:

- A resurgence of ethnic cultures and languages (such as Welsh or Basque)
- The creation of cross-cultural management contexts, in multi-cultural teams, international managerial postings and global 'virtual' organisations.

It may also be argued that people management values and practices are less likely to converge than, for example, production, quality or supply chain techniques, owing to the strength of culturally derived preferences. Managerial orientations such as flexibility and diversity recognise the continuing differences.

6.19 Susan C Schneider and Jean-Louis Barsoux *(Communicating Across Cultures)* argue that 'rather than knowing what to do in Country X, or whether national or functional cultures are more important in multi-cultural teams, what is necessary is to know how to assess the potential impact of culture, national or otherwise, on performance'. Anne Marie Francesco and Barry A Gold *(International Organisational Behaviour)* similarly note that: 'Managers must develop organisational systems that are *flexible* enough to take into account the meaning of work and the relative value of rewards within the range of cultures where they operate.'

6.20 There is a vast range of potential differences and appropriate responses: managers will have to monitor and address them as they go. However, it is worth being aware that cultural differences may raise issues in the following areas.

- **Teamworking**. 'Collective' working styles may be more congenial to some cultures than to others. Differences in social customs (gender roles, eating habits, business etiquette) may initially get in the way of co-operative working. Individual rewards and incentives may be ineffective in a collective culture geared to team rewards.
- **Communication**. There may be language barriers within a team or business relationship: allowances must be made for differences in fluency and understanding. There may also be different norms in regard to such matters as: the meanings attached to body language; the acceptability of displays of emotion; attitudes to conflict and consensus and so on.
- **Participation and involvement**. Some cultures prefer to raise issues or ideas one-to-one rather than in a group. Some have a problem with questioning or offering ideas to people in positions of respect or authority. In addition, there may be a need to encourage and balance diverse contributions within a cross-cultural group, to make sure that no viewpoints are excluded.
- **Conflict resolution**. Different cultures tend to have different norms and preferences in regard to the appropriateness of assertiveness, criticism or argument; the need to compromise or reach consensus; the value of competition and so on.

- **International issues**. There may be additional logistical issues in working across different time zones, developing 'virtual' teams and so on.

6.21 We will discuss the management of diversity, and how cross-cultural awareness can be fostered in organisations, in later chapters of this Course Book.

Organisational culture

6.22 Organisational culture has been defined as 'a pattern of beliefs and expectations shared by the organisation's members, and which produce norms that powerfully shape the behaviour of individuals and groups in the organisation' (H Schwartz and S Davis, 'Matching corporate culture and business strategy', in *Organisational Dynamics*). It has been summed up as 'the way we do things around here' (Edgar H Schein, *Organisational Culture and Leadership*).

6.23 Johnson, Scholes and Whittington *(Exploring Corporate Strategy)* use the **cultural web** as a way of representing 'the taken-for-granted assumptions, or paradigm, of an organisation, and the behavioural manifestations of organisational culture': Figure 1.4.

Figure 1.4 *The cultural web*

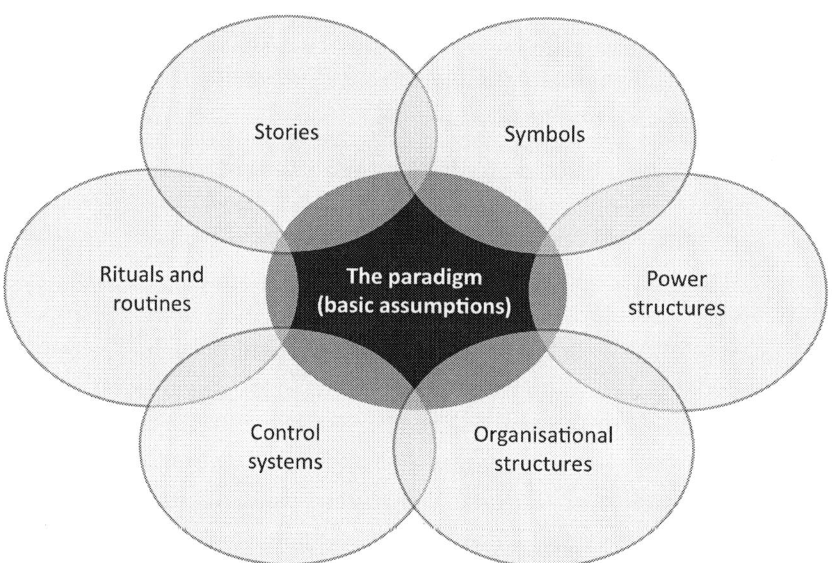

6.24 The elements of the web can be used as a framework to analyse organisational culture in a wide range of settings. (Note that all the elements are interlinked: any one can influence the others to change the culture.)

- The **paradigm** may include assumptions about customer satisfaction, quality, risk, innovation or employee relations; the importance of values such as integrity (and how that is defined), empowerment or teamhood; and how the organisation sees itself in general.
- **Stories** form the 'mythology' of the organisation: tales of past successes or failures, heroes and villains, how challenges were met, how things came to be the way they were. Organisations 'see' themselves in terms of these stories.
- **Routines** include formal procedures; 'short-cuts' developed in practice; informal norms (such as familiarity or formality with colleagues); and customs (such as 'pizza Fridays' or monthly 'dress down' days). **Rituals** are more symbolic behaviours, including business formalities (eg exchange of business cards), ceremonies (eg performance awards) and rites of passage (eg celebrating promotions or project completions).
- **Control systems** refer to ways in which control is exercised: performance monitoring, supervision, rewards and sanctions and so on. A culture based on the assumption that workers dislike work and

resist authority (which *Douglas McGregor* called 'Theory X') will use close supervision, detailed rules, and a carrot-and-stick approach to discipline. A culture believing in individual responsibility and initiative ('Theory Y') will facilitate self-control and reporting by exception.

- **Organisational structure**: centralised or decentralised; formal or informal; encouraging collaboration or competition.
- **Power structures** refer to how power is distributed; whether it is based on formal authority, charismatic leadership, democratic consensus or respect for expertise; and who the influential individuals and groups are.
- **Symbols** include formal logos and trade marks, as well as things which take on symbolic value – reflecting status (like office size or a car-park spot) or recognition (like 'employee of the month' plaques, team badges and so on).

Factors shaping organisational culture

6.25   An organisation's culture is often shaped by its history. Since cultures develop over time and are not easy to change, they often reflect the values of the era in which the organisation was founded (hence the persistence of 'old-fashioned' bureaucratic cultures) and/or of the organisation's founder. Myths and stories about the 'heroic' early days (or 'Golden Ages') of the organisation give further power to original values.

6.26   An organisation's culture is partly shaped by its environment, as it will adopt elements of the other cultural spheres (nation, region and industry sector) in which it operates. It will also embrace some of the cultural values of influential individuals and groups within the organisation: the cultures of particular professional or occupational groups, social classes and so on. *Charles Handy* noted that: 'Organisations are as different and varied as nations and societies of the world. They have differing cultures … affected by events of the past and the climate of the present, by the technology of the type of work, by their aims and the type of people who work in them.'

6.27   Managers and leaders can have a strong influence on organisational culture, because they are in a position to model values and behaviours – and they have the power to influence the behaviours (and sometimes also the underlying attitudes) of subordinates. This is the basis of deliberate culture-change initiatives, as we will see later in the chapter. At the same time, organisations with a strong culture tend to recruit managers who conform to that culture, so that the 'management culture' reflects – rather than shapes – the culture of the organisation.

A model of cultural types

6.28   R Harrison ('Understanding your organisation's character': *Harvard Business Review)* suggested that organisations could be classified into four types, differentiated by their structures, processes and management methods – and possessing, as a consequence, distinct cultural features: Table 1.4. The classification was later popularised by Charles Handy (*Gods of Management)* using the analogy of different ancient Greek gods.

Table 1.4 *Harrison/Handy's four cultural types*

CULTURE	KEY FEATURES	ADVANTAGES/DISADVANTAGES
Power culture (Zeus)	• Power centred in a key figure, owner or founder • Control through direct personal communication Little formalisation, rules or procedures	• Suits small, entrepreneurial organisations of like-minded people • Enables the organisation to adapt quickly in response to change
Role culture (Apollo)	• Classical, rational organisation (bureaucracy) • Formalised, impersonal: authority based on position, function; conformity to rules and procedures	• Efficient for large organisations in stable environments • Inability to change or innovate, owing to rigidity
Task culture (Athena)	• Management directed at outputs and results • Team-based organisation: horizontally structured, flexible • Valuing expertise, communication, collaboration	• Fosters focus on results and customer • Involves and empowers staff • Can be expensive (securing expertise, consensus decision-making)
Person culture (Dionysus)	• Serves the interests of individuals: eg barristers working through chambers • Management function administrative and supportive, rather than directive (eg bursars or registrars)	• Supports individual talent and interests • Rare in practice

6.29 One important point to note about this classification is the link between structure and culture. A bureaucratic structure will reflect (and be reflected by) a formalised, impersonal culture. A project structure will reflect (and be reflected by) a results-focused, collaborative culture and so on. It is not easy to change culture without addressing structural issues – and *vice versa*.

6.30 Another important point to note is that these are only classifications. Not every organisation will correspond to a particular 'type' – and different cultures may develop in different parts of the same organisation. The procurement and supply function may be a role culture – while the design or marketing department is more of a task culture, say.

The value of 'strong' culture

6.31 The importance of organisation culture for management was highlighted by Tom Peters and Robert Waterman, in their influential study of successful corporations: *In Search of Excellence* (1982). One of the key features of excellent companies (which consistently produce commercially viable new products and respond effectively to change) was their use of organisation culture to guide business processes and to motivate employees.

6.32 Both *Peters and Waterman* and *Terence Deal and Alan Kennedy* argued that cultural strength is a powerful tool for shaping the behaviour and success of an organisation. Not all organisation cultures are 'strong' – but those that *are* contribute to improved business performance.

6.33 This school of thought defined 'strong' cultures as those in which key values were widely shared and intensely held, and in which employees allowed themselves to be guided by them. In other words, as summarised by *Huczynski and Buchanan*: 'Strength refers to the degree to which employees share a commitment to a range of goals and values espoused by management, and have a high level of motivation to achieve them.'

6.34 So how does 'strong' culture improve business performance? Peters and Waterman argued as follows.

- A handful of widely shared, strongly held guiding values can replace rules, guidelines and supervision: focusing employees' attention on strategic aims such as quality, innovation and customer service, and empowering them to take initiative and responsibility in pursuit of those aims. This reduces rigidity, increases flexibility, enables change (on the basis that if values change, behaviour will follow) and develops people.

- Strong culture increases employee job satisfaction, loyalty and commitment. People need both to feel part of something meaningful and to 'shine' as stars in their own right: strong culture can satisfy both needs, by emphasising the 'family' nature of the enterprise, by building myths to reinforce the 'heroic' nature of the enterprise and by using value-laden symbols as rewards and incentives.

6.35 Strong culture is an attractive and influential idea, but empirical research has failed to show any strong correlation between strong culture and economic success. In other words, strong-culture organisations were not significantly more successful than weak-culture organisations. Nor was there any proof that culture was the determining factor in 'excellent' companies, as opposed to other organisational, market or environmental factors.

How do you change a culture?

6.36 Cultures which are negative, unsuited to changing requirements or otherwise failing or dysfunctional can be changed. The key tools of cultural change include the following.

- Consistent expression and modelling of the new values by management (from the top down), leaders and influencers (who may need to be co-opted to the initiative by those in authority)
- Changing underlying values and beliefs, through communication, education and involvement of employees in discussing the need for new ideas and behaviours: spreading new values and beliefs and encouraging employees to 'own' them (through incentives, co-opting people to teach others and so on); and reinforcing the change (through implementation, recognition and rewards).
- Use of human resource management mechanisms to reinforce the changes: making the new values and behaviours criteria for recruitment and selection, appraisal and reward; including them in competency profiles and learning needs assessments for training and development planning; and so on. (These mechanisms are important because the organisation may need to bring in new people who will 'fit' the new culture – and squeeze out those who don't 'fit'.)

Chapter summary

- An organisation is a social arrangement for the controlled performance of collective goals.
- Organisational behaviour includes the behaviour of the people within an organisation, but also the processes of management and leadership, the systems operating within the organisation, and factors in the outside environment.
- There is a psychological contract between an organisation and its employees, describing the expectations of each party.
- Effective management involves satisfying the needs of people at work, creating a positive organisational environment, and achieving strategic objectives.
- Gareth Morgan identifies eight metaphors, each of which highlights an aspect of organisations: machine; biological organism; brain; culture; political system; psychic prison; flux and transformation; instrument of domination.
- An organisation's structure is 'the sum total of the ways in which it divides its labour into distinct tasks and then achieves co-ordination among them'.
- The external environment exerts an influence on an organisation in three ways: it presents threats; it is the source of resources; it contains stakeholders.
- Culture is 'the collective programming of the mind which distinguishes the members of one category of people from another'. Organisational culture is 'a pattern of beliefs and expectations shared by the organisation's members, and which produce norms that powerfully shape the behaviour of individuals and groups in the organisation'.

Self-test questions

Numbers in brackets refer to the paragraphs where you can check your answers.

1 Define 'organisational behaviour'. (1.5)

2 List ways in which organisations interact with their external environments. (1.18)

3 In relation to the 'psychological contract', list ways in which (a) employees and (b) employers may be expected to act. (2.5, 2.6)

4 Explain how the changing business environment has led to changes in the psychological contract. (2.12, 2.13)

5 List Fayol's five functions of management. (3.4)

6 List Mintzberg's ten managerial roles. (Table 1.1)

7 List reasons why people form organisations. (4.2)

8 List some modern trends leading to increasing flexibility of organisational structure. (4.16)

9 Explain three ways in which an organisation is affected by its external environment. (5.4)

10 What are the seven categories of environmental factors referred to by the acronym STEEPLE? (Table 1.2)

11 Sketch the elements of culture as identified by Trompenaars. (Figure 1.3)

12 List the seven elements in the cultural web (J, S & W). (6.23)

CHAPTER 2

Theories of Organisation and Management

Assessment criteria and indicative content

1.3 Analyse the origins of management and organisational behaviour

- Classical approaches to organisational behaviour and management
- The development and application of scientific management
- Bureaucracy in organisational design and structure
- The human relations approach

1.4 Analyse the main contemporary approaches to management and organisational behaviour

- Organisations as a 'socio-technical' system
- The systems approach to organisational behaviour
- The contingency approach
- Postmodernism in organisations

Section headings

1. Overview of organisation and management theory
2. Classical approaches
3. The human relations approach
4. The systems approach
5. The contingency approach
6. The postmodern organisation

Introduction

In the previous chapter, we introduced some of the key elements and concepts in organisational behaviour. We also noted that theories and perspectives on organisation and management have developed over time.

In this chapter we trace some of the major developments in organisation and management theory and research – what we might call 'schools' of management thought – in order to explain the origins of today's focus on ideas (and practices) such as teamwork, leadership, motivation, employee development and change management.

We will start with an overview, and then explore the major strands of thinking in more or less chronological order, as they developed: drawing out core themes and their relevance for modern management.

1   Overview of organisation and management theory

1.1   In this chapter we will look at some of the key developments in organisational theory over time, and their influence on how organisations are configured and managed. The general flow of these developments has been via:

- A focus on universal principles to achieve the 'one best way' of organisation, primarily directed at production efficiency ('classical' organisation approaches, such as bureaucracy) *towards*
- A focus on adapting the organisation to changing environments and demands, primarily through key values of human relations and flexibility ('modern' approaches, including the human relations and contingency schools of thought).

1.2   Huczynski and Buchanan (*Organisational Behaviour*) argue that 'postmodern' organisation is now developing as a new paradigm, in response to the increasingly turbulent external environment. Although it is more an ideal concept than an existing reality, it embodies maximising structural and cultural flexibility through a focus on information flow, employee empowerment and responsiveness.

1.3   Huczynski and Buchanan summarise the general development of organisation theories and forms as a reflection of the 'classical', 'modern' and 'postmodern' thinking of different eras: Table 2.1.

Table 2.1 *Classical, modern and postmodern organisational forms*

	CLASSICAL	MODERN	POSTMODERN
Approximate period	1880–1970 (the industrial age)	1970–1990 (the technological age)	1990– (the information age)
Organisation metaphor	Machine	Open system	Flexible tool
Organisation structure	Rigid, hierarchical chain of authority	Decentralised: delegated authority and local units	Not important: action, not 'design'
Focus	Internal processes	Human relations	Adaptability and innovation
Production focus	Mass production: efficiency	Customisation: meeting customer demands	Time to market: speed of response
Work organisation	Routine, repetitive work	Teamworking	Entrepreneurial units
Human resource	Full-time employees	Flexible working patterns	Networks, sub-contractors
Control mechanisms	Direct supervision, rules and procedures	Decentralisation: local problem-solving	Not important: results, not rules
Key values	Control and predictability	Quality, customer service	Change, flux, quick decisions
Approach	Find the 'one best way' (prescriptive approach)	Find 'best fit' (contingency approach)	Maximise responsiveness
Strategy for uncertainty	Avoid	Manage	Exploit

1.4   Mullins similarly gives a broad survey of dominant paradigms (belief systems) in organisational behaviour, sourced from Hamid Bouchikhi & John R Kimberly ('The Customized Workplace', in *Management 21C*): Table 2.2.

Table 2.2 *Changing paradigms of management principles and techniques*

	19TH CENTURY	20TH CENTURY	21ST CENTURY
Theory of personhood	Interchangeable muscle and energy	A subordinate with a hierarchy of needs	Autonomous and reflexive individual
Information and knowledge	The province of management alone	Management-dominated and shared on a limited basis	Widely diffused
The purpose of work	Survival	Accumulation of wealth and social status	Part of a strategic life plan
Identification	With the firm and/or with the working class	With a social group and/or the firm	The disenfranchised self
Conflict	Disruptive and to be avoided	Disruptive but tolerated and can be settled through collective bargaining	A normal part of life
Division of labour	Managers decide, employees execute	Managers decide, employees execute thoughtfully	Employees and managers decide and execute
Power	Concentrated at the top	Limited, functional sharing and empowerment	Diffused and shared

1.5 In practice, as Huczynski and Buchanan note, change is never this clear-cut, in terms of dates or features. It would be wrong to think of a smooth, linear progression from one position to another according to well-defined environmental demands. Elements of 'classical' organisation exist today (bureaucracies, for example, are surprisingly resilient), and the 'postmodern' idea of multi-skilled, empowered, entrepreneurial, networked teamworking is not yet much in evidence. Nor (as we will see) would it necessarily be the most appropriate organisational form in all circumstances.

1.6 We will now look in more detail at some of the main approaches or 'schools' of organisation and management theory, in broadly chronological order: Figure 2.1.

Figure 2.1 *Developing 'schools' of organisation and management*

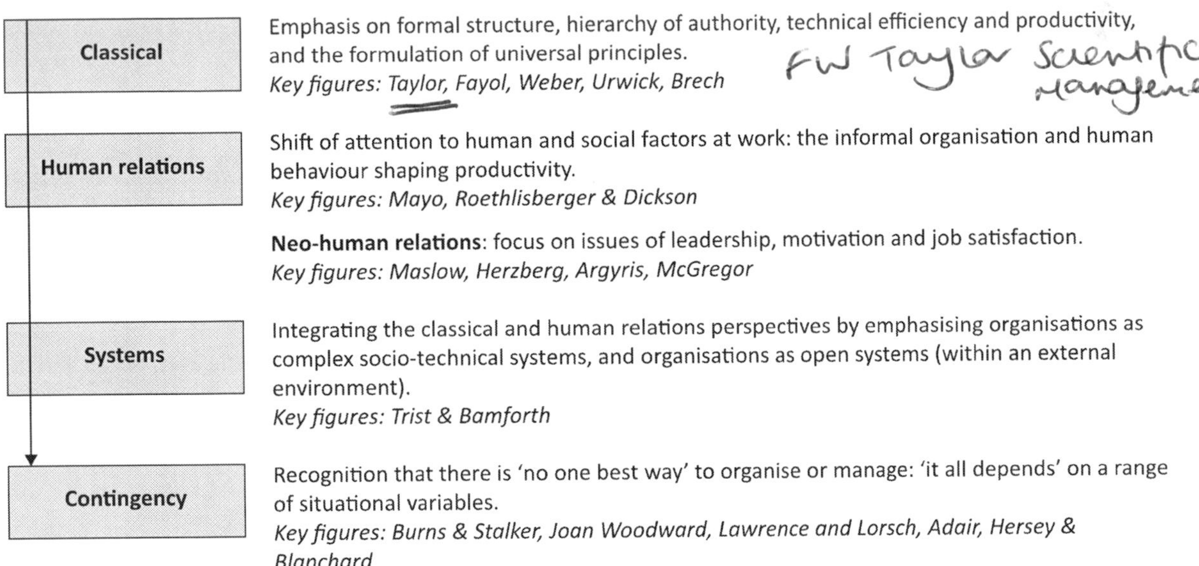

Classical
Emphasis on formal structure, hierarchy of authority, technical efficiency and productivity, and the formulation of universal principles.
Key figures: Taylor, Fayol, Weber, Urwick, Brech

Human relations
Shift of attention to human and social factors at work: the informal organisation and human behaviour shaping productivity.
Key figures: Mayo, Roethlisberger & Dickson

Neo-human relations: focus on issues of leadership, motivation and job satisfaction.
Key figures: Maslow, Herzberg, Argyris, McGregor

Systems
Integrating the classical and human relations perspectives by emphasising organisations as complex socio-technical systems, and organisations as open systems (within an external environment).
Key figures: Trist & Bamforth

Contingency
Recognition that there is 'no one best way' to organise or manage: 'it all depends' on a range of situational variables.
Key figures: Burns & Stalker, Joan Woodward, Lawrence and Lorsch, Adair, Hersey & Blanchard

2 Classical approaches

2.1 The 'classical' school is identified with writers such as FW Taylor, Henri Fayol and Max Weber who were pioneers of organisation and management theory. They were primarily interested in work organisation (division of work, specialisation, roles and responsibilities, co-ordination and so on), organisation structure (the hierarchy of authority and formal organisational relationships) and the formulation of universal principles of management, based on rationality and the pursuit of order, control, productivity and efficiency.

Scientific management: FW Taylor

2.2 The emphasis in this period (1880–1930) was on the efficiency of physical production. Organisations were continually looking for ways to become more efficient and prevent waste: focusing on increasing the productivity of individual workers, mainly through the structuring of work and the use of monetary incentives linked to output. The industrial revolution resulted in standardisation of production and the introduction of the assembly line: a time of large-scale industrial re-organisation, the emergence of large organisations, and the development of industrial technology.

2.3 Fredrick W Taylor pioneered the ideas of scientific management as a management consultant to the Bethlehem Steel Corporation. The ideological underpinnings of scientific management can be illustrated using the following quotes from Taylor.

- 'Management should be a science, resting on well organised, clearly defined and fixed principles, instead of depending on more or less hazy ideas'.
- 'The principal object of management should be to secure the maximum prosperity for the employer, coupled with the maximum prosperity for each employee.'
  (If productivity were increased then both employer and employees could enjoy a larger piece of a larger cake: piece-rate pay systems were designed with this in mind. Taylor firmly believed that workers had a purely economic or instrumental orientation to work.)

2.4 The key features of scientific management were as follows.

- Recognise a clear-cut division of responsibility and work between management (planning and organising) and workers (executing work).
- Develop a science for each element of work, to replace the old rule-of-thumb method: the best way of doing a job.
- Apply work-study techniques to establish the most efficient operations, motions and processes by which a task could be accomplished.
- Redesign jobs so that each worker carried out only one job operation (rather than sequences of operations within the task) as a specialised job: the assembly-line approach, also identified as the 'micro-division' of labour.
- Scientifically select and train workers to ensure all of the work being done is in accordance with the principles of scientific management.

2.5 Taylor's methods led to spectacular results in terms of efficiency and output, and focused attention on the 'science' (systematic formulation of principles and techniques) of organisation and management. Later management writers appraised scientific management as follows.

- It has contributed a useful philosophy of worker and work. 'As long as industrial society endures, we shall never lose again the insight that human work can be studied systematically, can be analysed, can be improved by work on its elementary parts.' (Drucker, *The Practice of Management*) Drucker also argued that Taylor's ideas on output-related rewards, the removal of physical strain from work, the development of workers to undertake their tasks efficiently, and the duty of management to help workers provided a useful orientation to positive industrial relations.
- However, the micro-division of labour has been found to be profoundly unsatisfying to workers (owing

to rigid control, removal of discretion, and de-skilling of the work) – despite financial incentives. 'By the end of the scientific management period, the worker has been reduced to the role of an impersonal cog in the machine of production. His work became more and more narrowly specialised until he had little appreciation for his contribution to the total product' (Hicks). Early trials of scientific management were followed by strikes, and attitude surveys revealed hostility to the methods used.

- The rigidity and depersonalisation of the approach precludes concepts such as leadership, empowerment, flexibility and commitment, which are now considered essential in the successful management of *change*. Managers effectively 'affirmed efficiency over collaboration, quantity over quality and cost controls over customer service' *(Kenneth Cloke & Joan Goldsmith, The End of Management)* – directly contrary to the values underpinning competitive advantage and added value in the modern environment.

2.6 Nevertheless, elements of scientific management practice can still be seen in modern management and organisation, for example in:

- The use of efficiency studies and work-study techniques, to improve the efficiency of processes and procedures, and the application of ergonomics to remove physical strain from work tasks and motions
- Assembly-line production processes, machine tool automation and systematic production control (eg Six Sigma methods)
- The use of payment-by-results (PBR) schemes
- The continuance of intrinsically unsatisfying jobs (with molecularised work design, minimal training, close supervision and tightly timed work activities), justified by purely financial productivity incentives (piece-rates or performance-related pay). You might argue that this can be seen in fast-food outlets (with programmed cash registers, precise procedures, timed operations, training of workers to do operations under specified and close supervision) and call centres (where calls are scripted, timed and monitored, discretion is eliminated by administration software, and staff are closely controlled).

2.7 Call centres have been explicitly classified as 'white collar Taylorism', and even as the 'dark, satanic mills' of the 21st century (*People Management*, 1999). Even the more progressive approaches to call centres continue to be based on careful selection and training of individuals to 'fit' the intensity of the environment and the highly programmed work (rather than addressing these issues), and to rely on financial incentives to attract and retain staff. As Huczynski and Buchanan note, there is less talk of 'quality of working life' when there is little work to be had … .

Principles of management: Henri Fayol

2.8 Henri Fayol (1841–1925) was a French industrialist who popularised the concept of the 'universality of management principles'. His focus was the structure and processes of the formal organisation, and the rational principles by which it could be most effectively directed.

2.9 Fayol suggested that management consisted of five functions: planning, organising, 'commanding' (managing staff), coordination and control. This classification is still used to discuss the role of management in organisations – although later approaches have emphasised the need to supplement 'commanding' with more complex interpersonal processes such as communicating and motivating, inspiring and influencing.

2.10 Although Fayol recognised that 'seldom do we have to apply the same principle twice in identical conditions' and that 'allowance must be made for different changing circumstances', he proposed fourteen rational principles of organisation and management.

- *Division of work.* Work should be divided and allocated rationally on the basis of skill or resource specialisation, in order to produce more and better outputs.
- *Scalar chain of authority.* Authority should flow vertically down a clear 'chain of command', running from the top of the organisation to the bottom, via defined lines which are also the organisation's formal channels of communication.

- *Correspondence of authority and responsibility:* authority (the right to make and implement decisions) should be commensurate with responsibility (the liability to be called to account for the results of decisions).
- *Appropriate centralisation.* Decisions should be taken at the top of the organisation, where appropriate, and should 'cascade down' to lower levels.
- *Unity of command.* For any action, a subordinate should receive orders from only one boss. Fayol saw dual command as a disease (whether caused by imperfect demarcation between departments or by superiors ignoring the proper channels of authority).
- *Unity of direction.* There should be one head and one plan for each activity, so that efforts can be coordinated towards the same objective.
- *Initiative.* Employees should be encouraged to use discretion, within the bounds of their authority.
- *Subordination of individual interests.* The interest of any one employee or group should not prevail over the interests of the organisation as a whole.
- *Discipline.* Expected standards of conduct should be clearly formulated and understood, with fair and systematic disciplinary policies to encourage compliance.
- *Order.* People and resources should reliably be where they are supposed to be, and behave in agreed ways.
- *Stability of personnel.* There should be continuity of employment, where possible, to maintain consistency of performance.
- *Equity.* Policies for the treatment of people at work should be just and fair.
- *Remuneration.* Rewards should be fair and equitable, and should satisfy the needs of the employee (for an adequate livelihood) and the employer (enabling the organisation to attract, retain and motivate good quality people).
- *Esprit de corps.* Harmony, co-operation and teamwork are essential to promote both discipline and morale.

2.11 Lyndall Urwick, the leading British proponent of classical management principles, suggested a similar set of organisation principles: specialisation; the scalar chain; unity of command; the correspondence of authority and responsibility; the span of control (an optimum number of subordinates reporting to each superior to enable effective management); reporting by exception (decisions to be taken as far down the scalar chain as possible, with reference back limited to deviations from plan); objective (structures and processes should only exist if they contribute to the organisation's objectives and purposes); and scientific method (decisions to be taken rationally on the basis of data).

2.12 You might note that some of the key principles of classical management have been challenged by modern concepts such as: cross-functional project working; matrix structures (eg product or brand management); self-managed teamworking and empowerment; multi-skilling; and a more general recognition that order and rationality are limited in turbulent, people-based business environments.

Bureaucracy: Max Weber

2.13 Max Weber, a German sociologist, is the writer most associated with the concept of bureaucracy as an organisational form. He defined it as 'a continuous organisation of official functions, bound by rules'.

2.14 Bureaucracy is a pure application of rational organisational principles and of a rational and legal understanding of authority as the function of a role and position in the organisation – not an interpersonal process. Although the word has unpleasant associations to the modern ear, Weber *(The Theory of Social and Economic Organisation)* claimed that bureaucracy is technically the most efficient form of organisation: 'from a purely technical point of view, capable of attaining the highest degree of efficiency and … in this sense formally the most rational means of carrying out imperative control over human beings.'

2.15 Interest in bureaucracy was stimulated by the growth in size and complexity of organisations, creating a demand for administrative order, efficiency and control.

2.16   Weber specified several general characteristics of bureaucracy.

- *Hierarchy of authority:* each lower office is under the direct control and supervision of a higher one. There are distinct levels of managerial authority, and a clear distinction between management and workers.
- *Specialisation:* work is divided into technically specialised functions, allocated as official duties to defined positions in the organisation structure.
- *System of rules:* employees work within laid-down rules and regulations, according to formal procedures. This achieves consistency and uniformity of decisions and actions, and supports co-ordinated activity.
- *Impersonality:* There is nothing 'personal' or subjective about the application of authority, decisions made, or the distribution of resources and privileges: they are rationally and objectively determined by the system of rules.
- *Rationality:* 'jurisdictional areas' (areas of authority) are determined rationally. The hierarchy of authority, duties and responsibilities and measures of performance are clearly defined (eg in job descriptions).
- *Uniformity:* standardised performance of tasks is expected, regardless of who carries them out.
- *Technical ability:* employment by the organisation is based on technical qualification.
- *Stability:* rules, structures and continuity (irrespective of change of membership) removes ambiguity and creates a stable environment.

2.17   Weber emphasised the technical superiority of such a system. 'Precision, speed, freedom from ambiguity, knowledge of files, continuity, discretion, unity, strict subordination, reduction of friction and of material and personal cost – these are raised to the optimum point in the strictly bureaucratic administration.' You might also recognise the advantages of bureaucratic principles for public sector organisations, where there is a need for public accountability, procedural regularity and consistent treatment. However, Weber himself also acknowledged the 'deadening' effect of bureaucracy as a culture, deploring an organisation of 'little cogs, little men, clinging to little jobs and striving towards bigger ones'.

2.18   The very strength of bureaucratic organisation in creating rationality and stability may be seen as a weakness in environments characterised by ambiguity and change. Common criticisms of bureaucracy include the following.

- Long channels of authority and communication (referring decisions back to the top) lengthen the decision-making process, making bureaucracies notoriously inflexible and poor at responding to customer demands.
- Conformity and uniformity create ritualism and formalism, which create further rigidity and unresponsiveness, and suppress creativity, initiative and innovation.
- The personal growth of individuals is inhibited, because there is no room for discretion, initiative or trial-and-error learning. Chris Argyris *(Integrating the Individual and the Organisation)* argued that bureaucracy restricts the psychological growth of individuals (fostered by responsibility, challenge, commitment, opportunities for development and so on), causing frustration and de-motivation. (However, it should be recognised that bureaucracies tend to attract, select and retain people with a tolerance for such conditions.)
- The rigidity of centralised decision-making makes it insensitive to feedback, unable to learn, and unable to respond to changing demands and environments. Michel Crozier *(The Bureaucratic Phenomenon)* suggests that bureaucracies adjust only when forced to do so by serious problems – by which time, change is difficult, traumatic and resisted by the culture.
- Rules originally designed for efficiency take on a significance which is unrelated to the organisation's objectives. Rules and 'red tape' (record keeping and paperwork) are adhered to for their own sake, even if unhelpful.
- People tend to justify poor service by citing rules, procedures and job descriptions. They do not feel personally responsible for quality or customer satisfaction.

- Reliance on positional authority and impersonal relationships can lead to inflexible, stereotypical behaviours and lack of responsiveness to human factors.

2.19 In fast-changing and competitive environments, the dysfunctions of bureaucracy must be addressed to some extent. This has created a trend towards greater flexibility (which we will discuss further, later in the chapter) through strategies such as:

- Downsizing organisations, or 'chunking': breaking organisation structures down into smaller units such as teams or autonomous local branches.
- Decentralising authority, or delegating – especially to customer-facing units, in order to increase initiative and responsibility, and to shorten decision-making processes. This may also involve the removal (or reappraisal) of rules and controls.
- Decreasing the rigidity of specialisation, eg by using multifunctional teams, multi-skilling, and role or competence analysis as an alternative to job descriptions.
- Improving structural communication mechanisms in all directions (eg with cross-functional teamworking and meetings, performance management systems, and so on).
- Emphasising quality, customer service and flexibility as key cultural values (at least in customer-facing units of the business), reinforced by staff selection, development and reward.

2.20 Bureaucracy has been identified as a 'mechanistic' style of organisation (taking the metaphor of the organisation as machine) in contrast to a more flexible 'organic' or 'organismic' style (the organisation as a living organism), in the terminology of Burns and Stalker (discussed in Section 4 of this Chapter).

3 The human relations approach

3.1 The human relations approach developed to a large extent as a reaction to the dehumanising aspects of the approaches previously described. In the early 1920s, managers and academics were becoming increasingly aware of signs of worker alienation in the face of impersonalisation and standardisation. Elton Mayo's work on the famous Hawthorne experiments gave birth to the human relations movement which dominated the field of organisational behaviour during the 1940s and 1950s.

Elton Mayo and the 'Hawthorne Effect'

3.2 Experiments were carried out between 1927 and 1937 at the Hawthorne plant of the Western Electric Company by Fritz Roethlisberger and William J Dickson, under the general direction of Harvard academic Elton Mayo (1880–1949). These experiments have become known as **The Hawthorne Experiments**.

3.3 The experiments arose from an attempt by Western Electric to find out the effects on morale and productivity of changes in lighting intensity (*The Illumination Studies*). A group of female operatives (the experimental group) were placed in a room with variable lighting, while others (the control group) were placed in a room with normal, consistent lighting, To the astonishment of management, productivity shot up in both rooms. When the lighting was then worsened in the first room, not only did productivity continue to rise in that room – but it also rose still further in the control room. Mayo was called in to investigate the 'mystery factor' at work in the groups.

3.4 The Hawthorne Studies consisted of four stages.

- **The Relay Assembly Room.** Six women were segregated in a different room, where they were observed under varied working conditions. Records were kept of working conditions, lighting, heating and rest periods, and the women's private lives. In most cases, the women were consulted in advance about each change. Productivity rose – whether the changes were positive or negative. It was apparent that changes in conditions could not account for the changes in output. Mayo identified what was later called 'the Hawthorne Effect': productivity and morale appeared to be affected by the women's sense of being a group singled out for attention and consultation. 'Management, by consultation with the girl workers, by clear explanation of the proposed experiments and the reasons for them, by accepting the workers' verdict in several instances, unwittingly scored a success in two most important human matters – the girls became a self-governing team, and a team that co-operated wholeheartedly with management.' (Mayo).

- **Interview programme.** The company surveyed attitudes towards supervision, jobs and working conditions. The major conclusion was that relationships with people at work were important to employees – and that they valued the opportunity to have their voice heard by management.
- **The Bank Wiring Observation Room** (Roethlisberger & Dickson). Fourteen men were segregated from the department, and observed working under more or less normal conditions. The group developed a keen sense of its own identity, and developed its own norms of behaviour and standard amount of output (regarded as 'fair' for the pay received, rather than maximising potential earnings through the incentive scheme). Its behaviour became oriented towards its own group interests – 'fiddling' output reports to show constant volumes of daily production; using social pressure to control the output of over-performing and under-performing members; and sabotaging the efforts of an unpopular supervisor. The group had developed into a powerful, self-protecting informal organisation, which had to be carefully managed in order to secure its commitment to company goals.
- **Employee counselling.** Employee counselling was used to work through problems, and to improve relationships and personal adjustment at work, on an ongoing basis.

3.5 The Hawthorne Studies were the first major attempt to undertake genuine social research, and to redirect attention to the human factor at work. They proved the importance of employees' attitudes to work, to supervision and to working in groups – and the importance of managerial behaviour in worker motivation and performance.

3.6 The human relations school argued that an organisation was more than a formal structure or arrangement of functions. Mayo wrote: 'An organisation is a social system, a system of cliques, grapevines, informal status systems, rituals and a mixture of logical, non-logical and illogical behaviour'. The approach highlighted the need for managers to:

- Pay more attention to the needs of workers, not just tasks and processes
- Realise that the satisfaction that individuals gain from group membership may be equal to any rewards or incentives offered by management
- Organise and reward work around groups (or teams).

3.7 This approach has been enduringly popular, not least because of its apparent simplicity and a straightforward (and enthusiastically promoted) message. By modern standards of research, however, the Hawthorne studies were 'less than rigorous in many respects' (GA Cole, *Personnel Management)*. They have also been criticised for their narrow view, over-simplified theories and lack of awareness of additional factors (such as the different responses of the female and male groups due to gender power imbalances). A balanced evaluation of the studies' value admits that:

- The studies have had practical impact on organisation practice, in the application of human resource management approaches such as employee involvement, teamworking, facilitative leadership and positive employee relations.
- Mayo's human relations ideas were applied in the Western Electric Company – but didn't work! Once the counselling service was rolled out organisation-wide, the Hawthorne Effect appeared to be diluted (there was no longer a sense of special status arising from participation in an experiment). There was a general decline in productivity, and the counselling programme eventually dwindled for lack of enthusiasm.

3.8 Huczynski & Buchanan also address the question of whether a 'happy' group is also a productive one, as the human relations approach suggested. 'The Hawthorne studies signalled the birth of the human relations school of management... It was not until some time had passed that people started to question this relationship between productivity and satisfaction. Perhaps it had been a fortuitous coincidence rather than some iron law? Sociologists who reviewed the findings and compared them with other data swung to the former explanation.'

The neo-human relations approach

3.9 By the early 1960s the term 'organisational behaviour' began to emerge and a behaviouralist approach to management was pioneered by psychologists such as Abraham Maslow, Douglas McGregor, Chris Argyris and Frederick Herzberg. The 'neo-human relations' school differed from human relations in two important respects.

- It was concerned both with organisations (structure, tasks, reporting relationships) *and* people.
- It explored a wider range of human needs and motivations than simply social belonging, turning attention to the 'higher order' needs of people to develop themselves and fulfil their potential.

3.10 **Abraham Maslow,** for example, suggested a theory of individual motivation based on innate human needs, proposing that behaviour is driven by the need to satisfy those needs. **Frederick Herzberg** developed a more complex needs-based theory of motivation which emphasised the importance of the intrinsic rewards of work (variety, challenge, responsibility, development, self-actualisation) in motivating employees. He suggested that extrinsic rewards (such as pay, incentives and working conditions) could not satisfy or motivate workers in the long term, and developed alternative methods of job design to offer greater intrinsic rewards: job rotation (doing different jobs), job enlargement (building more task variety into a job) and job enrichment (building more challenge, responsibility and discretion into a job – ie empowerment).

3.11 **Douglas McGregor** criticised scientific management and bureaucracy on the grounds that they reflected simplistic managerial assumptions about workers and their motivations. He contrasted two extreme sets of assumptions, which he called Theory X and Theory Y.

- *Theory X* asserts that the average human being dislikes work and must be coerced, controlled, directed and/or bribed or threatened with punishment in order to get him to expend adequate effort towards the achievement of organisational goals. This is what the worker prefers: he avoids responsibility in favour of security.
- *Theory Y* asserts that the average human being does not dislike work, which can be a source of satisfaction. People can exercise self-direction and self-control to achieve objectives to which they are committed, and – if encouraged – will not only *accept* but *seek* responsibility.

3.12 McGregor's point is that such assumptions are self-fulfilling prophecies: managerial assumptions lead managers to treat people in a certain way – and people learn to behave according to how they are treated. If you treat employees as if Theory X were true (using rules, detailed supervision, low-discretion jobs and so on), they will begin to behave accordingly: it is negative experience at work that fosters lack of ambition and the need for security. If you treat people as if Theory Y were true (delegating responsibility, consulting and involving), they will rise to the challenge.

3.13 Recognition of people as the key organisational resource focused attention on organisational configurations which offered greater job satisfaction and harnessed the energy, ability and commitment of employees for the benefit of organisational efficiency, flexibility and innovation.

- *Flatter organisation structures*, with fewer layers and authority decentralised to lower levels.
- *Teamworking*, to fulfil social needs and create the synergy of pooled skills and expertise.
- *Cross-functional and multi-skilled working*, allowing workers to perform larger and more meaningful parts of the task.

3.14 We will discuss a number of neo-human relations theories in Chapter 5.

4 The systems approach

Organisations as open systems

4.1 Ludvig van Bertalanffy, a pioneer of general systems theory in the 1950s, defined a 'system' as 'an organised or complex whole' and 'organised complexity'. A system might also be defined as 'an entity which consists of interdependent parts', so that viewing an organisation as a system emphasises the inter-relationships of these interacting parts and processes.

4.2 General systems theory makes a distinction between open and closed systems.

- A closed system is one which is isolated from its environment and independent of it, so that no external influences affect the behaviour of the system (the way it operates) nor does the system exert any influence on its environment.

- An open system is a system which is connected to and interacts with its environment. It takes in as inputs influences (or 'energy') from its environment (or outputs from other systems) and converts these into outputs (or inputs to other systems). Feedback enables a system to change its behaviour in order to stay stable in a changing environment: a process called 'homeostasis'.

4.3 As we saw in Chapter 1, an organisation can be seen as an open system. Such a system must remain sensitive to its external environment, with which it is in constant interaction: it must respond to threats and opportunities, restrictions and challenges posed by external environmental factors. Changes in inputs will influence the conversion process, which in turn will influence outputs.

Organisations as a 'socio-technical' system

4.4 Eric Trist and his associates at the Tavistock Institute of Human Relations developed the proposition that an organisation is a 'structured socio-technical system'. Such a system consists of at least two major subsystems: a technological system (including task organisation, methods, tools and technology) and a social system (the people in the organisation and how they behave and interact). Organisation should aim to find a 'fit' that will maximise technical efficiency *and* human needs.

4.5 Mullins suggests five basic sub-systems as the basis for analysing work organisation and activities, within the context of the external organisational environment.

- **Task**: the nature of the organisation's inputs and outputs and the work activities to be carried out as part of the conversion process
- **Technology**: the manner in which organisational tasks are carried out: the materials, equipment, systems and procedures used in the conversion process
- **Structure**: the patterns of organisation, division of labour, co-ordination, authority relationships and communication channels by which activities are carried out
- **People**: the nature of the people undertaking the activities: their personality, attitudes, competencies, needs and expectations, relationships, behaviours and so on (including dynamics such as teamworking, communication, motivation and leadership)
- **Management**: the co-ordination of the other sub-systems, and the direction of organisational activities as an integrated whole.

Eric Trist and Ken Bamforth

4.6 Trist *et al* (*Organisational Choice*) based their ideas on a study of the effects of changing technology in the Durham coal mines (the Longwall Coal Mining Study). Miners had been used to working in small autonomous teams. Each had its own place at the coal seam and was responsible for cutting coal, loading it into tubs for removal and propping up the roof as they advanced: each miner in the team was an all-rounder and could perform any of these tasks. Each team was paid as a group.

4.7   The Coal Board introduced new coal-cutting equipment, capable of cutting a long stretch of wall at a time – and changed the work organisation to match the technology. A new 'conventional longwall system' introduced three shifts (doing away with teams): one shift did the cutting; a second loaded the coal onto a moving conveyor belt; and a third moved the coal cutting equipment and conveyor forward and propped up the roof.

4.8   Immediate problems emerged. Within each specialised shift, some miners were more willing and able than others to carry out the work, and there were problems co-ordinating the work of the three shifts, requiring closer supervision. There was industrial unrest and a fall in productivity – and Trist *et al* were appointed to investigate.

4.9   Trist *et al* knew that productivity was linked to worker job satisfaction and motivation, and the ability of workers to associate their own extra effort with extra reward. 'It is difficult to see how these problems can be solved efficiently without restoring responsible autonomy to primary groups throughout the system and ensuring that each of these groups has a satisfying sub-whole as its work task, and some scope for flexibility.' They advocated an approach which they called 'composite autonomous group working': 'composite' in terms of the range of skills in the group as a whole (ie multi-skilling) and 'autonomous' in terms of self-determination (in regard to task organisation and allocation).

4.10   In the Durham coalfields, this took the form of the 'composite longwall method'. The new technology was retained, but the workforce was no longer divided for the three separate tasks. The team as a whole was given responsibility for the whole task and for assigning individuals to particular jobs: the group was given autonomy, self-regulation, multi-skilled roles and a 'whole' task to perform. This was psychologically and socially more rewarding – and also more efficient.

4.11   The socio-technical approach developed the understanding that:

- Although the new technology necessitated some change in work organisation, the advantages of technological improvements were offset by employee resistance to loss of the psycho-social benefits of working in groups.
- Work organisation is not wholly determined by technology, but by *organisational choices*: the social system has properties independent of the technical system, and can be designed so as to meet both technical demands *and* human needs. In other words, any given technical system can be operated by different social systems.
- The organisation must attempt to balance economic, technological and psycho-social needs, in its strategic decision-making about work organisation and methods.

Contribution of the systems approach

4.12   The contribution of the systems approach is as follows.

- It draws attention to the dynamic nature of organisations.
- It creates awareness of subsystems, each with goals which must be integrated. (Sub-optimisation, where subsystems pursue their own goals to the detriment of the system as a whole, is a feature of organisational behaviour.)
- It creates awareness of the inter-relatedness of aspects of the organisation, and a focus on the needs of the system as a whole. The socio-technical systems approach, in particular, focuses on the recognition that the 'people system' of the organisation is crucial in realising value from all its other subsystems (including technology), and that the psycho-social implications of organisational decisions must be taken into account.
- It focuses attention on the interrelationship between the organisation and its external environment. This may be particularly important in focusing attention outward (eg to customers). It also teaches managers to reject the deterministic idea that doing A will always cause B to happen, because of the unpredictability and uncontrollability of many inputs.

- It integrates the insights of the formal classical approach (focusing on technical and organisational requirements) and the informal human relations approach (focusing on psycho-social or human aspects), by seeing these as inter-related subsystems.

4.13 Systems thinking is based on an analogy, and as such cannot be stretched too far. However, it has an imaginative appeal, and provides a useful framework for thinking about the implications of environmental factors, structure and work organisation.

5 The contingency approach

5.1 The contingency approach developed as a reaction to the prescriptive ideas of the classical and human relations schools. Research by Tom Burns & Graham Stalker, Joan Woodward, P R Lawrence & J W Lorsch and others indicated that different forms of organisational structure could be equally successful, depending on the circumstances. Mullins suggests that the contingency approach can be seen as a form of 'if-then' relationship: 'If certain situational factors exist, then certain variables in organisation structure and systems of management are most appropriate'.

5.2 Contingency theory does not ignore the lessons learned from other schools, but suggests that the best way to manage and organise work depends on the circumstances – there is no 'one best way'. Contingency approaches seek to identify the internal and external variable factors that influence the effectiveness of organisation structures, cultures and leadership, and to explore how they can be adjusted for a 'best fit' with the demands of the particular situation.

5.3 As Huczynski & Buchanan put it: 'With the coming of contingency theory, organisational design ceased to be "off-the-shelf", but became tailored to the particular and specific needs of an organisation.' In essence, contingency theory is about organisational flexibility.

- Lawrence & Lorsch compared the structural characteristics of a 'high-performing' container firm, which existed in a relatively stable environment, and a 'high-performing' plastics firm which existed in a rapidly changing environment. They concluded that in a stable environment the most efficient structure was one in which the influence and authority of senior managers was high and of middle managers low. The *opposite*, however, was true of the dynamic environment.
- Joan Woodward's research with firms in Essex highlighted the importance of technology as a major factor contributing to variances in organisation structure: 'It appeared that different technologies imposed different kinds of demands on individuals and organisations and that these demands have to be met through an appropriate form of organisation'.

5.4 Contingency approaches to organisation assert that organisations may be structured in a variety of ways (as we saw briefly in Chapter 1), and the most appropriate organisation structure for a given situation will depend on factors such as the organisation's history and ownership; its size; the type of people it employs; the nature of its activity and associated technology; the demands of its market; and a range of factors in its external environment.

5.5 We will consider various contingency theories of this type in relation to management style, conflict handling and team leadership, in later chapters of this Course Book.

Burns and Stalker

5.6 Tom Burns and Graham Stalker (*The Management of Innovation*) argued that organisation structures and cultures should be adaptive: differing according to how stable or dynamic their market environments were. They categorised organisations along a continuum ranging from *mechanistic* to *organic*. Neither was intrinsically functional or dysfunctional; a structure's suitability depended on the stability of the market and the speed of change in the technology of the production process.

5.7 Mechanistic ('machine-like') organisations are bureaucratic. As discussed earlier, they are highly technically competent and efficient in stable conditions – but unsuited to conditions of change, because of their rigidity. They tend to delay (referring decisions 'higher up'), and to create new jobs, departments and committees to deal with new challenges and problems, perpetuating the structural complexity and formality.

5.8 Organic ('oganism-like') organisations can adapt more easily to changing conditions. They are typified by structural and cultural fluidity and flexibility, involving:

- A 'contributive' culture of information and skill sharing, encouraging versatility (rather than specialisation) and teamworking (rather than functional departmentation)
- A 'network' structure of authority and communication, allowing decentralisation and a range of lateral relationships (crossing functional boundaries) for coordination and self-control
- Job design that allows flexible definition of tasks according to the needs of the team and changing demands
- Focus on goals and outputs rather than processes.

The contribution of contingency theory

5.9 Awareness of the contingency approach will be valuable in the following ways.

- Encouraging managers to identify and define the particular variables in the situation they need to manage, and to devise situationally appropriate ways of handling them. A belief in universal principles and prescriptive 'off the shelf' solutions can hinder problem-solving and decision-making by obscuring some of the available alternatives – and by preventing managers from developing flexibility and judgement.
- Encouraging responsiveness and flexibility to changes in environmental factors through organisational structure and culture. Task performance and individual and group satisfaction are more important design criteria than permanence or unity of design type. Within a single organisation, there may be bureaucratic units side by side with task-focused, multi-skilled, self-managing teams (for example in the R & D function) which can respond to particular pressures and environmental volatility.

6 The postmodern organisation

6.1 According to Mullins, 'Postmodernism rejects a rational systems approach to our understanding of organisations and management and to accepted explanations of society and behaviour... The possibility of any kind of complete and coherent body of management knowledge has increasingly been brought into question... The idea of postmodernism... is arguably more of a generalised sociological concept rather than a specific approach to organisation and management, and ... appears to be of little interest or appeal to the practical manager.'

6.2 However, a postmodernist orientation can be helpful in:

- Recognising different viewpoints and paradigms in organisations: encouraging 'thinking outside the box' on organisational issues, and the consideration of divergent perspectives (potentially contributing to the management of diversity)
- Emphasising the need for organisations to be responsive, fluid and tolerant of turbulent change (without the trauma and frustration of trying to retain control over uncontrollable forces).

6.3 Huczynski and Buchanan argue that 'postmodern' organisation is developing as a new paradigm, in response to the increasingly turbulent external environment. Although it is more an ideal concept than an existing reality, it involves maximising structural and cultural fluidity through mechanisms such as:

- Multi-directional information flows, through networking (rather than formal communication channels).

- Permeable boundaries with the environment: organisational information-gathering, learning and responsiveness; use of subcontractors, freelance workers, networks, alliances.
- Downsizing and delayering to shorten decision processes and decentralise authority to front-line responsive units.
- Staff flexibility and empowerment: multi-skilling, team autonomy, motivation for commitment (rather than compliance), encouragement of entrepreneurship.
- Cultural tolerance of ambiguity, change and flexibility: de-emphasising rules, channels, procedures, job descriptions.

6.4   Huczynski and Buchanan describe *adhocracy* as 'a type of organisation design which is temporary, adaptive, creative – in contrast to bureaucracy, which tends to be permanent, rule-driven and inflexible.' Adhocracy would typically involve a loosely constructed network of temporary, flexible, multidisciplinary project teams. It is associated with innovation, creative thinking and organisational learning ('adhocracies explore, while bureaucracies exploit') – but also with disorder, ambiguity and possible loss of coherence and identity.

6.5   This pushing of organisational flexibility to extremes (what Tom Peters calls 'thriving on chaos') may be identified with the idea of the 'postmodern organisation', proposed in Section 1 of this chapter. Peters himself *(Thriving on Chaos)* advocates approaches such as 'chunking' and 'ungluing' structures – not just flattening the organisation structure, but destroying it! He cites successful businesses such as McKinsey and CNN as examples of loose networks of small, functionally versatile units that join and disband flexibly according to requirements; that find their own customers and generate their own projects; that continuously re-educate themselves through information-gathering.

Chapter summary

- In the 20th century, schools of management theory developed from classical (eg Taylor, Fayol), through human relations (eg Mayo) and systems theories (eg Trist and Bamforth), to contingency approaches (eg Burns & Stalker, Hersey & Blanchard).
- Classical theories included the scientific management approach pioneered by FW Taylor, the principles of management laid down by Fayol, and the bureaucratic model described by Weber.
- The human relations approach (Mayo) developed as a reaction to the dehumanising aspects of scientific management. There was a new emphasis on social aspects of the workplace.
- Trist and Bamforth developed the idea of organisations as socio-technical systems, drawing on their study of technology in the Durham coal mines.
- Eventually there was a reaction against the idea that one particular view of organisational management is superior in all circumstances. A number of researchers instead favoured a contingency approach: 'it all depends on the circumstances'.
- This trend has been taken even further in the postmodern view of organisations. This view emphasises the importance of maximising structural and cultural fluidity.

Self-test questions

Numbers in brackets refer to the paragraphs where you can check your answers.

1 Summarise the development of organisational management through the classical, human relations, systems, and contingency approaches. (Figure 2.1)

2 List key features of the scientific management approach. (2.4)

3 What are the five functions of management, according to Fayol? (2.9)

4 List as many of Fayol's 14 principles as you can. (2.10)

5 List general characteristics of bureaucracy, as identified by Weber. (2.16)

6 List the lessons for managers suggested by the human relations school. (3.6)

7 Distinguish between Theory X and Theory Y. (3.11)

8 An organisation can be regarded as a closed system. True or false? (4.3)

9 List contributions achieved by the systems approach to organisational management. (4.12)

10 Distinguish between mechanistic and organic organisations (Burns & Stalker). (5.7, 5.8)

11 List characteristics of the postmodern view of organisations. (6.3)

CHAPTER 3

Individual Difference and Diversity

Assessment criteria and indicative content

 Assess how the different behavioural characteristics of individuals can impact on their management in the procurement and supply function

- Understanding the differences among individuals
- Uniqueness and similarities between individuals
- Idiographic approaches to the development and measurement of individuals
- Emotional intelligence
- Diversity in organisations
- Managing diversity

Section headings

1   Individual differences
2   Personality and behaviour
3   Models of personality
4   Emotional intelligence
5   Diversity in organisations
6   Factors in individual work performance

Introduction

In this chapter, we begin our discussion of key variables and processes in individual behaviour at work – before going on to explore *group* behaviour in Chapters 6 and 7.

We start with some general comments on the nature of individual differences and similarities, and the implications of individual uniqueness for managers.

We then explore the concept of personality, which is one of the ways in which differences and similarities between individuals are described. The nomothetic approach to personality emphasises observable similarities (such as personality traits and types) which makes it possible for managers to deal with people 'in general', and to understand and possibly even predict their behaviour. The idiographic approach emphasises individual uniqueness and the development of personality over time, which may help managers to appreciate diversity.

Next, we turn to the issue of diversity (or difference), and how it can be effectively managed. Diversity is a much broader concept than 'equal opportunity' (which is covered in Chapter 11 on the regulatory framework), but we also focus here on issues of gender in the workplace.

Finally, we survey some of the factors that affect individual work performance, as an introduction to the following chapters on learning and motivation.

1 Individual differences

Individual uniqueness and similarity

1.1 It should be obvious from your own experience that people differ from each other, and that this presents a significant challenge to managers. People differ on many dimensions: their beliefs, values and attitudes (what they think and feel about things); their perceptions (how they 'see' things); how they behave in different situations (what they do and say); all arising from differences in their genetic and psychological pre-dispositions; ethnic origin; age; gender; upbringing; intelligence, aptitudes, education and interests; motivation; culture; present circumstances – and so on.

1.2 Some of these characteristics and background factors will be shared within a group. For example, a team may contain people of the same gender or age, from the same educational or professional background and culture. But the full range of inherited (nature) and environmental (nurture) factors interact in complex and diverse ways, accounting for individual differences.

1.3 Mullins argues that: 'Managers are required to be competent at selecting the individuals who will be valuable to the organisation. They need to be observant about the individuals who are performing well and have the potential to develop within the organisation. They also need to be able to value individual difference and be sensitive to contrasting needs. Finally, managers need to know themselves and understand their [own] uniqueness and the impact their personality has on others.'

1.4 One of the key attributes of so-called 'transformational' leaders is that they give people 'individual consideration' – and we will be looking specifically at managing diversity later in this chapter. But the fact is that managers cannot respond to individual uniqueness in its full complexity all the time. Fortunately, it is possible to identify ways in which people behave alike – and more or less consistently – so that we can deal with them in work and social situations. One of the concepts that allows us to do this is personality.

1.5 Even so, some psychological models focus on shared features and areas of largely inherited similarity between people (such as gender, intelligence or ability), attempting to identify personality 'types', and measure and compare individuals on these consistent dimensions. Others see all individuals as basically unique combinations of features and personality-shaping experiences, and seek only to describe each unique 'self' and its unique interaction with, and interpretation of, the world.

2 Personality and behaviour

2.1 Huczynski and Buchanan define personality as 'the psychological qualities that influence an individual's characteristic behaviour patterns, in a distinctive and consistent manner, across different situations and over time.' This raises several points which are important to an understanding of the concept of personality.

- It is an integrating concept, embracing how the individual relates to the environment in terms of psychological predispositions, learning, motivation and behaviour patterns.
- It focuses on stable or consistent properties: those that are 'characteristics' of an individual in different situations and at different times. Occasional or random behaviours do not demonstrate a 'tendency' which is useful to the consideration of personality.
- It focuses on the distinctive behaviour patterns of individuals, which may be identified and used consistently in comparisons between them.

2.2 There is an ongoing 'nature-nurture' debate about whether or how far the factors of heredity or environment influence personality. Theorists disagree on the relative importance of each factor and how (if at all) they relate to each other.

- Some psychologists (taking a nomothetic approach: see below) believe that personality is part of an individual's genetic endowment, and not significantly alterable by experience of social or environmental influences. People simply have certain psychological predispositions or preferences: however, they can still adapt their *behaviour*, learning and becoming skilled at practising behaviours which are not 'natural' to their personality, if required.

- Others (taking an idiographic approach: see below) suggest that as individuals experience life and interact with other people, their personality is shaped: behaviour is influenced by environmental, cultural and social factors. Individuals become 'socialised' to fit in with their environment, especially through early learning experiences: personality is both adaptive (designed to help the individual cope with environmental challenges) and adaptable (amenable to change).

2.3 There are two main – and fundamentally different – approaches to the study of personality.
- The **nomothetic** (law setting or law giving) approach
- The **idiographic** (writing about individuals) approach

Although the syllabus only explicitly mentions the idiographic approach, several of the concepts included in the indicative content are drawn from the nomothetic approach, so we will cover both here.

The nomothetic approach

2.4 The nomothetic approach is based on generalisation, to emphasise 'laws' or regularities in human behaviour, enabling personality characteristics to be identified, described and measured – with a view to understanding and (cautiously) predicting behaviour. Such an approach is useful in the selection, management, training and development of individuals in work organisations, as well as in making swift generalised judgements about people in interpersonal situations.

2.5 The nomothetic approach generally proceeds in the following way.

- Identifying the main areas or 'dimensions' in which personality can vary (eg introversion or extroversion, emotional stability or instability) – *assuming* that these are constants (qualitatively the same in any individual)
- Testing the personalities of groups of individuals, using self-response questionnaires, to derive scores for the personality dimension under analysis
- Constructing a personality profile for the individual. Scores on each dimension are compared with averages, to identify 'average' personalities and any pronounced deviation from the norm (in a statistical sense) in particular characteristics
- Formulating principles of personality and behaviour – *assuming* that personality is largely inherited and impervious to environmental factors

2.6 Nomothetic attempts to describe how personality works focus on two broad concepts: personality **traits** (attributes or qualities in an individual's personality which create a tendency to behave in certain ways) and personality **types** (distinct patterns or clusters of characteristics which reflect the psychological preferences of the individual).

- If we say that someone is 'sociable', for example, we are identifying a personality trait, which will make them respond to situations in predictable ways.
- To say that someone is 'an extrovert', however, is to identify a personality type, which brings with it a whole cluster of characteristics (sociable, expressive, impulsive, practical, active and so on).

2.7 Type theories of personality divide people into categories, which are defined as possessing common behaviour patterns. The trouble with 'types' is that they are too general, and do not do justice to the complexity and subtlety of individual differences. Most type models, however, recognise this, and emphasise (a) that preferences need not dictate behaviour, and (b) that no one 'type' is 'better' than another.

2.8 Trait theories of personality identify dispositions to behave in a particular way, or any consistently observable behaviour. (If you say a team member is 'always late', for example, you are identifying traits in their personality.) This assumes that there is a range of common traits which may be identified and compared, as like to like, in different individuals – but it also admits that different individuals possess different traits, and different individuals possess different strengths of the same traits. This may offer a more accurate reflection of the complexity of personality.

The idiographic approach

2.9 The idiographic approach is a dynamic and holistic approach which individualises, aiming to build up a detailed, complex picture of the individual's personality. It describes personality as a unified whole, and in terms of a person's own image and understanding of himself. Individuals are subjected to in-depth study, with data drawn from interviews, observation, letters, diaries, life histories and so on. Information from the individuals themselves is very important, using writing and talking, free association (such as inkblot tests), the interpretation of dreams and analysis of the imagination (eg 'thematic apperception tests' based on writing short imaginative stories in response to pictures, designed to allow the individual to project his personality onto the pictures through the stories).

2.10 The approach focuses on:

- The *uniqueness* of individuals: 'personality assessment', using traits and types, is regarded as insufficient to understand how individuals understand and respond to the world
- The *development* of the 'self' or self-concept through learning and adaptation to the environment. Idiographic theory assumes that people behave according to a self-understanding developed largely through social interaction: that is, through our evaluation of the effect of our behaviour on other people, and their expectations of, and attitudes and behaviours towards, us. This is a useful approach for understanding work-relevant processes such as learning, motivation and team relationships.

2.11 The idiographic approach focuses primarily on understanding *why* (or how) people are 'who they are'. The nomothetic approach focuses primarily on describing 'who' or 'what' people are. Mullins argues that in a work context, we tend to be more interested in understanding the 'what' of personality than the 'why', and the impact of various personality characteristics on performance at work. Most of the models of personality widely utilised in the workplace context are therefore nomothetic models, and we will look at some of the ones highlighted by the syllabus.

3 Models of personality

Eysenck's three dimensions of personality

3.1 British psychologist Hans Jurgen Eysenck *(Personality and Individual Differences)* developed a popular and influential nomothetic model of personality based on:

- Universal personality traits, measured using personality test questionnaires
- Trait clusters: the proposition that individuals who possess one particular trait are likely to possess certain other 'compatible' traits
- Personality types, formed by the pattern or cluster of traits.
- For Eysenck, personality is inherited, fundamentally unalterable and physiologically based: ie associated with the nervous system and other genetic and biological factors.

3.2   Eysenck's research identified two major areas in which variations in individual personality occur.

- The **'E' dimension:**
  - *Extroversion* (focusing attention on inner experiences). This includes traits such as expressiveness, impulsiveness, risk-taking, sociability, practicality, irresponsibility, activity
  - *Introversion* (focusing attention outward). This includes traits such as inactivity, carefulness, responsibility, control, reflectiveness, unsociability and inhibition
- The **'N' dimension:**
  - *Neuroticism* (emotional instability). This includes traits such as anxiety, guilt, obsessiveness, hypochondriasis (imaginary illness), unhappiness, lack of autonomy and low self esteem
  - *Stability*. This includes traits such as calm, freedom from guilt, casualness, sense of health, happiness, autonomy and high self esteem.

3.3   The Eysenck Personality Questionnaire (EPQ) asks mainly 'yes or no' questions for each dimension (plus some 'lie scale' questions to test the subject's overall honesty in answering questions). The scores on 'E' and 'N' are not correlated: you could be introverted and *either* neurotic or stable. This leads to four basic personality types:

- Sanguine (stable extrovert): talkative, responsive, lively, carefree (traits) – leading to a predisposition to certain types of behaviours (eg confident rapport building in a group situation)
- Choleric (unstable extrovert): impulsive, changeable, restless, excitable, aggressive
- Phlegmatic (stable introvert): calm, even-tempered, thoughtful
- Melancholic (unstable introvert): anxious, moody, pessimistic.

3.4   Questionnaires attempt to find questions that discriminate between individuals (not using those that everyone answers in the same way) and that *correlate* (appear to be measuring the same thing).

3.5   Despite this 'statistical' method, however, there is inevitable subjectivity involved in the wording of questions and interpretation of results. There are other limitations to the use of such tests. The hypothetical yes/no question may be irrelevant to the individual's experience, and inaccurate as a reflection of complex thought processes. The conditions of 'being tested' may falsify the response (eg where individuals give what they think is the 'normal', desirable or expected response). And the data are not, in any case, designed to *predict* individual behaviour (which would be most useful to a manager), but for *comparison.*

Cattell's 16PF Questionnaire

3.6   Raymond Cattell *(The Scientific Analysis of Personality)* uses another nomothetic approach focused on personality *traits*, rationalising the personality trait spectrum of trait theory pioneer Gordon Allport. He rated a large sample of individuals on 171 identified traits, and then used factor analysis to identify closely related terms – whittling the list down to sixteen key personality factors, which are regarded as the basis of personality. This data was the basis for a very widely used personality assessment instrument, called the Sixteen Personality Factor Questionnaire (16PF).

The 'Big Five' trait dimensions

3.7   The 'Big Five' is another nomothetic trait-based theory, based on research (RR McCrae & PT Costa, *Personality in Adulthood)* suggesting that just five major personality factors are sufficient to account for the range of differences in personality. In various versions, these trait clusters are the basis of personality questionnaires, deriving positive or negative scores on each dimension. The personality factors or trait dimensions (sometimes known by the acronym OCEAN, although different labels are used in some versions) are as follows.

- **Openness** ('Explorer') with subsidiary traits such as: fantasy, aesthetics, feelings, actions, ideas and values. (A negative score would be a 'Preserver': practical, conservative, confirming, liking routine, expert, efficient, no-nonsense and preferring things clear cut.)

- **Conscientiousness** ('Focused'), with subsidiary traits such as competence, order, dutifulness, achievement, striving, self discipline and deliberation. (A negative score would be 'flexible': unorganised, careless, frivolous, spontaneous, fun-loving, experimental, messy, open-ended, easily distracted and procrastinating.)
- **Extroversion** ('Extrovert'), with subsidiary traits such as: warmth, gregariousness, assertiveness, activity, excitement seeking and positive emotions. (A negative score would be 'introvert': private, independent, quiet, reserved, working alone, pessimistic and thoughtful.)
- **Agreeableness** ('Adapter'), with subsidiary traits including trust, straightforwardness, altruism, compliance, modesty and tender-mindedness. (A negative score would be a 'Challenger': oppositional, aggressive, tough, sceptical, self-interested, abrupt, cold and independent.)
- **Neuroticism** or **Negative emotionality** ('Reactive'), with subsidiary traits including emotional, anxious, insecure, depressed, self-conscious, alert, discouraged, eager, easily embarrassed and distracted. (A negative score would be 'Resilient': unflappable, calm, secure, self-assured, contented, unresponsive, guilt-free, up-beat and confident.)

3.8 As with the other personality models, some researchers have challenged the descriptors used, the subjectivity of the process, and the value judgements attached to use of the scales: you may have noticed the positive and negative connotations of some of the terms used. There is no attempt to describe personality as a dynamic interplay of the five factors, or to analyse their influence on each other. And the five 'clusters' of traits are inevitably generalised. ('Openness', for example, includes 'feelings', 'actions' and 'ideas' – whereas, as we will see in Chapter 4, other models suggest that individuals have preferences for operating on one or other of these areas, and in different 'styles'.)

3.9 However, the Big Five model arguably integrates a wide range of personality instruments, specifically in the workplace assessment field. It does not claim to be definitive, but is accepted as the best approximation of the basic trait dimensions of personality. 'If you could ask five questions about the personality of a stranger... querying where the person is on these five dimensions would be most revealing' (David Myers, *Exploring Psychology*). High scores for conscientiousness and stability have been found to correlate positively with high levels of job performance *(*Murray R Barrick & Michael K Mount, 'The Big Five Personality Dimensions and Job Performance: a Meta Analysis', in *Personnel Psychology)* – as you might perhaps expect.

Erik Erikson's stages of personality development

3.10 Erikson *(Identity and the Life Cycle)* regarded personality development as a life-long process, as individuals resolved personal tensions or conflicts at different phases of their lives. Successful resolution of conflicts produces a healthy personality and self-concept, whereas unresolved conflicts or blockages can result in dysfunction later in life.

- Stage 1 (1 year old): basic trust vs mistrust. Developing trust is the first task of the ego, and is never complete.
- Stage 2 (2–3 years old): autonomy (independent action) vs shame (arising from self-consciousness) and doubt.
- Stage 3 (4–5 years): initiative v guilt. Initiative develops the quality of planning and undertaking a task, but the child may feel guilt over its goals and actions.
- Stage 4 (6–11 years): industry (the desire for productive action) vs inferiority.
- Stage 5 (12–18 years): identity v role confusion (or diffusion). Adolescents are concerned with how they appear to others. 'Ego identity' is the developing confidence that one's inner sense of self is matched by one's meaning for others: the inability to settle on a school or occupational identity is disturbing.
- Stage 6 (young adult): intimacy v isolation.
- Stage 7 (middle age): generativity (a concern for establishing and guiding the next generation, having socially-valued work etc: producing a legacy) v stagnation

- Stage 8 (old age): integrity v despair. 'Ego integrity' is the continuing sense of one's capacity for order and meaning. Despair may arise from a fear of one's own death, as well as the loss of self-sufficiency and of loved partners and friends.

3.11 This is an example of the idiographic approach. We would hope that the detail is beyond the scope of this syllabus, being largely irrelevant to management in the workplace. However, elements of this approach can be seen in management theories which recognise individuals' changing needs, interests and orientations at different life stages (eg different 'career anchors' or orientations to work, depending on family and economic stages of life).

The Myers Briggs Type Indicator (MBTI)

3.12 The Myers-Briggs Type Indicator (MBTI®) model is one of the best known and most used personality type models in the business world. It is often classed as 'outside' both the nomothetic and idiographic approaches, being based on its own personality development framework, although as a type inventory, you might think of it as a broadly nomothetic methodology.

3.13 Carl Jung *(Psychological Types)* pioneered the concepts used by the model. He suggested that people use their minds for two basic activities.

- Perceiving (P): taking in information from the environment. We prefer to do this in one of two ways:
  — Sensing (S): taking in concrete (real, present, current) sensory information
  — Intuition (N): seeing the 'big picture', connections and future possibilities.
- Judging (J): drawing meaning and conclusions from what we perceive. We prefer to do this in one of two ways:
  — Thinking (T): stepping back in a situation to make objective evaluations of facts and underlying principles and concepts
  — Feeling (F): identifying with people in a situation, to make decisions based on needs, values and relationships.

3.14 We also tend to perform these activities differently, according to whether we prefer to direct our energies outwards (and are energised by people, experiences and activities) or inwards (being energised by our internal ideas, memories and emotions). Jung called these two orientations:

- Extroversion (E): energy directed to action and the external world.
- Introversion (I): energy directed to reflection and the inner world.

3.15 Some of the characteristics of these various dimensions are outlined in Table 3.1.

Table 3.1 *Extroverts and introverts*

Extrovert (E)	Introvert (I)
• Prefer oral communication	• Prefer written communication
• Sociable and expressive	• Private and reserved
• Impulsive	• Controlled or inhibited
• Learn through practical/'hands-on'	• Learn through reflection
• Wide ranging interests and activities	• Fewer, more in-depth, less active interests
Sensing (S)	**Intuitive (N)**
• Observe physical details of events	• Observe patterns and insights
• Learn through practical application	• Learn through ideas and theories
• Place trust in experience	• Place trust in insight and hunches
Thinking (T)	**Feeling (F)**
• Guided by reason, explanation	• Guided by values and impacts on people
• Make decisions with heads	• Make decisions with hearts
• Aspire to be 'reasonable'	• Aspire to be 'compassionate'
Judging (J)	**Perceiving (P)**
• Prefer to be organised, methodical	• Prefer to be flexible, casual, spontaneous
• Structured: detailed plans, schedules	• Keep options open
• Like certainty, achievement, closure	• Like ambiguity, uncertainty, change

3.16 The Myers Briggs website outlines the difference as follows.

- **Favourite world:** Do you prefer to focus on the outer world (Extroversion) or on your own inner world (Introversion)?
- **Information:** Do you prefer to focus on the basic information you take in (Sensing) or do you prefer to interpret and add meaning (Intuition)?
- **Decisions:** When making decisions, do you prefer to first look at logic and consistency (Thinking) or first look at the people and special circumstances (Feeling)?
- **Structure:** In dealing with the outside world, do you prefer to get things decided (Judging) or do you prefer to stay open to new information and options (Perceiving)?

3.17 The Myers-Briggs questionnaire analyses individual preferences on each of the four dichotomies (E-I, S-N, T-F and P-J) to produce a complex portrait of personality type: you may be an INTJ or an ESTP and so on. It is important to realise that no type is better than another: each can make its own contribution to a work task and team. Personality models are designed to help people understand areas of difference between them (which might otherwise be a source of misunderstanding) and to enable individuals and teams to improve their performance by appreciating the strengths of different operating styles.

3.18 Perhaps the most useful insight for managers, from this very brief survey, is the need:

- To allow for differences in working styles, without judging them. (You may think that an extrovert is 'better' than an introvert in a negotiating team, but an introvert can contribute deep insights and creative ideas.)
- To adapt your behaviours to those of others, in order to build rapport or influence. (If you are an extrovert, you may anticipate that your introverted subordinate would be more comfortable receiving feedback in an email, so that he can reflect on it, rather than in a face-to-face comment.)
- To utilise the strengths of each type, and the way they complement each other within the team. (For example, a perceptive type might be invited to lead a brainstorming meeting, because he is slower to shut down options. A judging type might be asked to take the lead in closing a meeting or negotiation, in order to push for resolution.)

The DISC model

3.19   Another example of a practical, personality-profiling model is known as **DISC**. DISC stands for dominance, influence, steadiness and conscientiousness (or caution). All individuals are considered to have each of these four traits, but for each individual the mix will be different.

- **Dominance** is concerned with control, power and assertiveness. People who score highly in this area tend to be very active in dealing with problems and challenges. A low score in this area indicates an individual who is conservative, cautious, and mild.
- **Influence** is concerned with social situations and communication. People who score highly in this area tend to influence others by talking and use of emotion. A low score in this area indicates an individual who is more likely to influence by facts rather than feelings.
- **Steadiness** is concerned with patience, persistence and thoughtfulness. People who score highly in this area are averse to sudden change and instead prefer a steady pace and a secure working environment. A low score in this area indicates an eager, impulsive individual.
- **Conscientiousness** is concerned with structure and organisation. People who score highly in this area like to do high quality work and get it right first time. A low score in this area indicates an individual who is likely to be careless of detail and perhaps heedless of rules.

Type A and Type B personalities

3.20   One personality type theory may be particularly useful in regard to the management of workplace stress, as well as team management. Meyer Friedman & Ray Rosenman (*Type A Behaviour and Your Heart*) identified recurring personality patterns in people suffering from premature heart disease.

- Type A individuals are typically competitive, dynamic, impatient, restless, tense and sensitive to pressure.
- Type B individuals are typically 'laid back', patient and calm. They may still have ambition and initiative – but work steadily and in a more relaxed, less 'driven' way.

3.21   Type A people 'thrive' on hard work and long hours, and are the self-starters and innovators in organisations – but their behaviours are also associated with a range of unhealthy symptoms, including: high blood pressure, high cholesterol, smoking and alcohol abuse. They are far more likely to suffer from heart disease under work-related stress than Type B people.

3.22   Moreover, Type A people tend to be stressed in work groups with Type B colleagues, who have less of a sense of urgency, efficient time management and the motivating effect of deadlines. Type A's time-urgent behaviours can impose strict schedules and reduce the team's ideas generation, creativity, learning and innovation (Lynda Gratton, *Hot Spots)*.

The use of personality assessments

3.23   Personality assessment instruments potentially have a useful role:

- In recruitment and selection, as a supporting tool for (more subjective) interviewing. It has been argued that personality tests have low validity in predicting work behaviour; that there is inevitable cultural bias and discrimination in tests; that tests infringe individual privacy; and that seeking 'desirable personality traits or types' simply leads to the 'cloning' of employees, without the potential for fresh viewpoints and contributions or support for diversity. We will discuss this further in Chapter 9.
- In personal and career development: initiating developmental discussions about individual strengths and weaknesses; 'diagnosing' learning or counselling needs for coaching sessions; and planning learning and development interventions and activities that take into account people's learning preferences and styles.

- In team building and team management: to highlight individual differences, the value of diversity and the contribution of different personality types; to help understand conflicts and team maintenance issues; to audit strengths and weaknesses in the team's mix and balance of personalities; and to plan learning and operating methods to optimise the contribution of different strengths.
- In employee counselling programmes and disciplinary interventions, to diagnose and address the personality-based causes of dysfunctional attitudes and behaviours; and to help employees to develop more successful personal and interpersonal behaviours and coping skills.

4 Emotional intelligence

4.1 Mullins notes that 'until recently, workplaces were seen as rational, logical places where emotions were excluded or seen in a negative light.'

4.2 'Intelligence' has always been prized in the work context – often defined in terms of cognitive abilities (that is, mental processes such as perception, mathematical ability, verbal fluency and reasoning) and measured by IQ or Intelligence Quotient. However, the work of Howard Gardner (*Frames of Mind)* challenged the narrow definition of IQ, arguing that it oversimplifies the wide range of intelligent behaviours observable in individuals. Gardner developed a model of 'multiple intelligences' which included new categories such as spatial capacity (design awareness), kinaesthetic ability (physical ability) and musical ability. He also introduced the category of 'personal intelligences'.

- *Intrapersonal intelligence*: knowing one's inner world; the ability to form an accurate self-concept and to be able to use that model to operate effectively in life
- *Interpersonal intelligence*: the ability to understand other people, what motivates them and how to work co-operatively with them

4.3 The concept of personal intelligences was further developed (eg by Peter Salovey & John D Mayer, and by Daniel Goleman) specifically to include feelings and emotions, which were said to express processes occurring in different parts of the brain than purely intellectual or cognitive processes. This gave rise to the concept of 'emotional intelligence'.

The work of Daniel Goleman

4.4 Daniel Goleman has popularised the argument that leadership success does not only depend on technical ability and mental dexterity (IQ), but on emotional awareness and maturity: the ability to be aware of and regulate one's emotions – and to manage relationships with a sensitivity to what others are feeling.

4.5 A basic definition of emotional intelligence is 'the capacity for recognising our own feelings and those of others, for motivating ourselves, and for managing emotions well in ourselves as well as others' (Goleman, *Emotional Intelligence*). 'Emotional intelligence' is often abbreviated to EI or (by analogy with IQ) to EQ.

4.6 Goleman's five basic components (or 'domains') of emotional intelligence are explained in Table 3.2.

Table 3.2 *Goleman's domains of emotional intelligence*

Self awareness	'Knowing what we are feeling in the moment, and using those preferences to guide our decision making; having a realistic assessment of our own abilities and a well-grounded sense of self-confidence'
Self regulation	'Handling our emotions so that they facilitate rather than interfere with the task at hand; being conscientious and delaying gratification to pursue goals; recovering well from emotional distress'
Motivation	'Using our deepest preferences to move and guide us toward our goals, to help us take initiative and strive to improve, and to persevere in the face of setbacks and frustrations'
Empathy	'Sensing what people are feeling, being able to take their perspective, and cultivating rapport and attunement with a broad diversity of people'
Social skills	'Handling emotions in relationships well and accurately reading social situations and networks; interacting smoothly; using these skills to persuade and lead, negotiate and settle disputes, for co-operation and teamwork'

4.7 Goleman defines **emotional competence** as a *learned capability* which translates emotional intelligence into skilled behaviours, resulting in effective work performance *(Emotional Intelligence at Work)*. Working with the Hay Group, Goleman developed the Emotional Competency Inventory (assessment instrument): a questionnaire measuring emotional competencies relevant to organisational management and leadership, as shown in Table 3.3. This may be used as a framework for leadership recruitment and selection, and management and leadership development.

Table 3.3 *The emotional competency inventory framework*

DIMENSION	COMPETENCIES
Self awareness	Emotional self-awareness Accurate self-assessment Self-confidence
Self management	Emotional self-control Transparency Adaptability Achievement orientation Initiative Optimism
Social awareness	Empathy Organisational awareness Service orientation
Relationship management	Developing others Inspirational leadership Change catalyst Influence Conflict management Team work and collaboration

4.8 The concept of EI links strongly to relevant skills for managers.

- Emotional intelligence underpins a range of leadership qualities such as confidence, perseverance, tolerance of stress, behavioural flexibility and so on.
- Social skills explicitly underpin leadership tasks such as inspiring, persuading, motivating, leading, negotiation, conflict management and teamworking.
- Emotional intelligence supports effective change management, because it helps a manager to change the beliefs, attitudes and values underlying people's behaviour – rather than merely getting people to change their *behaviour* (often temporarily).
- Goleman suggests that emotional aptitude is a meta-ability, determining how well we can use *whatever* other skills we have.

EQ in procurement and supply

4.9 Malcolm Higgs and Andrea Reynolds (*Do Purchasing Professionals Need Emotional Intelligence?*, 2002) have adapted this model for a procurement setting as follows.

- **Self-awareness:** the awareness of your own feelings and the ability to recognise and manage these
- **Emotional resilience:** being able to perform well and consistently in a range of situations and when under pressure
- **Motivation:** the drive and energy which you have to achieve results, to balance short-term and long-term goals, and to pursue your goals in the face of challenge and rejection
- **Interpersonal sensitivity:** the ability to be aware of the needs and feelings of others, and to use this awareness effectively in interacting with them and arriving at decisions impacting on them
- **Influence:** the ability to persuade others to change their viewpoint on a problem or issue
- **Intuitiveness:** the ability to use insight and interaction to arrive at, and implement, decisions when faced with ambiguous or incomplete information
- **Conscientiousness and integrity:** the ability to display commitment to a course of action in the face of challenge, to act consistently and 'in the line'.

5 Diversity in organisations

The meaning of diversity

5.1 Diversity is the 'visible and non-visible differences [between people] which will include sex, age, background, race, disability, personality and work style. It is founded on the premise that harnessing these differences will create a productive environment in which everybody feels valued, where their talents are being fully utilised, and in which organisational goals are met.' (Rajvinder Kandola & Johanna Fullerton, *Diversity in Action: Managing the Mosaic*).

5.2 As an HRM policy, diversity reflects the belief that the make-up of an organisation's workforce should broadly reflect that of the external labour market or society as a whole – and ideally, therefore (from a strategic point of view), that of the target customer base – in order to be able to meet the challenges posed by those environments.

5.3 Workforces are becoming increasingly diverse, not just in terms of national and ethnic backgrounds, but in: the wider representation of women in the workforce; the wider variety of educational experiences and pathways leading to employment; and legislative support for the recognition of workers' rights to equality of opportunity, regardless of sexual orientation, religious affiliation, family structure, age and disability.

5.4 A 'managing diversity' orientation argues that an organisation should proactively seek to understand, appreciate and manage the needs of a diverse workforce. This may mean: supporting tolerance of individual differences (and outlawing discrimination and harassment); taking diversity into account when designing reward systems (eg offering flexible menus of benefits) and development programmes (taking into account potential education and qualification issues); adjusting work arrangements and environments in order to accommodate diverse family responsibilities and disabilities; and enhancing employee communications.

5.5 Two related, but somewhat narrower, concepts are equality and inclusion.

- **Equality:** the principle that people should be treated fairly and without bias or discrimination in their access to rights and benefits, compared to other groups. It is particularly applied to the equal rights of minority, or under-represented, groups in society and the workplace.
- **Inclusion:** positive action to include all employees and potential employees in planning and decision making by reducing inequalities suffered by the least advantaged groups, closing the 'opportunity gap' and ensuring that support is given to those that need it most.

5.6   'Diversity management goes beyond what is required by legislation designed to promote equal opportunities and prevent discrimination. It comprises an approach which recognises and values differences and aims to make positive use of the unique talents and perspectives within the workforce. The focus is on individuals, rather than minority groups' (Chartered Management Institute).

Characteristics of diversity

5.7   Hellriegel, Slocum & Woodman (*Organisational Behaviour*) include 'Diversity competency' as a core competency for management, alongside self-competency, across-cultures competency, communication competency, teams competency and change competency. They define 'diversity competency' as 'the knowledge, skills and abilities to value unique individual, group and organisational characteristics, embrace such characteristics as potential sources of strength, and appreciate the uniqueness of each'. Diversity competency enables individuals, teams and organisations to be effective in:

- Fostering an environment of inclusion of people who have different characteristics
- Learning from individuals, teams or organisations with different characteristics and perspectives, to stimulate creativity and innovation
- Developing awareness, attitudes and behaviours that support diversity in the workplace
- Demonstrating commitment to work with team members and value their contributions, regardless of personal attributes or differences.

5.8   Hellriegel *et al* suggest that individuals may vary on a wide range of characteristics, which may affect individual, team and organisational behaviours. They propose a categorisation of diversity characteristics (based on the work of Sunny Bradford's Fourteen Dimensions of Diversity) commonly faced in organisations: Figure 3.1.

Figure 3.1 *Hellriegel, Slocum & Woodman's characteristics of diversity*

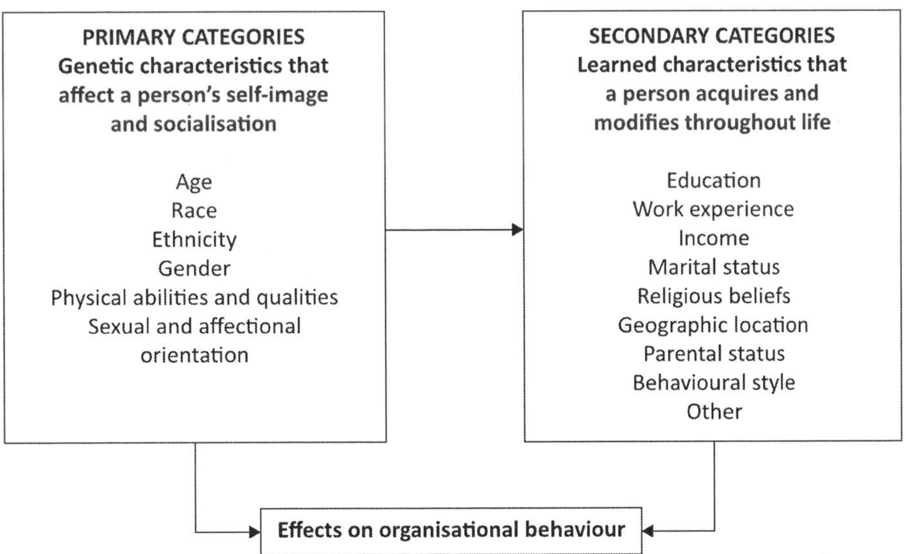

Advantages of diversity

5.9   The benefits claimed for developing a diverse workforce include the following.

- Widening the recruitment pool: giving the organisation access to more skills (particularly in the face of regional or specific skills shortages) eg from women returning to work, older workers and so on. There may be specific benefits from some of these previously underutilised skill sectors: older workers, for example, may offer experience and loyalty which more than compensate for age-related loss of performance.

- Performance benefits of being able to draw on (and support full contribution from) people with diverse skills, experiences and viewpoints. As discussed in Chapter 6, a diverse team or workforce can support better communication, decision-making, learning, change and innovation.
- Reflecting the diversity of external stakeholders. Employing representatives of different groups, cultures and viewpoints allows the organisation to anticipate the needs and concerns of similarly diverse stakeholders. This is most obviously beneficial in being able to anticipate the needs of the market and customer base (to target market and customer segments more effectively). However, it may also be beneficial in building rapport and relationships within the supply chain – particularly in areas such as cross-cultural negotiation and contract management.
- Benefits for staff morale and performance, as previously under-represented groups feel supported and valued, and are able to contribute fully
- Enhanced customer satisfaction and loyalty, both among minority groups (better represented in customer service teams, and more likely to have their needs taken into account in marketing strategies) and among consumers generally (who increasingly demand corporate ethics and responsibility over and above mere compliance with legislation)
- Enhanced employer brand (as an ethical and diverse employer): the ability to attract and retain quality talent
- Compliance with equal opportunities legislation and codes of practice
- Enhanced flexibility and learning. 'The more open we are to difference, the greater is the learning potential and the greater the ability to embrace change and development. Difference and diversity therefore hold the key to many of the aspirations of leadership. (Mike Pedler *et al: A Manager's Guide to Leadership*)

5.10 The benefits of diversity can be summarised as: legal, moral and social benefits; business benefits (better understanding of market segments; positive employer brand; attraction and retention of talent); and employee benefits (more representative workforce; value and respect for people; opportunity to contribute fully; enhanced creativity).

5.11 Conversely, an organisation which does *not* take proactive measures to develop and support diversity will suffer corresponding potential consequences: inability to target key market segments; reputational damage (affecting the employer brand, corporate image and business relationships); reduced staff morale, loyalty and contribution; inability to attract and retain talent in competition with other employers; and an impoverished organisation culture (lacking key ethical and social responsibility values, and based on a mono-cultural identity). Not to mention the potential for lawsuits, arbitrations and appeals as a result of claims of discrimination!

Disadvantages of diversity

5.12 Potential drawbacks of diversity are based on the idea that difference presents a challenge to organisation and management. However, these should be seen clearly as management challenges – *not* arguments against diversity.

- Burdens and costs of formulating and administering diversity policies and practices (including policy task forces, diversity monitoring, training, more extensive recruitment and more rigorous selection processes, implementation of job evaluation for equal pay and so on)
- Difficulties of managing and communicating effectively in ethnically diverse teams: differences in cultural values and norms, language, and interpersonal styles (for example, in negotiation or management style) – compounded by the difficulties and costs of training team leaders to cope
- Difficulties and costs of managing a workforce with increasingly diverse family structures and responsibilities (introducing flexible working; equal rights for part-time workers; child care support and so on)
- Confronting issues of literacy, numeracy and differences in different nations' qualification and training schemes (with implications for recruitment, training and development)

- Adapting the work environment, processes and task organisation to support contribution from disabled employees. (Adjustments may also have to be made to support an increasingly aged workforce.)
- Potential for misunderstanding, miscommunication and conflict arising from differences which have not been effectively managed.

5.13 Some of these disadvantages are simply costs that must be absorbed as an investment in the potential benefits. Others, however, can be minimised by effective management, as we will see in the final section of this chapter.

Diversity management in practice

5.14 At the organisational level, there should be a plan to evaluate the dimensions of diversity and to implement programmes to encourage: managerial and employee awareness of areas of difference and sensitivity; behavioural flexibility (being able to use multiple-solution models rather than 'one best way' approaches); and constructive communication, team-building, conflict resolution and problem-solving.

5.15 Diversity training may be required to ensure that managers and staff appreciate the value of diversity, respect individual differences and treat all team members with respect. Like any culture change initiative, there will have to be sponsorship and support from top management, in order to secure buy-in and embed diversity as a core value of the organisation.

5.16 It may be necessary or desirable to reinforce communication and awareness training with guidelines or Codes of Conduct for cultural sensitivity and respect for diversity. Other mechanisms of organisation culture may also be used: using diversity awareness criteria in recruitment, selection, appraisal and reward; planning diversity learning experiences as part of training and development programmes; and so on.

5.17 Mullins offers 'ten practical ideas' for managing diversity: Table 3.4.

Table 3.4 *Mullins's 'ten practical ideas for managing diversity'*

1	Test assumptions about people before acting on them
2	Ensure that organisational policies related to discipline and grievance are clearly understood
3	For all employees, but particularly new recruits, make sure that written and unwritten diversity policies are understood and acted upon
4	Maintain open channels of communication to try to locate possible issues before they become problems
5	Learn how to understand the views of all staff members and encourage open approaches
6	Be prepared to listen to varying methods of solving work-based problems
7	Learn about and have regard to any strongly held beliefs (such as religious observances, food, relationships) that are held by individuals
8	Acknowledge all contributions to improving working environments and processes, whatever the source
9	Know your own cultural diversity biases – and work at not letting them affect the workplace
10	Take care that any workplace based social events can be enjoyed by all workers – especially relevant (but not restricted) to those with physical disability

Gender in organisations

5.18 Gender is one of the most obvious 'dimensions' of difference between people, and as such is the basis on which individuals are easily categorised – and stereotyped. As Mullins asks: 'How does this perception affect our behaviour? What difference does it make if our work group is predominantly male or female? Do women and men have different experiences at work?'

5.19 Although the number of women in the workforce has increased in recent decades, they still do not have equal access to all occupations. The existence of predominantly 'male' or 'female' occupations is known as **gender segregation**.

- Horizontal gender segregation occurs where men and women are associated with different types of jobs. Research (such as the UK Labour Force Survey) suggests that 'women are much more likely than men to work as teachers, nurses or librarians than as doctors, judges or chartered accountants. They often do routine office work and shop work, but rarely do what is defined as skilled manual work. The reverse is true for men' (David A Buchanan & David Boddy, *Management: An Introduction*).
- Vertical gender segregation occurs when women are disproportionately distanced from positions of power and the exercise of formal authority: in other words, women are less represented in managerial positions than men. A survey *Sex and Power: Who Runs Britain?* found in 2007 that women made up just 10% of directors of FTSE 100 companies, and barely 20% of members of parliament.

5.20 Many cultural assumptions about women's attitudes to work, and capabilities for various types of work, are being re-examined. Maureen Guirdham (*Interactive Behaviour at Work*) argues that 'Sex and gender are not strong predictors of work behaviour. Even when gender differences are found, they typically account for only 1–5% of the variance for any given outcome. Recent research suggests that femininity and masculinity are independent dimensions and that each dimension has multiple domains within it, including appearance, behaviour, personality and interests. There is evidence that gender stereotypes are not very accurate, because they are more extensive than actual sex differences, and they contain information based on exaggerations of minor differences between the sexes.'

5.21 In other words, it is not helpful to view 'men' or 'women' as homogeneous groups: there are wide differences in individual characteristics of diversity within each gender. It is therefore difficult to make meaningful generalisations about men's and women's experience of work and working life. However, research attempts have been made to identify distinctive communication and negotiation styles; relationship styles; and management styles. Buchanan and Boddy cite the research of:

- Judy B Rosener (*America's Competitive Secret: Women Managers*), suggesting that male managers tend to adopt a transactional style of leadership (based on exchange and positional authority), while women tended to use a relational style (based on persuasion, encouragement, support and personal qualities). She argues that the female 'facilitate and empower' model of leadership is more suited to modern, turbulent conditions than the male 'command and control' style.
- Sally Helgesen (*The Female Advantage: Women's Ways of Leadership*), suggesting that women are better at developing co-operation, creativity and intuition than men; that women prefer to manage through relationships rather than positional authority; and that they listen and empathise more than men.
- David Knights and Fergus Murray (*Managers Divided*), suggesting that a predominantly male management undervalues the strengths of women's style of leadership, and prevents women reaching senior positions. 'Managers who emphasise the value of hard analytical skills above soft interpersonal skills support, perhaps unwittingly, the progression of men and discourage that of women. Stressing competitiveness, tension and long unsocial working hours has a similar effect.' (Buchanan & Boddy)

5.22 The position of women in the workplace is thus a culturally and historically conditioned issue. It is also an issue of gender politics. Mullins emphasises the extent to which 'emotions and politics surround the issue of gender', pointing out that:

- Some people may be over-sensitive to gender issues and interpret any and all negative comments as if they are intentional (or symbolic) acts of discrimination
- Some people may be under-sensitive to gender issues, and may unwittingly perpetuate stereotyping, bias and discrimination

Finding a balance between these extremes is an important skill in managing people at work. 'Perhaps the most positive approach to take is for an organisation to acknowledge the changing working pattern of *all* employees and to consider the best working practices for managing a diverse workforce as a whole.'

6 Factors in individual work performance

6.1 What makes people productive at work? Individual effectiveness may depend on: abilities, skills and knowledge; motivation, morale and commitment; the quality of leadership and management; the clarity of task goals and availability of feedback; the efficiency of systems, procedures and technology; resource availability; task organisation, co-ordination and teamworking – and so on.

6.2 Many different models may be used to describe the factors in individual performance. An easy-to-remember framework for this discussion is known as the 3Cs. You might use this framework as a checklist of factors to be considered if you encounter a poor-performing team (at work or in an exam scenario).

- Commitment: how willingly and energetically people approach their work
- Contribution: the conditions required to support effective working and task fulfilment
- Capability: the aptitudes, skills and competencies people bring to the work – and how they can be developed

Commitment

6.3 Commitment is an elusive concept, but Mowdray, Porter and Steers describe it as follows.

'Commitment is the relative strength of an individual's identification with and involvement in a particular organisation. It is characterised by at least three factors: a strong belief in and acceptance of an organisation's goals and values; a willingness to exert considerable effort on behalf of the organisation; and a strong desire to maintain membership of the organisation.'

6.4 Increasing employee commitment involves motivation and effective leadership.

Contribution

6.5 Individual and team contribution must be enabled and supported by organisational conditions (including leadership). Contribution must be:

- Commissioned: by clear task objectives and delegation of sufficient authority to perform them. People need to know what the organisation expects and backs them to do.
- Controlled: by clear values, policies, procedures (if necessary), targets and success criteria – and the feedback to adjust performance accordingly. People need to know where they stand, and where they're 'up to' in pursuing their objectives.
- Championed: by leadership support, acknowledgement and inspiration. People need their leaders to value their contribution, mobilise resources on their behalf, and model what is required.
- Co-operative: via mechanisms for co-ordination, information-sharing and team-working. Organisations are formed because there are limits to what individuals can accomplish alone – but integration is required if they are to achieve positive synergy, where the whole achieves more than the sum of its parts (2 + 2 = 5).

6.6 This idea of supporting and enabling people in giving their best underpins the concept of empowerment. It turns the organisational pyramid on its head, and argues that rather than workers supporting leaders in achieving their objectives, the role of leaders is to support workers in achieving *their* value-adding objectives.

Capability

6.7 Individual and team contribution depends on what people are 'able' to do.

- Capacity: what people are capable of, or able to learn: their qualities and aptitudes (things they are naturally good at or suited to)

- Competence: what people are able (or can learn) to do. This includes knowledge, skills (learned effective behaviours) and competencies (ability to perform specific tasks to a required standard).
- Creativity: the ability to do *new* things and formulate new ideas or combinations of ideas. This is a highly valued element in work performance in the modern environment.

6.8   One of the key tasks of leaders is to source and develop high-quality, flexible (and, if possible, distinctive) capabilities in their workforces and teams.

Chapter summary

- Managers must cope with the fact that members of their teams are unique individuals, differing in their beliefs, values, attitudes and behaviours.
- A nomothetic approach to personality emphasises predictable regularities in human behaviour. An idiographic approach emphasises the uniqueness of every individual.
- Influential nomothetic approaches include those of Eysenck, Cattell, Erikson and the 'Big Five' trait dimensions. The MBTI approach is also broadly nomothetic.
- Daniel Goleman, among others, has emphasised the limitations of a concept of 'intelligence' based solely on intellectual level. Emotional intelligence also has an important role in the workplace.
- Diversity in the workplace is to some extent imposed by law. However, many researchers have emphasised that organisations derive clear benefits from a diverse workforce.
- Individual effectiveness in the workplace can be measured by factors such as commitment, contribution and capability.

Self-test questions

Numbers in brackets refer to the paragraphs where you can check your answers.

1   Distinguish between nomothetic and idiographic approaches to personality. (2.4, 2.9)

2   How can a nomothetic approach be used to analyse personality? (2.5)

3   Explain what is meant by the 'E' and 'N' dimensions (Eysenck). (3.2)

4   What are the five trait dimensions in the OCEAN model? (3.7)

5   List characteristics of extroverts and introverts. (Table 3.1)

6   List possible uses of personality assessments. (3.23)

7   Define emotional intelligence. (4.5)

8   Explain how Higgs and Reynolds have applied the concept of emotional intelligence to the role of purchasers. (4.9)

9   List benefits of diversity in the workplace. (5.9)

10   List possible disadvantages of diversity. (5.12)

CHAPTER 4

Learning

Assessment criteria and indicative content

 **2.2** Analyse how the different learning styles of individuals in the procurement and supply function can impact on their management

- Learning as a formal and spontaneous process
- Explicit and tacit knowledge
- Cognitive theories of learning
- Approaches to knowledge management

Section headings

1 The learning process
2 Theories of learning
3 Learning styles
4 Knowledge management
5 The learning organisation

Introduction

In this chapter we continue our discussion of factors and processes in individual behaviour, by looking at learning and development. Specifically, we look at theories of how adults learn – developing knowledge, skills and competencies – and how this process can be managed to enhance individual, team and organisational capability.

We start by examining the learning process, and by distinguishing learning from 'training': emphasising the often informal and spontaneous nature of the learning process – and how this can be utilised to support continuous learning at work.

We explore two key theories of human learning (behaviourist and cognitive) and their implications for the design of learning, training and development interventions. We focus on the popular concept of 'learning styles' (the recognition that people have certain relatively stable personality preferences in regard to how they learn) and its implication for the management of learners.

Learning can take place at individual, group and organisational levels, and in Section 4 we recognise the concept of 'organisational learning', linking it to the process of 'knowledge management' in organisations.

Finally, we draw together some ideas on how managers can facilitate the learning of their team members on a day-to-day basis. This will be followed up in Chapter 10 on training and development as a process of human resource management.

1   The learning process

1.1   Learning has been defined as 'relatively permanent change in behaviour that occurs as a result of practice or experience' (Bernard M Bass & J A Vaughan, *Training in Industry: The Management of Learning).* It is also the *process* by which people change their behaviour through the acquisition of knowledge, capabilities and skills.

The outcomes of learning

1.2   Learning activities may be directed towards a range of desired outcomes.

- The development of a **skill**. A skill may be defined as 'a learned pattern of operations, or responses to stimuli, which allow the successful, rapid and apparently confident performance of a complex task.' People have natural aptitudes or abilities, but skills are complex behaviours which are acquired as a result of learning and practice. Effective work performance often depends on the exercise of skills.
- The acquisition of **knowledge.** In a workplace learning context, knowledge is often categorised as *know-that* (or 'propositional knowledge': knowledge *about* ideas, concepts, theories, methodologies and so on) and *know-how* (or 'practical knowledge': knowledge *of* something, or the ability to do something). Propositional knokwledge is often associated with formal education, and often underpins the use of skills (hence a 'Management' unit in your CIPS studies). Practical knowledge may be based on untaught, unverbalised (or 'tacit') knowledge, and is typically acquired through imitation and experience. At the end of this unit, you may know about management (how it should be done) – but actually managing a team is a rather different challenge. An organisation needs to develop *both* know-that (understanding of processes) *and* know-how (ability to apply processes effectively).
- The development of **competencies**. A competency may be defined as 'the combination of skill, knowledge and behaviours that need to be applied for effective performance in a work role and context.' Competency therefore integrates knowledge, skills and other attributes into the notion of overall 'ability', specifically in the context of workplace performance and proficiency.
- The shaping of **attitudes**. Attitudes are mental states that influence human behaviour: including beliefs, value judgements and the will, inention or motivation to act accordingly. Changing attitudes is an important part of changing behaviour: in Chapter 3, for example, we mentioned the need for anti-discrimination (or 'sensitivity') training. We also noted, in Chapter 1, the importance of the 'psychological contract' in shaping organisational behaviour: effective work performance often depends on people's attitudes to the employer, the task etc.
- The fostering of **awareness**. Another recently recognised area of personal development is aimed at encouraging individuals to gain insight into their own behaviour, and to try to change negative or restrictive thought processes that prevent the individual from being more effective. Many organisations use awareness training in areas such as: management development, assertiveness training, diversity training and emotional competence development.
- The development of **employability**. The concept of 'employability' embraces a portfolio of knowledge, skills, competencies and attributes which enhance an individual's potential mobility and value in the labour market. Socially responsible employers, recognising that they are unable to offer long-term job security, may seek to facilitate employees' eventual transition to other jobs – while benefiting from a flexible, multi-skilled workforce and clear psychological contract.

Formal and informal learning

1.3   Formal learning arises from planned, deliberate learning interventions, guided episodes of learning or the facilitation of learning. Formal learning processes may be implemented in an organisation with a view to meeting specific, identified performance improvement needs, or filling knowledge, skill or attitude gaps. Alan Rogers *(What is the Difference? A New Critique of Adult Learning)* calls this 'educative learning', where learning itself is the main task – rather than learning 'naturally' as a result of accumulated experience.

Formal learning experiences may include a wide range of 'study', education and training programmes; e-learning; on-the-job coaching or mentoring and so on. We. will discuss these in Chapter 10. They are often accompanied by testing or assessment of learning against defined learning objectives.

1.4   However, learning can be informal, as well as formal; *ad hoc* as well as intentional and systematic; a learner-managed process as well as a 'teacher'-managed process. Pedler, Burgoyne and Boydell (*The Learning Company*) suggest that: 'If asked to think about how we have learned, most of us may think first of when attempts have been made to *teach* us. If, on the other hand, we are asked about problems we have solved, we think about difficult situations we have faced and managed to overcome. However, in solving problems, we don't just deal with the immediate difficulty; we discover a solution whch we can use in some form, and we may also become better at solving problems generally. Problem solving is, to a large extent, learning.'

1.5   As we will see in our discussion of experiential and trial-by-error learning, later in this chapter, the learning process goes on continuously as individuals perform tasks, note the results, and adapt their behaviours to be more successful next time. The learner may not be aware of learning: he is focused on performing a task well or better. Various terms are used for these kinds of informal, self-directed learning processes.

- *Accidental* or unintentional learning occurs continuously as individuals go through life and work, accumulating experience. For example, people imitate the behaviour of a respected colleague, learn where things are in the office, and absorb 'the way we do things around here' at work.
- *Incidental* learning is more or less unconscious learning which happens in the course of some other activity (eg reading, surfing the internet, talking to colleagues or performing work tasks), but which can be captured and applied to other contexts. We 'absorb' a wide range of information in everyday life.
- *Opportunistic learning* is intentional learning, where individuals set out to learn something – but use experiences that come to hand (rather than formal education and training resources). Approaches to opportunistic learning include: coaching and mentoring; experiential learning; personal development journalling; and problem-based learning (group problem solving).

1.6   The encouragement of self-managed, informal and continuous learning is an important concept in modern learning and development – and distinguishes the concept of 'human resource development' from the more narrow, organisation-driven process of 'training'.

1.7   However, there is still a place for systematic, organisation-driven or manager-driven learning interventions, in order to meet the identified learning and development needs of the individual – and the organisation. Mullins notes: 'It is surprising to observe that in some organisations learning is still left to chance. The individual employee is expected to 'pick up' behaviour, attitudes and skills'. We will discuss a systematic approach to managing learning, training and development in Chapter 10.

Learning to learn

1.8   Peter Honey & Alan Mumford *(The Opportunist Learner)* suggest that: 'Learning is perhaps the most important of all the life skills, since the way in which people learn affects everything else. We live in the post-industrial information age, where data have a shorter shelf-life and where trnasformational changes are less predictable and occur more rapidly than ever before. Clearly, learning is the key, not just to surviving, but to thriving on all those changes...'

1.9   Learning to learn enables people to keep learning – beyond any particular Course Book, training course or coaching session. It is a framework for ongoing personal and professional self-development and 'lifelong' learning. New learning needs emerge all the time: learning to learn is about developing values, attitudes, strategies and methodologies that support continuous learning and improvement.

The development of learning technologies

1.10   Mullins notes that there is 'an increasing use of technology as a means of enhancing the learning situation'.

- ICT-enabled learning (such as podcasts, You Tube videos and learning 'apps') can facilitate access to learning resources – eg participation in 'virtual' learning groups or observing lectures and demonstrations, regardless of geographic location.
- Human-computer interaction is becoming increasingly sophisticated, allowing a range of learning experiences.
- Knowledge-sharing and knowledge communities are now global, facilitating instant access to 'crowd-sourced' knowledge, information and solutions to problems (such as Wikipedia and discussion boards).

1.11   **E-learning** (electronic learning) is defined as 'learning that is delivered, enabled or mediated by electronic technology for the explicit purposes of training in organisations. It does not include standalone technology-based training such as the use of CD-ROMs in isolation' (CIPD).

1.12   In other words, e-learning uses ICT networks such as the internet or a corporate intranet. Formal e-learning systems typically include: software packages which provide course content, interactive testing and feedback and so on; and learning support from online tutors or coaches, discussion boards, webcast seminars and so on. E-learning has become very influential in recent years, particularly for training in IT skills, and information and awareness based learning.

1.13   The term *blended learning* (or hybrid learning) is a popular approach to maximising the benefits of various methods and media. The term is used to describe learning or training activities where e-learning is combined with more traditional forms of training, such as classroom training or instruction. For example, theoretical content may be delivered by e-learning, prior to attendance at a training or revision course (for practice and group interaction). Or a demonstration or site visit may be supported by in-depth exploration using e-learning methods. Or a trainee may use e-learning in a classroom setting, while being coached or supported by a trainer.

1.14   A significant advantage of a blended programme is its flexibility: it allows a combination of focused self-study (at the individual's own pace) and options for group interaction, on-site application and so on. At the same time, it is an efficient use of training resources, minimising time spent on travel and external training activities – while maximising their effectiveness.

1.15   Mullins suggests that, despite the advances in the available technology, cultural barriers have hindered the widespread uptake of online learning. Individuals may lack time to engage in systematic e-learning, and may lack the motivation to complete programmes – particularly if unsupported by management. E-learning has, however, created major opportunities for personal development, with resources and computer or mobile applications including the ability to access lectures and classes from major universities, to user-generated demonstrations of basic skills.

1.16   We will discuss these issues further in Chapter 10 on training and development.

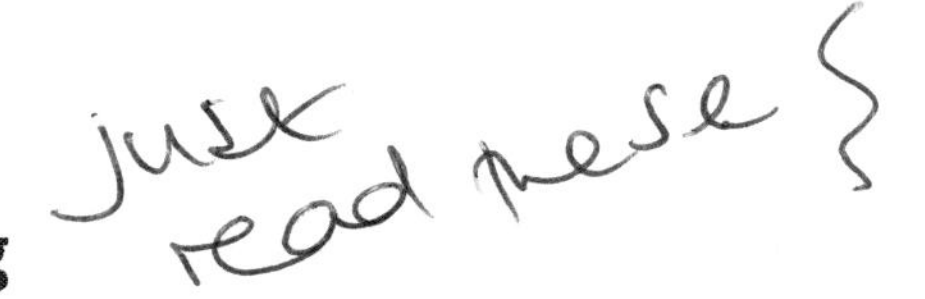

2   Theories of learning

2.1   Despite extensive research, there are still different ways of understanding what learning is, how the learning process works, and what we mean when we say that an individual 'knows' something. There are two basic schools of psychology which have focused on learning theory.

- **Behaviourist psychology** is based on an empirical epistemology (the view that the human mind operates purely on information obtained from the senses). It therefore focuses on observable behaviours, arising from the relationship between 'stimuli' (sensory experiences) and our 'responses' to those stimuli. Learning is interpreted as the formation of new connections between stimulus and response, on the basis of experience or 'conditioning': messages about the results of our behaviour ('feedback') are either an incentive ('positive reinforcement') or a deterrent ('negative reinforcement') to similar behaviour in future.
- **Cognitive psychology** is based on a rational epistemology (the view that the human mind imposes meaning and organisation on sensory data). It argues that we *process* (interpret and utilise) 'feedback' information on the results of our past behaviours in order to make rational decisions about whether to maintain successful behaviours or modify unsuccessful behaviours in future, according to our goals and our plans for reaching them.

Behaviourist learning theory

2.2   According to behaviourist theory, we learn to modify our responses to a given stimulus according to whether the feedback on the results of our previous experience was good (positive reinforcement: an incentive to repeat the behaviour) or bad (negative reinforcement: an incentive to modify the behaviour). The development of associations between stimuli and responses happens through a process called 'conditioning'.

2.3   **Classical conditioning** (or 'simple learning') was described by Ivan Pavlov in 1909, when he noted that a dog salivated not only at the sight of food, but at the appearance of the lab assistant brining it. There was a clear association between the stimulus of the food and the natural response of salivating – but the dog had, through repeated experience, also come to associate the appearance of the assistant with the food (conditioned stimulus) and responded by salivating on his appearance (conditioned response).

2.4   In follow-up experiments, by repeatedly ringing a bell while showing the dog the meat, Pavlov created an association between the sound and the meat: the dog became conditioned to salivate at the sound of the bell, even if the meat was not present. Classical conditioning therefore involves associating an established response with a new stimulus.

2.5   **Operant (or instrumental) conditioning** describes how new behaviours or responses become established through association with particular stimuli. It suggests that, in a particular context, any behaviour that is rewarded by positive results (reinforcement) will tend to be repeated in that context; any behaviour that is 'punished' by negative results will tend *not* to be repeated in that context; and any behaviour that is ignored will tend to die out.

2.6   BF Skinner demonstrated this in experiments with rats. A hungry rat is placed in a box with a lever which, if pressed, delivers a pellet of food. The rat is allowed to explore its surroundings at random. When the rat accidentally presses the lever, it is rewarded with food – reinforcing the behaviour. After a number of repetitions, the rat presses the lever deliberately in order to obtain food.

2.7   Operant conditioning differs from classical conditioning in that rather than deliberately linking a desired response with a particular (controllable) stimulus (as in classical conditioning), operant conditioning seeks to reward – and therefore reinforce – desired behaviours and punish (and therefore eradicate) undesirable behaviours when they occur. Skinner established the following results.

- Complex patterns of behaviour (such as skilled performance or desirable conduct and attitudes) can be built up by step-by-step reinforcement of individual actions or learning steps. This is known as 'behaviour shaping'. Organisations often seek to control the behaviour of members, in the interests of discipline, compliance and corporate image.
- Punishment is of relatively little value in encouraging learning: it only suppresses undesirable behaviours temporarily – and does not stimulate positive learning. Reinforcing desired behaviours with positive and valued rewards is more effective.
- Occasional reinforcement is sufficient to maintain learned behaviours, once they have been established. (As Huczynski and Buchanan note: why else do gamblers persist in playing?).

2.8 This is the basis of experiential or 'trial and error' learning, where some form of positive reinforcement or 'payoff' (the satisfaction of achievement, recognition, praise, reward) is consistently and immediately given for desired behaviours.

2.9 **Reinforcement** is a key concept in learning, and an important factor in designing effective training and development interventions, because it determines which new behaviours will be adopted for future use (learned) and which will be discarded. It is important to recognise – as we will discuss further in Chapter 5 on motivation – that positive reinforcement may be:

- *Intrinsic,* arising from the behaviour or learning itself: eg the satisfaction of success or mastery, or the interest of acquiring knowledge
- *Extrinsic,* arising from external sources. This need not mean monetary rewards: important intangible reinforcement may come from a manager's praise and recognition, or the future prospect of financial or career rewards as a result of learning attainments. Recognition and encouragement (eg commending learners or team members for making progress or completing tasks successfully) embeds correct learning and motivates further effort.

Cognitive learning theory

2.10 Cognitive psychology is concerned with the goals and plans individuals choose to pursue, the methods they adopt, and the effect of experience and thinking on those plans and methods. According to this theory, learning is the way in which human beings process and interpret feedback on the results of behaviour and experience – and make decisions about whether to maintain successful behaviours or modify unsuccessful behaviours, in pursuit of their chosen goals. In other words, we learn not simply new 'habits' (as behaviourist theory suggests) but ways of dealing with information and choosing alternative methods of reaching our goals.

2.11 Cognitive learning approaches suggest several useful concepts for learning in the workplace.

- Learning is likely to be most effective if people are encouraged to formulate clear **goals or desired outcomes** for their learning, and if they receive clear and immediate **feedback** that suggests whether the learned behaviour contributes to attaining those goals or outcomes. This information feeds into a kind of 'learning calculation': is the likely reward worth the effort of learning and change?
- Learning is likely to be most effective if learners are able to experiment, discover things and solve problems for themselves. **Participation and problem-solving** encourages the engagement of cognitive processes, which means that the learner is more likely to retain the skill or knowledge acquired, transfer it to other contexts, and use it when required. This is the basis for approaches such as discovery learning, workshops, and the use of role plays, case studies and simulations.
- Human beings develop 'learning sets': strategies for how to learn different types of skill and solve different types of problem. Training interventions may be more effective when directed at **learning how to learn** (reason, solve problems, gather and use data, formulate questions, get help etc), rather than focusing on 'content' outcomes of learning.
- An important goal of work-related training (particularly in off-the-job training) is the **transfer of learning**: the ability to transpose a solution from one learning experience (eg a course) to *other*

situations which are similar, but in a different context (eg at work). The Gestalt school of learning demonstrated, for example, that transfer of learning is maximised when something previously learned is built on, to create new learning: helping the brain to generalise, compare and make connections.

The cybernetic analogy

2.12 Cybernetic learning theories are drawn from the way machines use information and feedback to trigger adjustments to their settings or 'behaviour'. Chris Argyris & Donald Schon *(Organisational Learning: A Theory of Action Perspective)* use the term 'single-loop learning' to describe how people adjust their actions in response to feedback on the success of those actions in achieving a desired result. They compare this style of learning to an air conditioning system, in which the thermostat adjusts the degree of heating or cooling by comparing the current temperature of the room to the desired temperature of the room.

2.13 This analogy highlights the importance of **feedback** in individual learning. 'Feedback' is information about the results of behaviours, which may indicate *either* that those behaviours are successful in furthering one's goals (positive feedback) – in which case the behaviour should be repeated or continued – *or* that they are unsuccessful or counter-productive (negative feedback) – in which case the behaviour should be discarded or modified. Feedback information may include:

- The *observable results of a behaviour*: eg the team's response to a newly learned management technique. This is the basis of experiential learning, where you monitor the results of your behaviours and reflect on how you may need to do things differently next time to obtain a better result.
- Information *given by other people* on the impact of your behaviour. This is the basis of group learning activities (where participants are given feedback about how they 'come across' to others), and also coaching and self-managed learning (where learners seek feedback from others: eg asking team members to evaluate your leadership style).
- Information *given by learning facilitators* (eg coaches or team leaders) on your progress in relation to specific objectives and expectations. This is the basis of learning assessment and performance management.

2.14 Two main types of feedback should be given by managers on a regular basis, both of which are valuable in supporting learning.

- *Motivational feedback:* used to reward and reinforce positive behaviours, progress and performance, by recognising attainment and praising and encouraging the team member. The purpose of motivational feedback is primarily to develop *confidence.*
- *Developmental feedback:* used to identify particular areas of behaviour or performance which need to be changed or improved, and to suggest how this might be done. The purpose of developmental feedback is primarily to develop *competence.* Note that, unlike negative reinforcement, negative *feedback* about undesirable behaviours and areas for improvement, given constructively, is extremely helpful for personal and skill development.

Experiential learning

2.15 Experiential learning is learning by experience – or 'learning by doing'. David Kolb *(Experiential Learning)* is an influential proponent of the idea that effective learning could start, not just from abstract concepts or theories, but from concrete experience. He formulated the 'experiential learning cycle' to demonstrate how everyday work experiences can be used for learning, personal development and performance improvement, through the process of 'learning by doing': Figure 4.1

Figure 4.1 *The experiential learning cycle*

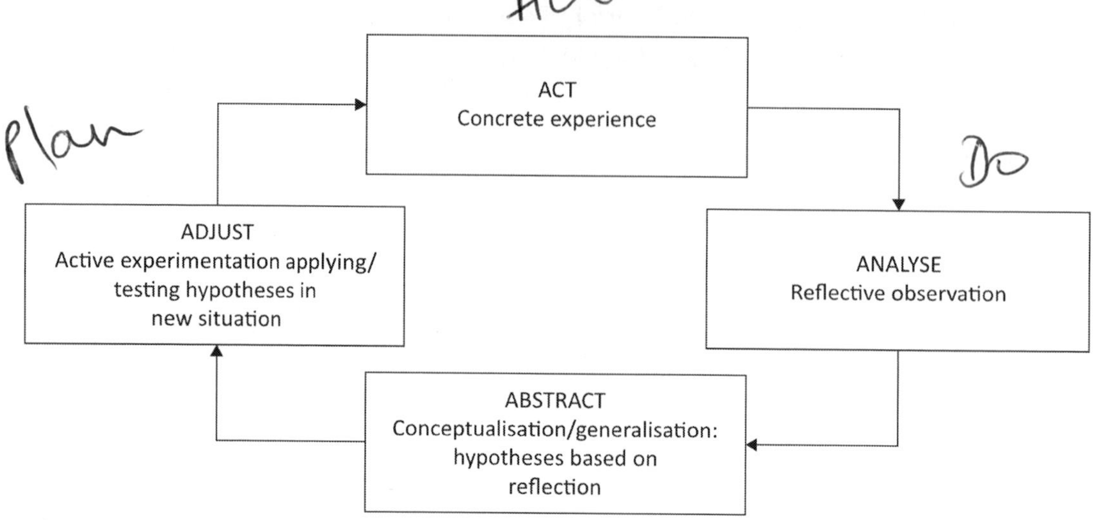

Act

Plan

Do

ACT
Concrete experience

ADJUST
Active experimentation applying/
testing hypotheses in
new situation

ANALYSE
Reflective observation

ABSTRACT
Conceptualisation/generalisation:
hypotheses based on
reflection

2.16 Working through the cycle:

- The learner has a concrete experience of the technique or concept to be learned. (For example, the trainee purchasing manager chairs a meeting of supply partners.)
- He thinks back over the experience later, perhaps using a personal development journal. (The trainee notes that the meeting split into side-issue arguments on several occasions, and ponders what sorts of behaviour may have allowed this to happen.)
- Using theory and experience, he develops some abstract concepts of what might have been going on, and sets up a hypothesis for future action. (The trainee realises that the facilitator is responsible for controlling a meeting, and that this can be achieved only by being the focus of all communications.)
- He applies and tests the hypothesis in a new situation. (The trainee plans to facilitate the next buying group meeting, in which he requests that all communications be routed via the chair.)
- The learner is thus supplied with a new or adjusted concrete experience, from which to begin the cycle again.

2.17 Trial and error is an important learning process. It basically involves doing something, and (if you do not get the results you wanted or expected), doing it again – *differently*. This is the foundation of experiential, spontaneous learning, where every work situation (particularly mistakes and problems) can become a learning opportunity. In facilitating trial-and-error learning, facilitators should be aware that:

- Learners require feedback on their performance (in order to identify errors)
- Learning steps should be small, to avoid frustration (through repeated failures) and wasted time (carrying on past potential correction and adjustment points)
- A safe environment is required, in order to allow practice and to genuinely encourage error-making as part of the learning process. Negative consequences for errors (eg costs, dangers or being 'shown up' in front of colleagues) demotivate learning – and create a downside risk for the organisation, where learning involves real-life tasks or resources. This is particularly important in cultures where 'face' (personal dignity) is valued, and in general, there will need to be a positive learning culture which tolerates errors in the course of learning.

2.18 Experiential learning allows any experience or situation to become an opportunity for learning and development, enabling the learner to manage his own learning. It also provides a systematic and effective approach to 'learning to learn', and emphasises the nature of learning as a continuous process or cycle. It engages different learning approaches, preferences and 'styles' (discussed below): experimentation, practice, theorising, watching and reflecting – and so on. And it builds in transfer or application of learning from the original learning context to other contexts: reinforcing and embedding learning on the job.

Thinking performers

2.19 The volatility of the business environment, and the need for flexibility, creativity and innovation, has created an increasing priority for organisations – not just to train people to perform a task (as set out in a job description), but to develop what Nancy Kline *(Time to Think)* called 'thinking performers'. Thinking performers are people equipped with the learning skills and behavioural flexibility to come up with different ways of performing tasks – or indeed to perform different tasks – in order to get results. 'In a rapidly changing environment, it is not possible to train everyone to do everything, particularly where time is important... People need to learn and use their knowledge and skills to see what needs to be done and to adapt rapidly' (Reid, Barrington & Brown, *Human Resource Development).*

The learning curve

2.20 A learning curve is a graph of an individual's competence over time, showing the relationship between time spent in learning and the level of competence attained. It is common for people to say that they are 'on a steep learning curve' when they have to acquire a lot of new knowledge in a short period of time.

2.21 The 'standard' learning curve is initially steep, levelling out towards proficiency. However, in practice, the curve typically shows a variable pace of learning. The curve for the acquisition of manual skills, for example, typically shows a slow start (the trainee has a lot to take in), then gains momentum. There may be one or more 'plateaus' where output levels off for a while, reflecting the trainee's need to consolidate what he has learned so far. Momentum then typically gathers again, until the trainee reaches proficiency level – where the curve will level off (unless there is an injection of new equipment or methods, or fresh motivation, to lift output again). Learning curves can go down as well as up: for example, if the learner is unable to apply newly acquired skills and forgets them, or suffers disorientation as a result of major job change. An up-and-down 'transition curve' is common in cases where an individual changes job roles or work methods.

3 Learning styles

3.1 David Kolb noted that individual learners tend to have a psychological preference for particular phases of his experiential learning cycle (Figure 4.1). The broad categories of preference identified by Kolb *(Experiential Learning)* are as follows.

- Converger: prefers the Abstracting/Generalising and Applying/Testing phases. Learns best by applying abstract generalisations in practical and specific ways (eg by experimenting)
- Diverger: prefers the Concrete Experience and Reflective Observation phases. Learns best by reflecting on a specific experience from different points of view (eg by generalising)
- Assimilator: prefers the Abstracting/Generalising and Reflective Observation phases. Learns best through concepts and abstract ideas (eg theorising)
- Accommodator: prefers the Concrete Experience and Applying/Testing phases. Learns best by doing (eg trial and error).

Honey and Mumford's learning styles

3.2 Like Kolb, Honey and Mumford *(The Manual of Learning Styles)* noted that: 'people vary not just in their learning skills, but also in their learning styles. Why otherwise might two people, matched for age, intelligence and need, exposed to the *same* learning opportunity, react so differently?' Honey and Mumford drew up a popular classification of four learning styles for which people may have a natural preference: Table 4.1. You might like to assess your own learning preferences and style(s), using this outline – or a copy of the Learning Styles Inventory, if your study centre has access to it.

Table 4.1 *Honey and Mumford's learning styles*

STYLE	LEARNING PREFERENCES
Theorists *('If it's logical, it's good')*	Need to understand underlying concepts prior to any hands-on attempt: their preferred approach is intellectual and rational. Are keen on principles, theories and models, and like to think problems through systematically and logically. Can be perfectionist and uncomfortable with lateral thinking and ambiguity. Learn best from activities which are intellectually challenging, structured and theory-based; which allow time for analysis and grasping underlying logic; and which allow generalisation of reasons for success or failure. Do not thrive on training which is experimental, skims over principles or appears intellectually disorganised.
Reflectors *('Look before you leap')*	Need to stand back and observe and think deeply about things (considering all angles and analysing all available data) before acting or coming to carefully-thought-out conclusions. Tend to take a back seat (while listening and observing others carefully): may appear disengaged. Learn best from activities which encourage observation and reflection; allow them to work at their own pace and with plenty of data; and help them to exchange views with others in a safe, structured way. Do not thrive on fast-moving, participative training.
Activists *(I'll try anything once')*	Need to work on practical tasks or problems, and want to 'get stuck in'. Prefer to tackle problems by brainstorming. Open-minded and enthusiastic – but easily bored by long-term implementation issues and consolidation processes: want to 'act first, think later'. Learn best from activities which are high on hands-on experience, immediate payoffs, excitement and variety; allow them to generate ideas without constraints of feasibility or structure; involve them with other people; and allow them to 'have a go'. Do not have patience with theory, consolidation, risk-analysis or constraints.
Pragmatists *('If it works, it's good – but there's always a better way')*	Need to see a direct link between the subject being studied and a real-world task or problem for which they are, or may be, responsible: see no point in learning for its own sake. Are eager to try out ideas, theories and techniques to see if they work in practice. Enjoy practical decisions and responding to problems as 'challenges'. Learn best from activities which: relate to work problems (eg on-the-job training); allow practice with coaching from a practical expert; allow them to concentrate on practical issues (eg tips, guidelines etc); and are followed up with immediate implementation opportunities. Tend to be impatient with open-ended theory or discussion.

3.3 Awareness of learning styles enables managers to devise learning activities that fit learners' natural preferences, and work to their associated strengths and limitations: in a training group, say, this may mean including a range of activities to engage all participants.

3.4 As with many style or type approaches, however, it is important to note that no style is 'better' than another – and that individuals can develop good skills in areas that are not their natural preference. All four styles are used in the learning cycle, for example: the pragmatist is strong in the 'act' stage, the reflector in the 'analyse' stage, the theorist in the 'abstract' stage, and the activist in the 'adjust' stage.

3.5 When developing learning activities for team members, therefore, a manager may:

- Include elements which will suit the learner's preferred style (for individual learning), or elements which will suit all four learning styles (for group learning). 'This avoids the likelihood of people being exposed to learning experiences in a form which they find unhelpful. It reduces frustration' (Honey & Mumford).

- Encourage learners to undertake activities which do *not* suit their preferred style, in order to stretch them. This builds a wider range of learning opportunities, by developing learners' competence in less preferred styles (which may be more appropriate for the development of a particular competency). Note that the fact that a learner has a strong preference for one style does not mean *either* that he uses that style effectively *or* that he cannot learn to learn using other styles. The opportunity for learning may be maximised by 'mixing it up'.

4　Knowledge management

4.1　Systems to capture and share individual knowledge and learning are increasingly recognised as important, so that every member of an organisation can contribute to the creation, management and dissemination of collective 'know-that' and 'know-how' throughout the organisation. The objective of knowledge management is to optimise the knowledge that is available in an organisation: creating new knowledge, and increasing awareness and understanding in the process.

4.2　Knowledge management may be defined as 'the systematic process that supports the continuous development of individual, group and organisational learning; involving the creation, acquisition, gathering, transforming, transfer and application of knowledge to achieve organisational objectives' (John P Wilson, *Human Resource Development*). Mullins identifies knowledge management both with organisational learning and with the ability of the organisation 'to make effective use of its intellectual assets'.

4.3　A holistic approach to knowledge management involves the following processes.

- *Acquiring* knowledge (eg from environmental scanning, market research, purchasing research, benchmarking, modelling, networking and so on)
- *Generating or creating* knowledge, through processes such as ideas generation (eg brainstorming and think-tanks); research and development; stakeholder consultation (eg suggestion schemes, quality circles, early supplier involvement); lesson learning (eg project reviews and learning capture); and cultivating supplier and workforce diversity (for diverse perspectives and information)
- *Transforming* information into new knowledge (eg by compiling, combining, analysing, interpreting or re-formatting)
- *Capturing* unspoken, internal (tacit) knowledge to convert it to open, stated (explicit) knowledge, so that it can be communicated, shared and used
- *Storing* knowledge effectively in information and knowledge management systems
- *Sharing* or disseminating knowledge throughout the organisation (eg via ICT networks, cross-functional teams)
- *Protecting* distinctive, value-adding knowledge for competitive advantage (eg via access controls, confidentiality agreements and intellectual property protections)
- *Applying* knowledge to develop core capabilities (such as innovation or agile supply) which cannot easily be imitated by competitors.

4.4　MP Kerr ('Knowledge Management'; *Occupational Psychologist)* identifies seven drivers for knowledge management in organisations.

- Business pressure for innovation
- Inter-organisational enterprises (eg mergers, takeovers)
- Networked organisations (including supply chains), and the need to co-ordinate geographically dispersed groups (eg in virtual organisations)
- Increasingly complex products and services with a significant knowledge component
- Hyper-competitive global markets (with decreasing product lifecycles and time to market, putting pressure on innovation and responsiveness)
- The digitisation of business environments and the ICT revolution (including an explosion of available knowledge, and tools for managing knowledge)
- Concerns about the loss of organisational knowledge, due to increasing downsizing, outsourcing and staff mobility.
- Explicit and tacit knowledge

4.5　According to Ikujiro Nonaka, the idea of organisations processing information in an 'input-transformation-output' model is too passive. He argues instead that organisational learning results from a process in which *individual* knowledge is transferred, enlarged and shared upwardly to the *organisational* level. In collaboration with Hirotaka Takeuchi *(The Knowledge-Creating Company)*, Nonaka developed this idea into a model based on the distinction between tacit and explicit knowledge.

- *Tacit knowledge* is innate 'know-how': deeply ingrained, taken-for-granted and often unconscious mental models and competencies. People 'just know' how to do things. Such knowledge is difficult to articulate, formalise or share with others.
- *Explicit knowledge* is formal, systematic, clearly articulated knowledge, which can be communicated and shared via tools such as product specifications, procedures or computer programs.

4.6 To increase organisational learning, a process of knowledge conversion is required, beginning at the individual level, and expanding through social interactions to include a diversity of perspectives that ultimately represent shared knowledge at the organisational level. Nonaka and Takeuchi illustrate this process as follows: Figure 4.2.

Figure 4.2 *The Nonaka-Takeuchi model*

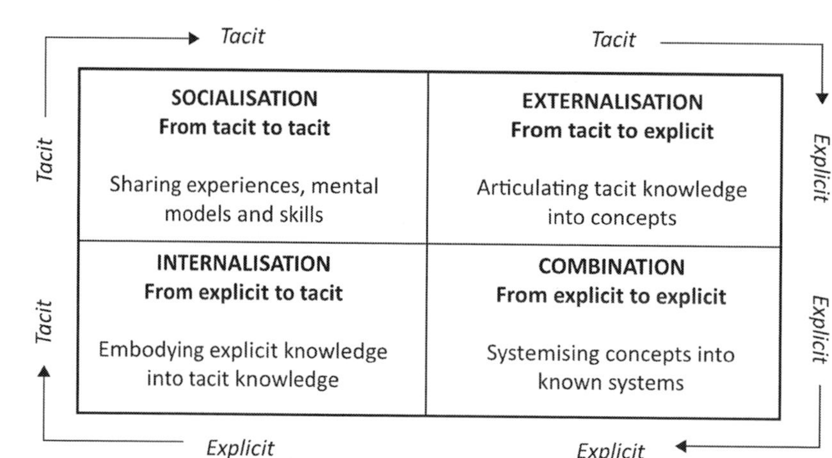

4.7 Taking each process in turn:

- **Socialisation** is the transfer of tacit knowledge through interactions between individuals, as when a master shares craft knowledge and skills with an apprentice, or a mentor with a mentoree. This may occur without the knowledge being verbalised: for example, through observation, imitation, and practice.
- **Externalisation** is the transformation of tacit knowledge into explicit knowledge, as one individual explains to another what he knows. Metaphors and analogies, for example, may be used to explain tacit concepts that are otherwise difficult to articulate.
- **Combination** is the aggregation of multiple, diverse pieces of explicit knowledge (eg during meetings or conferences), to form an enhanced body of understanding, which may be formalised or codified for further sharing and use.
- **Internalisation** is the conversion of explicit knowledge to tacit (embedded) knowledge, through a series of repetitions in which concepts become concrete – and ultimately absorbed into people's mental models as integral beliefs and values or unconscious competence.

4.8 This process is initiated at the level of the individual organisation member: individual commitment to knowledge creation and sharing is therefore critical. Managers may have an important role in creating the conditions within which this process occurs: stimulating the motivation to pursue new knowledge (eg problems to be solved, or environmental challenges and changes to be met); and providing the freedom to do so (creating an open communication climate, promoting trust and allowing time for knowledge creation processes).

Knowledge communities

4.9   A knowledge community is a group of individuals or organisations with a common interest, and a willingness to share ideas and experience. A knowledge community may exist within a single organisation. For example, there might be an area on the firm's intranet where different project teams could swap tips or request help from others who have met with similar problems in the past. (One example is the Xerox 'Eureka' Knowledge Base, through which Xerox copier technicians could share problems and solutions encountered in the field: tips, tricks, 'cheat sheets' and so on, organised in a central database.)

4.10   Alternatively, a knowledge community could involve a wide range of individuals and organisations, facilitated by ICT networks such as the internet. The term 'communities of practice' is often given to groups of people drawn together to facilitate learning and best practice sharing *other than* with immediate work colleagues. 'They are usually organised around a particular theme, field or 'knowledge domain', with which the volunteer participants identify. The community of practice is held together by a mutual interest in learning and knowledge development with a shared knowledge domain' (Etienne Wenger, *Communities of Practice: Learning, Meaning and Identity*).

4.11   Knowledge communiities and communities of practice offer a way of capturing (externalising and combining) tacit knowledge in an organisation or field. Many organisations now encourage, support and sponsor them, in order to benefit from the knowledge resource created.

4.12   The main incentive for organisations to invest in developing knowledge communities is the value that is placed on transferring knowledge between people. Organisations increasingly need their employees to become 'knowledge workers,' ie individuals who constantly draw on a wealth of knowledge to devise new responses and solutions for a rapidly changing market place. This means that employees need to be able to participate in a flow of knowledge that consists of not only documentation and online information sources, but the exchange of ideas with others who have experience and skill related to the same area of work.

4.13   Knowledge communities are also useful in orienting new employees; helping customer-facing staff to respond to customer problems and questions; saving time on the 'reinvention of the wheel' every time a common problem occurs; developing and disseminating best practice; and generating new ideas. It may be argued that they also encourage performance-focused communication, collaboration and problem-solving within an organisation and stakeholder network, which may improve relationships and decision-making.

Challenges of knowledge management

4.14   Different organisations and sectors will have their own particular issues with knowledge management. You might be aware, for example, of the current struggle of music, film, software and consumer electronics companies to protect their intellectual property (copyright, patents and designs). Generally, organisations may struggle to find a balance between the need to *protect* knowledge (confidentiality and intellectual property: requiring a culture of protection and control) and the need to *capture, share and disseminate* it (requiring a culture of trust and transparency).

4.15   Mullins cites a summary by Megan Santosus & Jon Surmacz ('The ABCs of Knowledge Management', *CIO Magazine*) of the problems associated with knowledge management initiatives.

- *Getting employees on board.* Many initiatives ignore the people and cultural issues, and fail to recognise the importance of tacit knowledge to the organisation
- *The role of technology.* Many initiatives allow techology (information systems) to initiate and dictate knowledge management – rather than asking important questions about what data is required (now and in the future) and why
- *Lack of business goals* for knowledge management

- *Lack of dynamism and flexibility.* Knowledge management needs to be a continuous process, as new issues and opportunities emerge, and knowledge needs to be updated: it is not a one-off process of data capture.
- *Confusion of information and knowledge.* Not all information is knowledge, and quantity does not equal quality. Information overload (and resulting 'analysis paralysis') is a problem in many organisations.

5 The learning organisation

5.1 Pedler, Burgoyne and Boydell *(The Learning Company: a Strategy for Sustainable Development)* popularised the term 'learning organisation' to describe an organisation 'that facilitates the acquisition and sharing of knowledge, and the learning of all its members, in order continuously and strategically to transform itself in response to a rapidly changing and uncertain environment'.

Characteristics of learning organisations

5.2 According to Pedler *et al,* learning organisations are good at certain key processes.

- **Experimentation.** Learning organisations systematically search out and test new knowledge. Decision-making is based on scientific 'hypothesis-gathering, hypothesis-testing' techniques: the plan-do-check-act cycle. *Application* of new information and learning, however, is the key: learning organisations support risk-taking and encourage innovation.
- **Learning from past experience.** In a learning organisation, all actions have two purposes: to resolve the immediate problem *and* to learn from the process. Learning organisations constantly gather and provide feedback on processes and results: they review their successes and failures, analyse them systematically and disseminate the lessons as widely as possible. Mistakes and failures are regarded as learning opportunities.
- **Learning from others.** Learning organisations encourage employees to seek information and learning opportunities outside the organisation. They recognise that the most powerful insights and opportunities come from looking 'outside the box' of the immediate environment, and support wide environmental monitoring, networking and borrowing of ideas (within legal constraints).
- **Transferring knowledge** quickly and efficiently throughout the organisation. Information is made available at all levels and across functional boundaries. Education, training and networking opportunities are constantly available.

5.3 Peter Senge *(The Fifth Discipline)* describes the learning organisation as one where people continually expand their capacity to create the results they truly desire; where new and expansive patterns of thinking are nurtured; where collective aspiration is set free; and where people are continually learning how to learn together. Senge identified five key disciplines of learning organisations: Table 4.2.

Table 4.2 *Senge's five disciplines*

DISCIPLINE	EXPLANATION
Personal mastery	Continually clarifying and deepening our personal vision, focusing our energies, developing patience, and seeing reality objectively
Mental models	Deeply ingrained assumptions, generalisations or even pictures or images that influence how we understand the world and how we take action
Shared vision	Unearthing shared 'pictures of the future' that foster genuine commitment and enrolment rather than compliance
Team learning	The capacity of team members to suspend assumptions and enter into a genuine process of thinking together
Systems thinking	The 'fifth discipline': a conceptual framework, a body of knowledge and tools to make patterns clearer and to help us see how to change them effectively

5.4   Yukl *(Leadership in Organisations)* proposes a number of features of learning organisations through the lens of effective management and leadership practices.

- Leaders developing methods for understanding and interpreting business processes
- People at all levels being empowered to deal with problems and suggest better working methods
- Knowledge being made available throughout the organisation and people being encouraged to apply it in their work
- Top management championing changes, and suggestions for change, initiated by lower levels of the organisation
- Resources being invested in the promotion of learning and entrepreneurship

5.5   Other characteristics of a learning organisation include the following.

- All actions have two purposes: to resolve the immediate problem *and* to learn from the process (by gathering and analysing feedback on processes and results, and disseminating lessons).
- Decision-making processes are continuously modified in the light of experience, avoiding rigid plans and procedures.
- Problem-solving is systematic and based on analysis rather than guesswork; utilising the 'plan-do-check-act' cycle (W Edwards Deming).
- Risk-taking, failures and mistakes are regarded as useful input to learning.
- Information and feedback are encouraged from all possible sources (including suppliers, customers and competitors).
- Knowledge is disseminated quickly and efficiently through the organisation. Burgoyne calls this 'informating': a combination of internal openness and the use of ICT for continual information sharing.
- Everything is open to challenge and questioning. No body of knowledge or procedure becomes 'enshrined' by practice.
- Learning and development activity focuses on learning how to learn, and continuous self-managed learning.
- Learning, education and training, and networking opportunities are supported.
- Evaluating the learning organisation

5.6   A number of difficulties have been recognised in the concept of the learning organisation.

- Despite the importance of a supportive learning culture or climate and infrastructure, it is not in itself sufficient to bring about learning. Learning depends on the personality, ability and motivation of individual learners. 'It is impossible to conceive of a learning organisation... which exists without individual learners. The learning organisation depends absolutely on the skills, approaches and commitment of individuals to their own learning' (Mumford, Individual and organisational learning: *Managing Learning*).
- The concept is based on a 'unitary perspective' of organisations: assuming that the goals of workers and management are broadly in alignment, and that willing and trusting collaboration is the norm. In fact, issues of politics, control and conflict may complicate the picture. Organisational politics may be based on the belief that 'knowledge is power', eroding trust and openness for knowledge sharing. Managers may resist learning, in order to preserve their power differential.

Chapter summary

- Outcomes of a learning process may include skills, knowledge, competencies, attitudes, awareness and employability.
- Two basic schools of psychology have focused on learning theory: behaviourist psychology and cognitive psychology.
- Experiential learning is 'learning by doing'. David Kolb is the most influential exponent of this technique, and he categorises learning styles as 'converger', 'diverger', 'assimilator', and 'accommodator'.
- Knowledge management is an increasingly important strategic tool in organisations. Systems to capture and share individual knowledge and learning are increasingly practised in organisations.
- Pedler *et al* have popularised the term 'learning organisation'. Such organisations are good at experimentation, learning from past experience, learning from others, and transferring knowledge throughout the organisation.

Self-test questions

Numbers in brackets refer to the paragraphs where you can check your answers.

1   List types of informal learning. (1.5)

2   What is meant by blended learning? (1.13)

3   Distinguish between behaviourist psychology and cognitive psychology. (2.1)

4   Describe BF Skinner's findings from his research on conditioning. (2.6)

5   What approaches to learning in the workplace are suggested by a cognitive approach to learning? (2.11)

6   Describe the stages in Kolb's experiential learning cycle. (2.16)

7   Describe the learning styles identified by Honey and Mumford. (Table 4.1)

8   List the processes involved in knowledge management. (4.3)

9   Describe the stages in the Nonaka-Takeuchi model. (4.7)

10   What are the five disciplines of learning organisations identified by Peter Senge? (Table 4.2)

CHAPTER 5

Motivation and Job Satisfaction

Assessment criteria and indicative content

2.3 Evaluate the main approaches to motivation in the management of individuals involved in the procurement and supply function

- The meaning of motivation
- Extrinsic and intrinsic motivation
- Frustration-induced and constructive behaviours
- Content theories of motivation
- Process theories of motivation
- Equity and goal theories of motivation

2.4 Analyse the major factors that can influence job satisfaction among individuals involved in the procurement and supply function

- The dimensions of job satisfaction
- Alienation at work
- Approaches to job design, enlargement and enrichment
- Flexible working arrangements

Section headings

1. What is motivation?
2. Content theories of motivation
3. Process theories of motivation
4. Job satisfaction
5. The impact of job design
6. The impact of management style

Introduction

The human relations school of management (as we saw in Chapter 2) shifted focus from employee 'compliance' with the directives of the organisation to employee 'commitment' to the objectives of the organisation. It is now widely recognised that employees must be not just instructed but *motivated* to give their best efforts. This chapter is about how managers can motivate their team members effectively.

Is motivation something we have or don't have, or a decision-making process we go through? What kinds of rewards or incentives should be offered to employees to gain their commitment and best efforts? Do the same rewards and incentives work for everyone? Will people work harder if offered more money, or greater job satisfaction? What *is* job satisfaction? In this chapter we will look at a number of these questions, citing some of the most influential theories and research studies – and building on this foundation to suggest how managers might practically improve motivation and commitment in the workforce.

1 What is motivation?

1.1 Motivation may be defined as:

- The mental process of choosing desired outcomes, deciding how to pursue them, assessing whether the likelihood of success is worth the required effort, and acting accordingly. Our 'motivation' to do something depends on this calculation.
- A social process by which the behaviour of an individual is influenced by others. 'Motivation' thus includes the various strategies organisations and leaders use to secure the efforts and commitment of their workers, from reward systems to leadership styles.

1.2 For a manager, motivation boils down to questions such as: how can we get people more excited about their work? How can we get them to achieve more? How can we recognise and reward achievements? What will make the work itself more meaningful, interesting and challenging for people? What can we do to help people grow and develop and take on more responsibility? What will the team or organisation gain from having committed, loyal people?

Motivation, job satisfaction and performance

1.3 You may be wondering whether motivation is really so important. It could be argued that if a person is employed to do a job, he will do that job – and no question of 'motivation' arises. If the person doesn't want to do the work, he can resign.

1.4 The point at issue, however, is *how* the job is done. It is suggested that if individuals can be 'motivated', by one means or another, they will work more efficiently (and productivity will rise) or they will produce a better quality of work, or will exercise their creativity and initiative in the service of organisational goals. They will work in a more committed fashion. Mullins emphasises that performance is a product of both ability level *and* motivation.

1.5 Job satisfaction is an even more controversial concept.

- It is often said that 'happy bees make more honey' – but this is difficult to measure and demonstrate in practice.
- Job satisfaction is difficult to define: it means different things to different people, and over time, according to needs and expectations.
- As Huczynski and Buchanan note, there is not so much talk about 'the quality of working life' when there is little work to be had.

1.6 On the other hand, low morale, dissatisfaction or demotivation can cause direct and indirect performance problems, through effects such as the following.

- Higher than usual (or higher than acceptable) labour turnover (resignations and transfers)
- Higher levels of absenteeism (whether through work avoidance or genuine stress-related illness)
- Deterioration in timekeeping and discipline
- Reduction in upward communication, proactive involvement (such as suggestions for quality improvements) and other benefits of employee commitment
- Higher incidence of employee disputes and grievances
- Restricted output quantity and/or quality (through lack of commitment or deliberate assertion of negative power).

1.7 You may gather that motivation is an art, not a science: it is a highly subjective phenomenon. Some models of motivation have highlighted the cultural dimension of motivational strategies. Managers will attempt to motivate their teams according to their own assumptions about what makes workers 'tick': what will encourage or force them to work better.

Theory X and Theory Y

1.8 Theory X and Theory Y (*Douglas McGregor*) are not 'types of people' but two extreme sets of managerial assumptions about what makes workers tick, at opposite ends of a continuum.

1.9 As we saw in Chapter 2, McGregor's point is that Theory X and Theory Y assumptions are, in essence, self-fulfilling prophecies. If employees are treated as if Theory X were true (using carrot-and-stick motivation systems, detailed rules and close supervision, low-discretion jobs and so on) they will begin to behave accordingly. It is negative experience at work that fosters lack of ambition, the need for security and intellectual stagnation. If employees are treated as if Theory Y were true (using empowered teamworking, employee involvement schemes and facilitative managerial styles) they will begin to behave accordingly and rise to the challenge.

Motivation theories

1.10 One way of grouping the major theories of motivation is by distinguishing between content theories and process theories.

- *Content theories* ask the question: '*What* are the *things* that motivate people?' They assume that human beings have a set of needs or desired outcomes that they pursue.
- *Process theories* ask the question: '*How* can people be motivated?' They explore the conscious or unconscious process of calculation by which individuals choose certain outcomes and the most advantageous or acceptable paths towards them.

2 Content theories of motivation

2.1 According to content theories, motivated behaviour is aimed at reducing the tension experienced as a result of an unsatisfied need or drive. The managerial task is therefore to offer the means of satisfying the individual's needs – or to create or awaken needs in the individual which the organisation is in a position to satisfy.

2.2 Needs vary between individuals and within the same individuals over time. It is, however, possible to identify various classes of need which are assumed to be innate: natural to all human beings. (Content theories are, in effect, need theories.)

Maslow's hierarchy of needs

2.3 Abraham Maslow *(Motivation and Personality)* described seven innate needs, arranged in a 'hierarchy of relative pre-potency' (summarised in Figure 5.1). Each level of need is dominant until it is satisfied (however incompletely): only then does the next level of need become the dominant motivating factor.

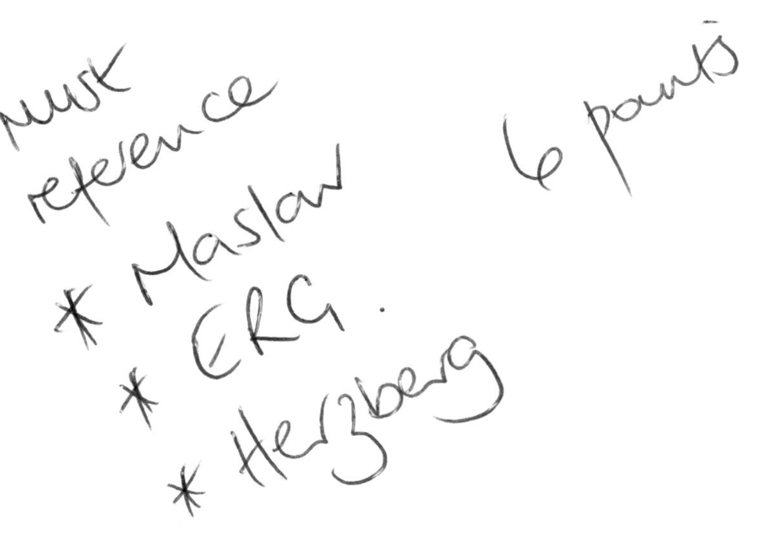

Figure 5.1 *Maslow's hierarchy of needs*

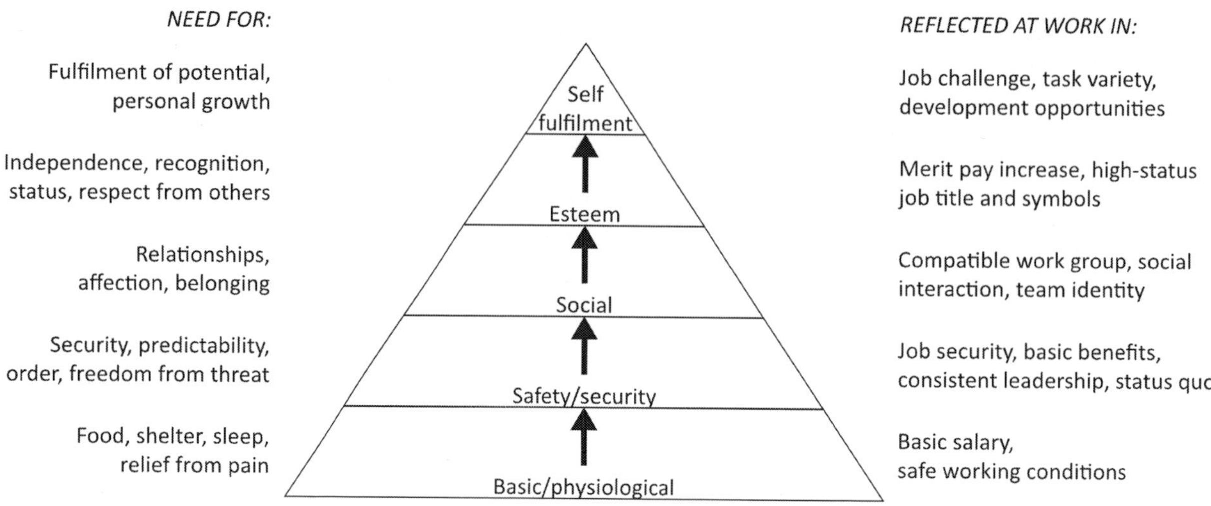

2.4   In addition, Maslow described two 'higher needs' which underpin all the others.

- Freedom of enquiry and expression needs (for social conditions permitting free speech, and encouraging justice, fairness and honesty)
- Knowledge and understanding needs (to gain knowledge of the environment, to explore and learn)

2.5   There is a certain intuitive appeal to Maslow's theory. After all, you are unlikely to be concerned with status or recognition while you are hungry or thirsty: primary survival needs will take precedence until they are satisfied.

2.6   However, it is difficult to use the hierarchy to predict employee behaviour. (Maslow did not intend it to be applied to the work context.) The boundaries between the needs are, in practice, indistinct and overlapping; different people emphasise different needs; and the same need may prompt different behaviours in different individuals. In some contexts, people are clearly able to suppress even their basic physiological and safety needs for the sake of a perceived 'higher cause' or for the sake of others. The role of pay is problematic, since it arguably acts as a 'stand in' for (or way of obtaining) other rewards. Self-actualisation is particularly hard to offer as an 'off the shelf' reward package, since it is highly subjective.

2.7   In addition, Huczynski and Buchanan suggest that 'Maslow may simply have reflected American middle class values and the pursuit of the good life, and may not have hit on fundamental universal truths about human psychology.' Research studies indicate that cultural values affect work behaviour and the success of management techniques. However, the hierarchy of needs offers a useful reminder to managers to adopt a flexible, contingency approach to motivating employees.

Alderfer's ERG theory

2.8   Clayton Alderfer simplified Maslow's need hierarchy down to three categories, along the same lines.

- The need for *existence*
- The need to *relate* to others
- The need for personal *growth*

He called this the 'Existence-Relatedness-Growth' (ERG) model.

2.9   ERG is also a hierarchical model (with individuals progressing through the hierarchy from existence to growth), but Alderfer points out that each individual may have different levels of each kind of need: lower-level needs do *not* have to be satisfied before a higher-level need emerges as the prime motivator. This means that if a person's needs are blocked at one level, managers can still motivate team members by attention to the satisfaction of needs at other levels. (If the job does not allow opportunities for promotion, say, the organisation can still attempt to provide greater teamworking satisfactions.)

McClelland's motivation theory

2.10   David McClelland measured motivation using Thematic Apperception Tests, in which individuals are shown pictures, and invited to describe what they think is happening and what the people in the picture are thinking. They project their dominant motivating needs onto the pictures as they interpret them. These tests identify three categories of need.

- The need for *power*. People with a high need for power usually seek positions in which they can influence and control others.
- The need for *affiliation*. People with a high need for belonging tend to be concerned with maintaining good personal relationships.
- The need for *achievement*. People with high achievement needs have a strong desire for success and strong fear of failure. McClelland identified this as the most important need for the country's economic growth and success. It correlates with: preference for moderate task difficulty (in order to maximise the likelihood of attainment); preference for personal responsibility for performance (in order to obtain success by their own efforts); the need for feedback (in order to determine success or failure); and innovation and an entrepreneurial spirit (in order to move on to the next task once one has been completed).

Herzberg's two factor theory

2.11   In the 1950s, Frederick Herzberg *(Work and the Nature of Man)* interviewed Pittsburgh engineers and accountants to find out what 'critical incidents' had made them feel good or bad about their work. Analysis revealed two distinct sets of factors: those which created satisfaction (which Herzberg called 'motivator factors') and those which created dissatisfaction ('hygiene' or 'maintenance' factors).

2.12   Herzberg highlighted two basic needs of individuals.

- The need to avoid unpleasantness, satisfied by **hygiene** factors
- The need for personal growth, satisfied at work by **motivator** factors only

2.13   Herzberg argued that: 'when people are dissatisfied with their work it is usually because of discontent with environmental factors.' These include company policy and administration, salary, style of leadership and supervision, interpersonal relations, working conditions and job security. Herzberg called them 'hygiene' factors because they are essentially preventive: they minimise dissatisfaction but do not give positive or long-lasting satisfaction, in the same way that sanitation minimises threats to health but does not give good health. An individual is much more likely to be dissatisfied with his pay, for example, than satisfied with it. He may temporarily be satisfied with a pay rise, but only until he begins to take it for granted or compare it to others'. Nevertheless, leaders must give attention to hygiene factors in order to minimise dissatisfaction.

2.14   Motivator factors actively create satisfaction and are effective in motivating individuals to superior performance and effort. They do this by offering personal growth and fulfilment, because, according to Herzberg, if 'dissatisfaction arises from environment factors – satisfaction can only arise from the job'. Motivator factors therefore include: advancement, recognition, responsibility, challenging and interesting work, achievement and growth in the job.

2.15   How interesting or challenging a job has to be, to be motivating, will depend on each individual: his ability and intelligence, his expectations and his tolerance of delayed rewards (eg his preparedness to start at the bottom and work up). Herzberg recommended various approaches to job design which would build motivator factors into the work: job rotation (increasing task variety by moving workers from one job to another in sequence); job enlargement (adding tasks to the job: effectively a 'horizontal' extension) and job enrichment (adding feedback, meaning, interest, responsibility, autonomy and discretion to the job: a 'vertical' extension which we might today call empowerment).

2.16 Herzberg argued that 'management cannot really motivate employees: it can only create the environment in which the employees motivate themselves.' They do this by ensuring that hygiene factors are adequate (to minimise dissatisfaction), and by maximising motivator factors in the work (to maximise satisfaction).

2.17 Although simple and accessible, and embracing a wide range of specific workplace factors, Herzberg's theory has been criticised on a number of grounds. His sample size was small and culturally specific; his methods were rather subjective; and verification of the assertion that motivator factors increase productivity has proved hard to find.

2.18 Nevertheless, Herzberg's work has been helpful in highlighting the concept of job satisfaction (the intrinsic rewards to be found in work itself) and thus contributing to job redesign (discussed later in this chapter) and the 'quality of working life' movement.

Intrinsic and extrinsic motivation

2.19 Herzberg's two factors also highlighted the two types of reward that can be offered to individuals at work.

- **Intrinsic** rewards arise from the work itself, and (in a sense) from within the worker: challenge, interest, team identity, pride in the organisation, the satisfaction of achievement and so on. These are mainly 'psychological' rewards.
- **Extrinsic** rewards do not arise from the work itself, but are within the power of others (typically, management) to award or withhold: wages or salary, bonuses, prizes, promotion, improved working conditions and so on. These are mainly 'tangible' rewards.

2.20 Mullins suggests a 'simplistic but useful' three-fold classification of the needs and expectations which underlie motivation at work.

- **Economic rewards** (such as pay, benefits, deferred pay such as pension rights, and job security) – which satisfy an 'instrumental' orientation to work, mainly concerned with 'other things'
- **Intrinsic satisfactions** (derived from the work itself, interest and personal development) – which satisfy a 'personal' orientation to work, mainly concerned with 'oneself'
- **Social relationships** (such as friendships, teamworking, belonging and status) – which satisfy a 'relational' orientation to work, mainly concerned with 'other people'.

Mullins argues that a person's motivation, job satisfaction and work performance will be determined by the comparative strength of these sets of needs and expectations and the extent to which they are fulfilled.

Pay as a motivator

2.21 The objectives of pay from the organisation's point of view are: to attract and retain labour of a suitable type and quality; to fulfil perceived social responsibilities; and to motivate employees to achieve and maintain desired levels of performance.

2.22 Pay occupies a central – but ambiguous – role in motivation theory. In Herzberg's theory, for example, pay is a hygiene factor rather than a motivator factor. Drucker noted that incentives such as pay, once regularly provided, come to be perceived as 'entitlements' and their capacity to create dissatisfaction, to become a deterrent to performance, outstrips their motivating power. Moreover, Edward E Lawler *(Motivation in Work Organisations)* suggested that in the absence of information about how much colleagues are earning, individuals guess their earnings and usually overestimate – and are then dissatisfied because they resent earning less than they *think* their colleagues are getting!

2.23 However, pay is the most important of the hygiene factors, according to Herzberg. It is valuable not only in its power to be converted into a wide range of other satisfactions but also as a consistent measure of worth or value, allowing employees to compare themselves and be compared with other individuals or occupational groups inside and outside the organisation.

2.24 Employees need income to live. The size of that income will affect their standard of living, but people tend not to be concerned to maximise their earnings. They may like to earn more, but are probably more concerned:

- to earn *enough* pay; and
- to know that their pay is *equitable* in relation to others and to the effort they are putting in.

2.25 Payment systems tread the awkward path between equity (an objective rate for the job, preserving pay differentials and so on) and incentive (offering rewards that will stimulate extra effort and attainment by particular individuals and groups).

2.26 Goldthorpe, Lockwood, Bechofer and Platt (*The Affluent Worker: Industrial Attitudes and Behaviour*) researched the supposed 'instrumental' orientation to work: the attitude that work is not an end in itself, but a means to other ends. In their research, the team found that highly paid Luton car assembly workers experienced their work as routine and dead-end. They had in fact made a rational decision to enter employment offering high monetary reward rather than intrinsic satisfactions.

2.27 The Luton researchers did not, however, claim that *all* workers have an instrumental orientation to work, but suggested that a person will seek a comfortable balance of:

- the rewards which are important to him and
- the deprivations he feels able to put up with in order to earn those rewards.

2.28 Even those with an instrumental orientation to work have limits to their purely financial aspirations and will cease to be motivated by pay if the deprivations – in terms of long working hours, poor conditions, social isolation, boredom or whatever – become too great: in other words, if the price of pay is too high.

2.29 There are a number of **difficulties associated with incentive schemes** based on monetary reward, or performance-related pay.

2.30 Increased earnings may, as we noted above, not be an incentive to all individuals. Moreover, workers are unlikely to be in complete control of results (especially a company's profitability). The link between effort and reward may be insufficient to act as a meaningful incentive – or may be a cause of frustration to workers, if they put in the effort and are not rewarded to the level of their expectation.

2.31 Even if employees are motivated by money, the effects may not be altogether desirable. An instrumental orientation may encourage self-interested performance at the expense of teamwork. It may encourage attention to output at the expense of quality, or the lowering of standards and targets to make bonuses more easily accessible. Workers often remain suspicious that if they achieve high levels of output and earnings, management will alter the basis of the incentive rates to reduce future earnings. Work groups therefore tend to restrict output to a level that they feel is fair but achievable.

2.32 A range of **non-financial rewards** and incentives may be offered in addition to monetary incentives. These often include benefits such as: company car, health insurance, above-statutory holiday time; access to facilities (social, sports); canteen or luncheon vouchers; gift certificates and so on. There has been a trend in recent years towards flexible benefit schemes, allowing employees a choice from a 'menu' of potential benefits: the element of choice increasing the perceived value (valence) of the reward or incentive, and supporting the motivation of an increasingly diverse workforce.

2.33 Non-cash incentive schemes are still based on extrinsic rewards. We will now look at some of the intrinsic rewards that can be offered to employees.

3 Process theories of motivation

Vroom's expectancy theory

3.1 Expectancy theory is a process theory of motivation, which states that the strength of an individual's motivation to do something will depend on the extent to which he expects the results of his efforts to contribute to his personal needs or goals.

3.2 Victor Vroom *(Work & Motivation)* suggested a formula by which human motivation could be assessed and measured, based on expectancy theory. He suggested that the strength of an individual's motivation is the product of two factors.

- The strength of his preference for a certain outcome. Vroom called this 'valence': it can be represented as a positive or negative number, or zero – since outcomes may be desired, avoided or regarded with indifference.
- His expectation that the outcome will in fact result from a certain behaviour. Vroom called this 'subjective probability' or 'expectancy'. As a probability, it may be represented by any number between 0 (no chance) and 1 (certainty).

3.3 In its simplest form, the expectancy equation may be stated as follows.

$F = V \times E$

where:

F = the force or strength of the individual's motivation to behave in a particular way
V = valence: the strength of the individual's preference for a given outcome or reward
E = expectancy: the individual's perception that the behaviour will result in the outcome or reward

3.4 In this equation, the lower the values of valence or expectation, the less the individual's motivation. An employee may have a high expectation that increased productivity will result in promotion (because of managerial promises, say), but if he is indifferent or negative towards the idea of promotion (because he dislikes responsibility), he will not be motivated to increase his productivity. The same would be true if promotion was very important to him, but he did not believe higher productivity would get him promoted (because he has been passed over before, perhaps).

3.5 Expectancy theory can be used to measure the likely strength of a worker's motivation to act in a desired way in response to a range of different rewards, to find the most effective motivational strategy.

Porter & Lawler's expectancy model

3.6 Lyman W Porter and Edward E Lawler developed a more comprehensive model of motivation which they applied primarily to managers: Figure 5.2.

Figure 5.2 *The Porter-Lawler model of motivation*

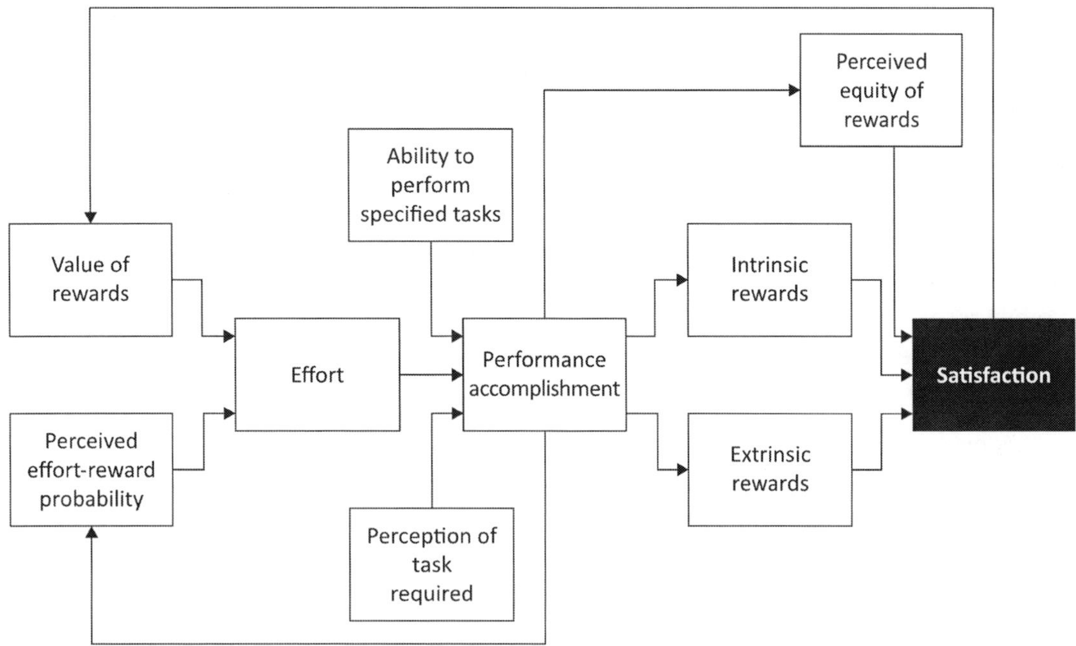

3.7 The model suggests that the amount of effort exerted depends on the value of a reward to the individual plus the amount of energy the individual believes is required to earn the reward, and the perceived likelihood of his receiving it. The last two factors are, in turn, influenced by a number of other factors, such as the actual rewards received for past performance.

3.8 Actual performance in the job is affected not only by the effort expended by the individual, but also by his understanding of the task and the extent of his ability to receive it.

3.9 The individual's perception of whether the extrinsic rewards for performance (such as pay) are equitable or not will affect his satisfaction in the job. At the same time, the intrinsic reward of satisfaction in the job will affect his perception of whether the extrinsic rewards are equitable.

3.10 This model urges a contingency approach to motivation. Managers should give attention to a number of factors.

- A balanced offering of intrinsic and extrinsic rewards for performance, relevant to the individual (with a focus on outcomes with high valence)
- Ensuring a clear link between performance and rewards
- Establishing clear yardsticks and measures of individual performance, and giving clear progress feedback.

3.11 At the same time, they need to recognise that:

- Motivation is not the sole influence on performance: attention must be given to intervening variables such as personality, ability and training, organisation and systems, and so on
- Motivation depends on the subjective perceptions of the team members as to the value of rewards, the perceived effort-reward link and the equity of the rewards offered
- The model is just a model (as recognised by Porter & Lawler): expectancy theory only applies to behaviours which are under the direct and voluntary control of the individual (the amount of effort and energy expended and the way in which they perform their work).

Equity theory: JS Adams

3.12   Equity theory focuses on people's perception of the fairness of their treatment, position, or rewards both in terms of *exchange* (outputs received in exchange for inputs of effort, energy, commitment and so on) and in terms of *comparison* (treatment compared with that of others in similar circumstances). When there is inequality or imbalance of reward or treatment, the individual experiences a sense of 'inequity' (lack of justice or fairness).

3.13   JS Adams ('Injustice in Social Exchange'; *Advances in Experimental and Social Psychology)* argued that a sense of inequity is created when people feel that the rewards obtained for their efforts are unequal to those received by others. A sense of inequity creates an unpleasant sense of cognitive dissonance or tension. The individual is motivated to remove the discomfort and restore a state of felt equity to the situation by various means.

- Changing inputs to match the outputs and rewards (reducing work to match unfairly low pay, say, or working extra hours without overtime to match unfairly high pay)
- Changing the outputs and rewards to match inputs (eg seeking extra pay or recognition to match perceived effort or contribution)
- Psychologically distorting the outputs or inputs to explain away the inequity (eg mentally glossing over how hard one is working compared to others)
- Changing the inputs or outputs of others (eg seeking to influence other team members to put in less effort, produce less or accept lower rewards)
- Changing the reference points for comparison (eg comparing oneself to a different group, which allows the inequity to be more readily explained)
- Leaving the situation (eg resigning, or requesting a transfer to another team, in order to find a more favourable balance).

3.14   Managers may attempt to reduce perceived inequity in a team by attempting to change an individual's inputs (persuading them to work harder, or, conversely, to cultivate better work-life balance) or outcomes (eg balancing rewards within the team). However, the inequity may only be in the team member's perception, and it may be necessary to offer a 'reality check' (eg in the form of more realistic comparisons).

Goal or goal-setting theory

3.15   Edward Locke ('Towards a Theory of Task Motivation and Incentives'; *Organisational Behaviour and Human Performance)* focused on the role of people's goals or intentions in motivating behaviour, and the importance of goal-setting as a motivational technique: Figure 5.3.

- The valence (perceived value) of an outcome or reward creates emotions and desires.
- In order to satisfy these emotions and desires, individuals formulate goals (or intentions).
- Pursuit of those goals directs the individual's actions – including work behaviour and performance.
- The level of effort the individual will expend on attaining the goal, however, depends on two factors: the perceived difficulty of attaining the goal, and the level of the individual's commitment to achieving the goal. People perform better if they have (a) specific, measurable, time-bounded goals and (b) challenging or 'stretching' (difficult but achievable) goals.
- Work behaviour and performance lead to results, consequences and feedback, which enables the revision of goals, and the calculation of expectancy for next time.

Figure 5.3 *Locke's goal-setting theory*

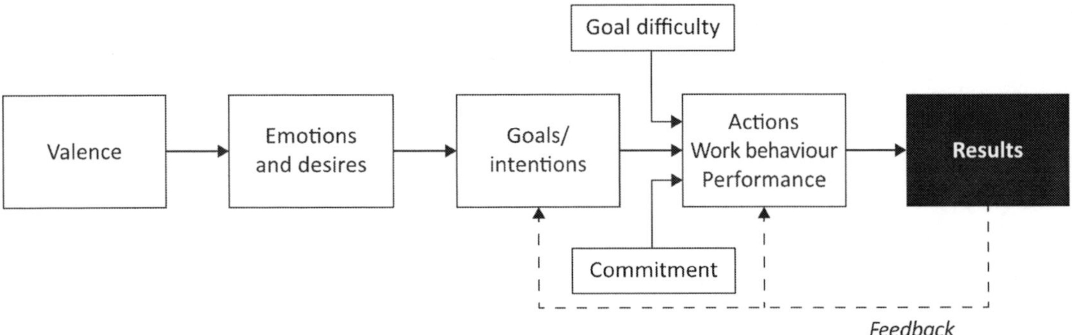

3.16 The goal-setting model has some clear implications for management practice. Specific, clear, measurable performance goals should be set in order to maintain motivation. Goals should be set at a realistic, attainable but challenging level. Timely, meaningful feedback on results should be given, to allow checking of progress on goal attainment. Other models have also emphasised that participation in the setting of goals may lead to higher motivation and performance.

Frustration of motivated behaviour

3.17 What happens if a person is unable to satisfy his motivating needs – because the path to his goals is blocked? Mullins suggests that two responses to frustration are possible.

- **Constructive behaviour**: a positive and adaptive response to blockage of the desired goal, based on:
  — *Problem-solving:* removal of the barrier (eg by finding alternative methods to reach the goal, such as going over the head of an unsupportive manager) *or*
  — *Restructuring:* formulating an adjusted or alternative goal (eg taking on part-time volunteer work to make up for lack of job satisfaction).
- **Frustration-induced behaviour**: a negative reaction to blockage of the desired goal, which may include:
  — *Aggression:* physical or verbal anger directed at a person or object (eg abusive language or sabotaging machinery or documents). It may be directed at the person or object responsible for the frustration – but if they are not identifiable (or not directly attackable, due to distance or risk of punishment) the aggression may be 'displaced' onto an easier or safer target (eg subordinates or colleagues). Individuals can be taught to manage aggression safely, channelling it into outlets that are safe or even constructive (eg physical exercise or hard work). They can also be taught skills of assertive communication (standing up for one's needs, wants and rights clearly and firmly, but *without* aggression).
  — *Regression:* reverting to childish or primitive behaviours (eg sulking or tantrums)
  — *Fixation:* persisting in behaviours which have no adaptive value, or continuing courses of action which have no positive results (eg repeatedly trying the same method in a task, even though it has proven ineffective)
  — *Withdrawal:* resignation, giving up or withdrawing energy and commitment from the task (eg poor time-keeping, absenteeism, avoiding decisions or people, leaving work to others, or leaving the job altogether).

3.18 The level of an individual's frustration at finding the chosen path to a chosen goal blocked will vary, according to circumstances: the strength of the need; the intensity of the individual's attachment to the goal; the strength of the individual's motivation; the perceived nature of the blockage (eg personal or impersonal; bad luck or intentional; fair or unfair); and the personality of the individual.

4   Job satisfaction

4.1   Work is a central feature of modern industrial societies. It occupies much of people's time for the majority of their lives. Work is sometimes viewed, simplistically, as a purely economic activity, but it occupies non-financial roles in people's lives as well.

4.2   Work has sociological importance. A person's occupation correlates strongly with social status and lifestyle, and 'places' the individual in social roles. Western cultural values assign a positive moral value to work (sometimes called 'work ethic'). The perception of a person's social worth and respectability is defined by paid employment, and being without paid work, for whatever reason, tends to reduce an individual's status and involvement in mainstream society.

4.3   Since work occupies so much of an individual's time and energy, it also has psychological importance. Work factors influence our relationships, self-image and self-esteem, sense of competence and power, opportunities for creativity and self-actualisation and so on. Sadly, research (eg by Robert Dubin) suggests that for many people, work satisfies relatively few of their needs, and satisfaction and interest are found only outside the workplace.

4.4   However, the expectations of workers in developed societies have become more sophisticated, with better education, comparative affluence, the demographic downturn (falling birth rates) and emerging skill shortages. Many organisations are making an effort to increase the quality of working life – and specifically, the intrinsic satisfactions of work – in order to attract and retain quality labour.

Dimensions of job satisfaction

4.5   J Richard Hackman & Greg R Oldham ('Motivation through the design of work', in *Organisational Behaviour and Human Performance)* focused on certain core job dimensions which contribute to job satisfaction and intrinsic motivation. Job satisfaction is related to the experience of three psychological states, each of which is aroused by key job characteristics: Table 5.1.

Table 5.1 *Hackman & Oldham's Core Job Dimensions*

STATE	JOB DIMENSIONS
Meaningfulness of work	*Skill variety*: the opportunity to exercise different skills and perform different operations – as opposed to micro-specialisation and repetition, which cause monotony and boredom *Task identity*: the integration of operations into a 'whole' task (or a meaningful 'chunk' of a task), as opposed to task fragmentation *Task significance*: the task has a role, purpose, meaning and worth, according to the values of the organisation and the individual
Responsibility	*Autonomy*: the opportunity to exercise discretion or self-management in areas such as target-setting, scheduling and choice of work methods
Knowledge of outcomes	*Feedback*: the availability of information by which the individual can assess progress and performance in relation to expectations and targets – and the opportunity to give feedback and have a voice in performance improvement.

4.6   Research by Paul Hill similarly suggests that the psychological requirements of a 'full job' for the individual are as follows.

- The content of the work should be reasonably demanding of the individual (in terms other than sheer endurance) and should have some variety.
- An individual should know what his job is, what are the standards of success and how he is performing in relation to them.
- There should be an opportunity to learn on the job and to continue learning.
- There should be some area of decision-making where the individual can exercise discretion.

- There should be some social support and recognition within the organisation.
- An individual should be able to relate his work and output to the objectives of the company and to his place in the community.
- There should be perceived potential for the job to lead to some sort of desirable future (though this does not necessarily imply promotion).

Alienation at work

4.7   Earlier, we discussed the frustration of goal-pursuing behaviour as a potential de-motivator. Mullins argues that job satisfaction can be seen as the opposite of frustration and alienation at work.

4.8   'Alienation' is the experience of separation or disengagement from some aspect of one's life, particularly one's work role. Karl Marx argued that the division of labour in capitalist society inevitably causes the worker to lose control over the conditions and fruits of his labour, with the result that he becomes estranged both from himself and from his fellow men (whether he knows it or not).

4.9   One of the main themes repeatedly emerging in accounts of unskilled work is the experience of alienation suffered by workers in mindless, routine, satisfaction-less jobs. Robert Blauner *(Alienation and Freedom)* identified four dimensions of alienation.

- Powerlessness – loss of control over work and conditions
- Meaninglessness – loss of the significance of work, due to standardisation and the division of labour
- Isolation – loss of a sense of belonging and relatedness, due to not belonging to an identified work group
- Self-estrangement – loss of personal identity, of any sense of work as a central life activity: work is solely a means of satisfying external demands, rather than satisfying in itself.

You should be able to see how the core dimensions of job satisfaction can be used to eliminate or reduce the experience of alienation at work.

4.10   Alienation has often been associated with automation and assembly-line work organisation, but Blauner's research indicated that *advanced* technology in fact reduces alienation in some circumstances.

- Where it allows teamwork and social contact
- Where it allows control over work pace
- Where it allows opportunities to learn about processes and develop technology-related skills

Participation and involvement as a motivator

4.11   There is substantial evidence that participation can improve the decision-making effectiveness of organisations. It is also suggested that people are more motivated to achieve targets they have helped establish and to put effort into solving problems that they have helped to identify: participation therefore acts as an incentive to performance. It is also a form of reward, since it offers enhanced status, job interest and recognition of employees' value to the organisation.

4.12   'Employee involvement' describes a number of policies and procedures which aim to increase employees' commitment and contribution to the organisation. David Guest describes five ways to get employees involved.

- Improving the provision of information to employees (eg through briefing groups or works councils)
- Improving the gathering of information from employees (eg through suggestion schemes and quality circles)
- Changing the structure and arrangement of work (eg through increased delegation and teamworking)
- Changing the incentives (eg introducing profit-sharing)
- Changing relationships (by more participative leadership and breaking down artificial status barriers between management and workers)

4.13   As Anthony G Hopwood noted, it is 'naïve to think that participative approaches are always more effective than authoritarian styles'. If there is no participation, most employees would still comply with orders, and in certain organisational contexts, this may be acceptable (for example, in authoritarian cultures) and sufficient to secure adequate performance (for example, where work is highly automated). However, there has been a shift in recent decades from systems of *compliance* to systems of *commitment*.

4.14   Commitment is an elusive concept, but Mowday, Porter and Steers describe it as 'the relative strength of an individual's identification with and involvement in a particular organisation. It is characterised by at least three factors:

- A strong belief in and acceptance of an organisation's goals and values
- A willingness to exert considerable effort on behalf of the organisation
- A strong desire to maintain membership of the organisation.'

4.15   Commitment may therefore be desirable where an organisation wants to foster goal congruence and harmonious employee relations; employee loyalty and retention; flexibility and maximisation of the labour resource; upward communication; a culture of continuous improvement, innovation and responsiveness; positive change management and so on.

4.16   Michael Armstrong suggests the following steps to increase employee commitment.

- Introduce programmes for increasing motivation (using any of the methods discussed above).
- Exercise more effective leadership.
- Develop identification with the organisation and its values by means of communication, participation, listening to employees' ideas, training and profit-sharing (or some other form of financial stakeholding for employees).
- Operate accountable management, ensuring that people know what they have to achieve and are aware of how their performance will be measured against agreed targets and standards.
- Introduce reward systems which partly link reward to individual performance.
- Care for employees: treat them as valued human beings, not machines.

Culture as a motivator

4.17   Organisation culture expresses the shared values, beliefs and self-image of the organisation: it can embrace positive or negative values towards work, performance, quality and so on.

4.18   Drucker speaks of the 'spirit of performance' which is the 'creation of energy' in an organisation. Peters and Waterman (*In Search of Excellence*) likewise argue that employees can be 'switched on' to extraordinary loyalty and effort through culture in the following ways.

- *The cause is perceived to be in some sense great.* Managers need to 'reaffirm the heroic dimension of work': emphasising that quality and customer satisfaction are worthwhile goals, celebrating successes (and heroic failures) and so on. 'Owing to good luck, or maybe even good sense, those companies that emphasise quality, reliability and service have chosen the only area where it is readily possible to generate excitement in the average down-the-line employee. They give people pride in what they do. They make it possible to love the product.'
- *People are treated as winners.* 'Label a man a loser and he'll start acting like one.' Repressive control systems and negative reinforcement (by threats, punishments and reprimands) break down the employee's self-image and confidence. Positive reinforcement (by reward, praise, recognition and attention) creates positive energy.
- *People are enabled to satisfy their dual needs:* to be a conforming, secure part of something bigger than themselves and to be a 'star' in their own right.

5 The impact of job design

5.1 A 'job' is a set of tasks or functions that are grouped together and allocated to an individual: his sphere of activity at work. For many employees, it seems as if jobs are just 'there' (or not). But the fact is that 'jobs' are the product of a great number of decisions about how the activities of the organisation can or should be divided up; what tasks naturally go together with others; how many different tasks an individual can perform effectively; whether it is more efficient or more motivating to have each individual perform a single task (repeatedly), or a variety of tasks (in sequence) – and so on.

5.2 Job design is the way in which tasks are divided or grouped to form the work responsibilities of a given job, and what decisions are made about specialisation, discretion, autonomy, variety and other job elements.

Early job design: efficient task performance

5.3 Frederick Taylor (discussed in Chapter 2) was an early exponent of systematic job design. His technique was basically as follows.

- Decide on the optimum degree of task fragmentation, breaking down a complex task into its most basic component parts, which would represent the whole 'job' of a worker or group of workers.
- Decide the most efficient way of performing each operation, using work study techniques and time and motion study to determine the simplest way to perform a task, eliminate wasteful motions (physical movements) and set standard times for all operations.
- Train employees to carry out their single task fragment in the most efficient way.

Jobs were therefore 'micro-designed': reduced to single, repetitive motions.

5.4 The micro-division of labour is based on a production line organisation of work and offers some efficiencies for this sort of work. Each task is so simple that it can be learned with little training; the effects of absenteeism and labour turnover are minimised; and tasks can be closely defined, standardised and timed, so output quantity and quality are more easily predicted and controlled. (You might recognise this form of design in packaging, quality inspection, assembly and other such jobs.)

5.5 Looking back on the scientific management period, however, Herbert Hicks wrote: 'the worker had been reduced to the role of an impersonal cog in the machine of production. His work became more and more narrowly specialised until he had little appreciation for his contribution to the total product.... Although very significant technological advances were made ... the serious weakness of the scientific approach to management was that it de-humanised the organisational member who became a person without emotion and capable of being scientifically manipulated, just like machines.'

5.6 Studies of human behaviour at work suggested that the existence of such micro-tasks also poses problems for management.

- Monotony, and the experience of boredom, is part of 'industrial fatigue', which interferes with the steady state in which workers work best. Tasks which provide little mental stimulation may result in inattention and preoccupation with social interactions and distractions: errors and accidents may result.
- High-workload, low-discretion jobs correlate strongly with stress. Its symptoms invariably affect performance.
- Motivation will suffer, and efforts to compensate workers with extrinsic rewards are unlikely to promote lasting satisfaction.
- If such tasks are perceived to be the lot of the worker ('us') under the control of and for the benefit of management ('them'), employee relations will be adversarial.

A human relations perspective: worker job satisfaction

5.7 The question of job design acquired its prominence when human relations theorists became interested in the motivational aspects of the job and the role of 'job satisfaction' in worker performance.

5.8 Motivation researcher Frederick Herzberg was among the first to suggest a systematic approach to job satisfaction and its relationship to job design. As we saw earlier in this chapter, Herzberg's theory suggested that the job itself can be a source of satisfaction, offering various ways of meeting the individual's needs for personal growth. Huczynski and Buchanan explain this by pointing out that 'the design of an individual's job determines both the kind of rewards that are available and what the individual has to do to get those rewards.'

5.9 Herzberg *(Work and the Nature of Man)* recommended three basic approaches to increasing worker satisfaction through job design: job rotation, job enlargement and job enrichment.

- **Job rotation** is the planned transfer of staff between jobs to give greater task variety. (The documented example quotes a warehouse gang of four workers, where the worst job was seen as tying the necks of the sacks at the base of the hopper, and the best job as being the fork lift truck driver: job rotation would ensure that individuals spent equal time on all jobs.) It is generally admitted that the developmental value of job rotation is limited, but it can reduce the monotony of repetitive work.
- **Job enlargement** is an attempt to widen jobs by increasing the number of operations or tasks in which the worker is involved. This is a 'horizontal extension' of the job (Argyris). The lengthened time cycle of repeated operations may reduce monotony. However, Herzberg himself noted that asking a worker to complete three separate tedious, unchallenging tasks is unlikely to motivate him more than asking him to fulfil one single tedious, unchallenging task.
- **Job enrichment** is a planned, deliberate action to build greater responsibility, breadth and challenge of work into a job. This is a 'vertical extension' of the job (Arygris), which is often equated with 'empowerment'. It may include removing controls over workers' actions; increasing responsibility and accountability; providing more regular feedback on performance; introducing new tasks; or allocating special assignments. This will clearly impact more powerfully on employees' experience in the core job dimensions discussed earlier.

5.10 It is worth getting this in perspective. Not all workers will need or want more challenging work. And, as Charles Handy points out, 'Even those who want their jobs enriched will expect to be rewarded with more than job satisfaction. Job enrichment is not a cheaper way to greater productivity. Its pay-off will come in the less visible costs of morale, climate and working relationships.'

5.11 It should also be noted that, however beneficial job enlargement or enrichment may be, it is not easy to redesign jobs in practice. The benefits of any such programme in relation to organisational objectives will need to be carefully justified in terms of increases in productivity, enhanced flexibility, improved worker commitment (leading to a reduction in undesired labour turnover), etc.

5.12 Job design can be very expensive in time and financial costs. It requires specialist work study and design techniques, and may involve the re-engineering of whole processes, systems and technologies. Training or retraining may be required, along with additional supervision in the short term. Productivity may be lost while job-holders readjust to new processes, reporting lines and responsibilities. People in enlarged and enriched jobs will expect greater remuneration for their additional tasks or responsibilities.

5.13 In addition, job redesign will not necessarily be welcomed by all workers. Some will fear the learning and accountability that accompanies extra responsibilities. Some will not be suited to the ambiguity and uncertainty that may accompany empowerment or multi-skilling. There may be collective resistance where the effect of job redesign is to make some positions redundant.

Empowerment

5.14   Empowerment involves both giving workers discretion to make decisions about how to organise their work and making workers accountable for achieving production and quality targets.

5.15   Empowerment is intended to enhance organisational effectiveness by increasing employees' job satisfaction; harnessing their creativity and 'front-line' expertise; and shortening response times at the interface with customers and suppliers.

5.16   However, there are acknowledged barriers to empowerment in practice.

- Not all employees desire more challenge or responsibility.
- Not all employees are capable of exercising greater responsibility or undertaking the necessary skill development.
- Managers may struggle to release control and/or to change role and style.
- Empowerment is not a substitute for other rewards: it must be reinforced by recognition and/or financial rewards for exercising increased responsibility.
- Empowerment may be perceived as a poor alternative to promotion or career development.

Teamworking

5.17   Teamworking is another key trend in job design. 'Team-based' job or role definitions allow individual skills to be pooled, and give workers the chance to be part of a whole meaningful task and social relationships. Teamworking is also often used in a context of shared decision-making, multi-skilling (see below), project work and empowerment – all of which offer significant job satisfactions and performance gains (as we will see in Chapter 6).

Multi-skilling

5.18   Multi-skilling is an alternative approach to functional flexibility. Rather than pooling different skills (eg in a multi-functional team), each individual is able to perform a number of different tasks, flexibly, as required. This involves the erosion of traditional demarcations between functional specialisms: workers are trained, organised and encouraged to operate across the boundaries of their job or craft. Instead of jobs being 'owned' by particular groups, the most appropriate individual to do a particular job should be able to do it.

5.19   Multi-skilling offers the organisation a cost-effective, efficient way of utilising a 'leaner' workforce, particularly under the constantly changing pressures of competition, technological innovation and customer demands. If it can be achieved with the co-operation of employees and their representatives, it can end costly demarcation disputes, redundancy packages and other consequences of seemingly 'rational' job design. Multi-skilling also offers the employee greater task variety, discretion and job satisfaction. It may also offer job security and material benefits, since a versatile, mobile employee is likely to have a higher value in the current labour market.

5.20   All these approaches require the kind of flexible, horizontal structures we introduced briefly in Chapter 1. In the words (quoted by Tom Peters) of a Motorola executive: 'The traditional job descriptions were barriers. We needed an organisation soft enough between the organisational disciplines so that... people would run freely across functional barriers or organisational barriers with the common goal of getting the job done, rather than just making certain that their specific part of the job was completed'.

Work-life balance and flexible working arrangements

5.21   Work-life balance reflects the increasing diversity of the workforce (especially women in work) by attempting to create flexible working patterns which enable employees to balance the demands of work with the demands of home life (particularly the need to care for dependent children or the elderly). It also recognises that overwork and stress are a cause of work-related ill health, and attempts to balance the desire for productivity with the need to manage work demands in a healthy and sustainable way.

5.22 Elements in work-life balance programmes (in addition to education and training in time management, delegation, stress management and so on) include the following.

- Flexible contracts (eg annualised hours or term-time contracts) to allow employees to plan hours around family responsibilities
- Flexi-time systems (with core periods and discretionary periods, during which hours may be debited or credited on a daily, weekly or monthly basis)
- Part-time working and job sharing

5.23 Such measures have been supported in recent years by family-friendly and equal opportunity legislation. In the UK, for example, parents of children under six years old have the right to have their requests for flexible working arrangements (changing total hours worked, when and where) seriously considered.

6   The impact of management style

6.1 Reward and motivation systems such as pay, benefits, promotion and job design may be determined at a department-wide or organisation-wide level. However, the motivational theories we have discussed suggest several ways in which a team leader can contribute to the motivation of the team.

Leadership as a motivator

6.2 Clear **goals and objectives** are essential in order for individuals to calculate how much effort a task will require (and whether it is worth it, given the rewards on offer). They also provide yardsticks by which individuals can measure and feel good about their progress.

6.3 **Participation and involvement** are powerful motivators – as well as potentially improving the quality of decision-making. If team members can be involved in setting goals, and articulating values, they are more likely to own and pursue them in a committed way. A team 'charter' or contract may even be drawn up to clarify the team's commitment to each other: what the team wants to accomplish, why it is important, and how the team will work together to achieve results.

6.4 Ongoing formal and informal **feedback on progress** and results is essential for individuals to calculate what further effort is required; to build confidence and shared accountability; and to enable milestones to be celebrated.

6.5 **Praise and recognition** should not be underestimated as a reward and incentive to further effort. They are highly valued by employees – and yet they cost the manager nothing to give. Teamworking gurus such as Ken Blanchard advocate 'Keeping the accent on the positive'.

- Looking for (and rewarding) positive behaviours that reflect the purpose and values of the team
- 'Catching people doing things right' (or even 'approximately right') instead of wrong
- Redirecting people towards the goal, when they get things wrong, instead of punishing them
- Linking all recognition and rewards back to the team's purpose and goals

Management style

6.6 As we mentioned in Chapter 1, not all managers operate in the same manner. It is possible to identify a wide variety of behaviours which different managers use as their 'preferred' approach or 'style'. Mullins defines leadership style as: 'the way in which the functions of leadership are carried out; the way in which the manager typically behaves towards members of the group'.

6.7 Many attempts have been made both to classify styles and to identify which is the most effective style for a manager to adopt. Some of these models have attempted to suggest that there are effective and ineffective styles: that team members prefer some styles to others, and that teams work better under some styles than others. A manager who naturally uses one style should therefore attempt to develop the skills to use a more effective style.

6.8 Other models, however, have reflected the growing realisation that a range of different styles might be appropriate – depending on the management context. The 'right' style is the one that will work best for a particular task, team and situation. Terry Gillen *(Leadership Skills for Boosting Performance)* suggests that: 'Using only one leadership style is a bit like a stopped clock: it will be right twice a day, but the rest of the time it will be inaccurate to varying degrees. Leaders need to interact with their team in different ways in different situations. This is what we mean by "leadership style".'

6.9 Management style is not mentioned in the syllabus, but is an important underlying factor in motivation and team leadership. We will therefore look at some of the key style models, briefly.

Two-dimensional style models

6.10 The Ohio State University Studies (EA Fleishman, 'the description of supervisory behaviour': *Journal of Applied Psychology*) asked people to analyse and comment on the behaviour of their superiors. From their results it was easy to identify two major dimensions of managerial behaviour.

- Initiating structure – concern with organising the work to be done, the definition of roles and ways of getting jobs done
- Consideration – concern with the social organisation of the group, maintaining good relations and giving opportunities for group involvement and participation

This distinction, more commonly referred to today as the difference between a task-centred approach and a people-centred approach, has been very influential.

6.11 The Managerial Grid (Figure 5.4) was developed by Robert R Blake and Jane Mouton *(The Managerial Grid)* in the US. Managers are classified on the grid in terms of their concern for people and their concern for production.

Figure 5.4 *Blake and Mouton's managerial grid*

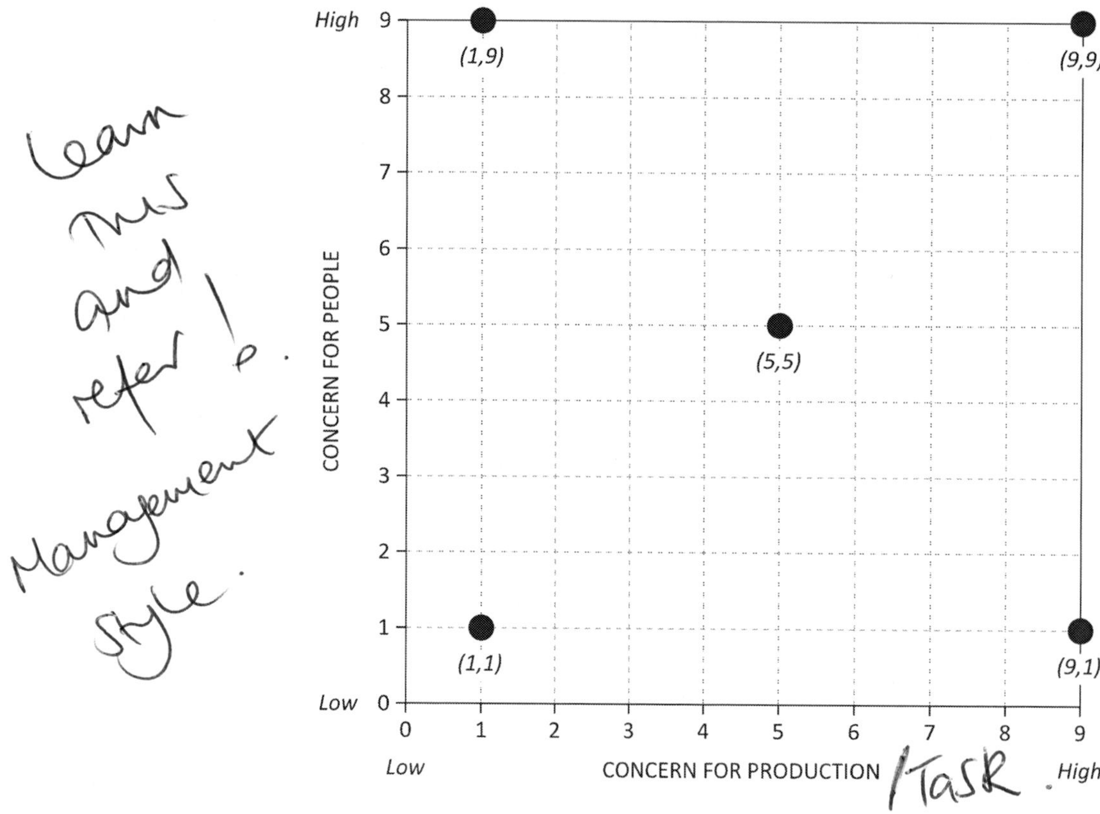

6.12 Key positions on the grid and can be explained as follows.

- 'Impoverished' (1,1): the manager exerts (and expects) minimal effort or concern for either staff satisfaction or work targets.
- 'Country club' (1,9): the manager is attentive to staff needs and has developed satisfying relationships and work culture – but with little attention to results.
- 'Task management' (9,1): the manager concentrates almost exclusively on achieving results. People's needs are virtually ignored, and work is organised so that human elements interfere to a minimal extent.
- 'Team' (9,9): the manager achieves high work performance through 'leading' committed people who identify themselves with organisational goals.
- 'Middle of the road' or 'dampened pendulum' (5,5): a manager achieves adequate performance through balancing the necessity to get work done with maintaining a satisfactory level of team morale. (Alternatively, the manager scores an *average* of 5,5 as a result of swinging from one extreme to another!)

6.13 The grid was intended as a tool for management appraisal and development. It recognises that management requires a balance between concern for task and people, and that there is no necessary correlation (positive or negative) between the two. However, it assumes that high concern for both is possible at the same time – and that this is the most effective style of management.

6.14 However, critics complain that the grid oversimplifies the management role and situation. Factors such as culture, technology, team members and the nature of the task are not directly considered. The model also assumes that (9,9) is the optimum style – but in some managerial contexts, this may not be so. A manager may find that a (9,1) approach is better in situations of crisis where survival is at stake, for example, or when urgent corrective action must be taken to get a project back on track.

Directive and facilitative leadership behaviour

6.15   The dual dimensions discussed so far underpin certain types of management behaviour.

- **Directive behaviours** (or management styles) are based on letting subordinates know clearly what the manager expects from them (targets and standards); giving specific guidance and instructions; asking subordinates to follow rules and procedures; scheduling and co-ordinating the work; and monitoring and controlling performance against specific criteria. A directive style may be effective when subordinates do not share the manager's objectives, or lack ability or confidence; when time is short and results critical; and when subordinates are willing to accept top-down authority.
- **Facilitative behaviours** (or participative or supportive behaviours) are based on giving team members the opportunity to take responsibility and initiative: jointly agreeing objectives and standards; delegating responsibility to the team for day-to-day planning and organisation, monitoring and control; being available as a resource for guidance, information and mediation if required; acting as a champion on behalf of the team (accessing information, resources, contacts and influence on its behalf); and performing the role of 'critical friend' to provide constructive and challenging feedback for individual and team development. A facilitative style may be effective where subordinates are willing, able and confident enough to participate in decision making; where subordinate input to (and acceptance of) decisions is important; and where the task or problem is relatively unstructured.

A range of management styles

6.16   SG Huneryager and IL Heckman *(Human Relations in Management)* identified three basic leadership styles in use in commerce and industry – and while there are many style models, these may still be a useful way of classifying and describing broad types of style.

- **Authoritarian** (or autocratic) style: power and authority for planning, organising and decision making are centralised in the hands of the leader, and all communication and interactions focus on or through him. The expectation of subordinates is simply compliance or obedience.
- **Democratic style**: decision-making is decentralised, shared by team members via participative processes, and there is greater group interaction. Leadership functions are distributed among group members: the manager or designated leader may take on a more facilitative role as part of the team.
- ***Laissez-faire* style**: the team is genuinely autonomous, organising its own work and making decisions (within defined boundaries, such as task objectives, budget spending limits and organisational policies, say). The manager adopts a coaching role within the team: deliberately supporting freedom of action – while being available to help if needed. (Note that this is not the same as an 'impoverished' manager who just abdicates responsibility.)

6.17   Other studies and models have identified different style classifications: you may have come across other labels and definitions in your reading. However, style models are often talking about more or less the same things: a range of behaviours on a continuum between completely task-focused, directive behaviours at one end, and completely people-focused, supportive and facilitative behaviours at the other end.

6.18   The research unit at Ashridge Management College carried out studies in UK industry and identified four styles, which are summarised in Table 5.2.

Table 5.2 *Tells, sells, consults, joins*

STYLE	STRENGTHS	WEAKNESSES
Tells (autocratic) *The manager makes decisions and issues instructions which must be obeyed without question*	• Quick decisions can be made when required • The most efficient type of leadership for highly-programmed work	• Communications are one-way, neglecting feedback and potential for upward communication or team input • Does not encourage initiative or commitment from subordinates: merely compliance
Sells (persuasive) *The manager still makes decisions, but believes that team members must be motivated to accept them in order to carry them out properly*	• Team members understand the reason for decisions • Team members may be more committed • Team members may be able to function slightly better in the absence of instruction	• Communications are still largely one-way • Team members are not necessarily motivated to accept the decision • Still doesn't encourage initiative or commitment
Consults (participative) *The manager confers with team members and takes their views into account, although he retains the final say*	• Encourages motivation through greater interest and involvement • Enhances the acceptability of the decision to team members • Decision quality may benefit • Creates upward communication	• May take longer (especially if consensus is sought) • Team input may not enhance the quality of the decision • Consultation can be a façade for a basic 'sells' style
Joins (democratic) *Manager and team members make the decision together on the basis of consensus*	• Fosters motivation and commitment • Empowers team members to take the initiative • Plus strengths of 'consults' style	• May undermine manager's authority • May lengthen the process • May cause 'political' decisions

6.19 The Ashridge studies showed a clear preference amongst subordinates for the 'consults' style of management – although managers were most commonly perceived to be exercising a 'tells' or 'sells' style. Team members also had more positive attitudes to their work under managers who were perceived to be exercising a 'consults' style. The least favourable attitudes to work, however, were not found among team members under a 'tells' style, but among those who were unable to perceive a *consistent* style in their manager. In other words, subordinates are unsettled by a boss who chops and changes between different styles.

A continuum of leadership styles

6.20 R Tannenbaum and WH Schmidt ('How to choose a leadership pattern': *Harvard Business Review)* proposed a continuum of leadership behaviours: Figure 5.5. The continuum format is a useful reminder that managers do not adopt extreme either/or styles, but select from a wide repertoire of behaviours.

Figure 5.5 *Tannenbaum and Schmidt: a continuum of leadership style*

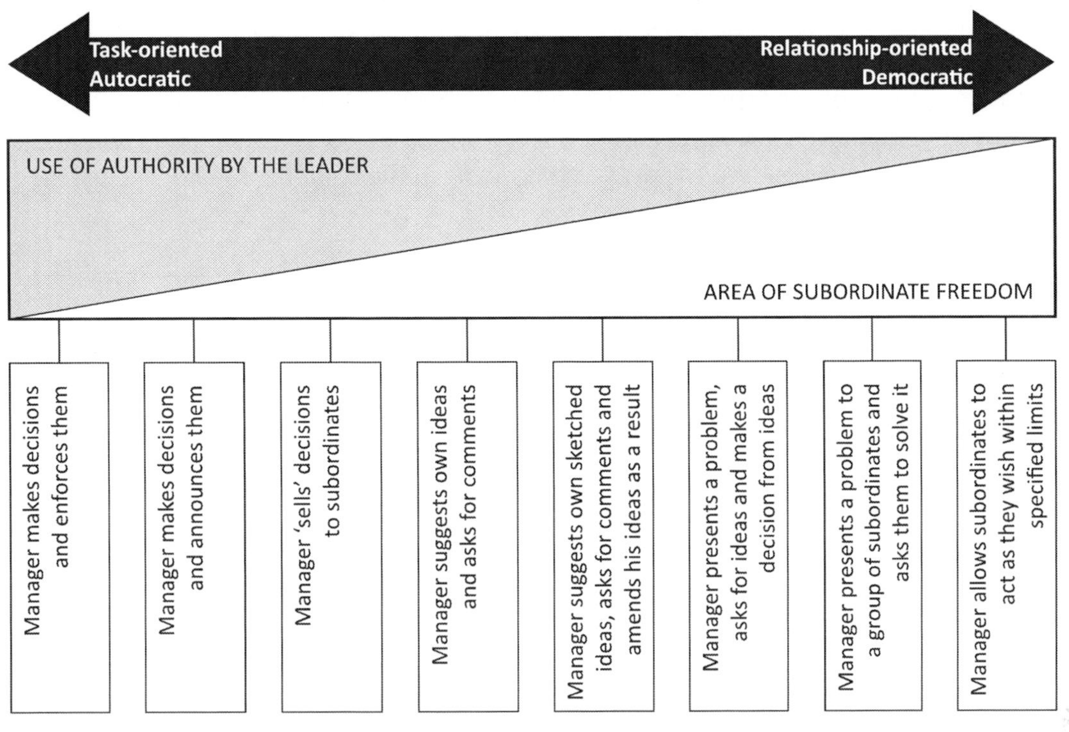

6.21 You should be able to see how these behaviours might be classified into the four basic styles discussed above. (Tannenbaum and Schmidt named their styles: telling, selling, consulting and coaching.)

Limitations of style models

6.22 The style approach to leadership has provided useful insights into the nature and processes of leadership. It has usefully stressed the value of democratic and participative styles and, in identifying styles, it has helped in the perception of leadership as a range of choices open to the manager rather than one limited and universal set of behaviours.

6.23 However, the approach is also subject to certain criticisms. Despite a level of agreement between different researchers, there are confusions as to style definitions. It has also been argued that the style approach does not consider all the variables that contribute to the operation of effective leadership. In particular:

- The manager's personality (or acting ability) may simply not be flexible enough to utilise style approaches effectively.
- The demands of the task, technology, organisation culture and other managers constrain the leader in the range of styles effectively open to him. (If the leader's own boss practises an authoritarian style, and the team are incompetent and require close supervision, no amount of theorising on the desirability of participative management will make it possible.)
- Consistency is important to subordinates. If a manager adopts a style suitable to the changing situation, subordinates may simply perceive him to be fickle, or may suffer insecurity and stress.

6.24 It is the consideration of this wider set of variables that has led to the development of contingency or situational approaches to leadership.

Situational leadership

6.25   Situational leadership models see effective leadership as being dependent on a number of variable or contingent factors. There is no one right way to lead that will fit all situations; rather it is necessary to lead in a manner that is appropriate to a particular situation. One of the most popular models in this school is the Situational Leadership model of P Hersey & K Blanchard (*Management of Organisational Behaviour: Utilising Human Resources).* We will discuss this model in the context of team leadership, in Chapter 6.

Chapter summary

- Theories of motivation are important in organisational management because of a perception that motivated employees perform their roles more effectively.
- Content theories of motivation attempt to identify needs experienced by individuals and then to seek means of satisfying them in the workplace.
- Process theories of motivation are concerned with how behaviour is initiated, directed and sustained. They place emphasis on the actual process of motivation.
- Many organisations nowadays attempt to increase the quality of working life. The idea is that this will help to attract and retain quality personnel.
- Approaches to job design have changed over the years in line with changes in organisational management theory (eg from scientific management to human relations approaches).
- Many researchers have studied styles of management, hoping to identify how such styles can impact on the motivation of team members.

Self-test questions

Numbers in brackets refer to the paragraphs where you can check your answers.

1. List adverse effects arising from low morale and demotivation. (1.6)

2. Distinguish between content theories and process theories of motivation. (1.10)

3. List the individual needs identified by Maslow. (Figure 5.1)

4. Explain what is meant by hygiene factors and motivator factors (Herzberg). (2.12–2.14)

5. According to Vroom, an individual's motivation is the product of what two factors? (3.2)

6. What are the two possible responses to employee frustration identified by Mullins? (3.17)

7. What are the three core job dimensions identified by Hackman & Oldham? (Table 5.1)

8. List possible ways of improving employee involvement. (4.12)

9. Describe FW Taylor's approach to job design. (5.3)

10. Distinguish between job rotation, job enlargement and job enrichment. (5.9)

11. Explain the key positions on Blake & Mouton's managerial grid. (6.12)

12. What are the three leadership styles identified by Huneryager & Heckman? (6.16)

CHAPTER 6

Work Groups and Teams

Assessment criteria and indicative content

3.1 Evaluate the importance of work groups or teams for effective performance in the procurement and supply function

- Groups, teams and teamwork
- Group values and norms
- Formal and informal groups

3.2 Explain the stages of development of work groups or teams in the procurement and supply function

- Reasons for the formation of groups/teams
- The work environment: size of the group, capability of the members, the nature of the task, physical setting, communications and the use of technology
- Theories on the stages of group/team development

3.3 Evaluate the characteristics of effective work groups or teams in the procurement and supply function

- Characteristics of an effective work group
- Perspectives on team roles
- Stages of group dynamics and development
- Self managed work groups/teams
- Virtual teams and remote working
- The benefits of cultural diversity

3.4 Analyse the nature of role relationships in work groups or teams in the procurement and supply function

- Intra group/team cohesion and conflict
- Developing effective groups/teams

Section headings

1 Groups and teams in procurement and supply
2 The value of teamworking
3 Team development
4 Team roles
5 Team dynamics and processes
6 Building effective teams
7 Managing diverse teams

Introduction

Although human beings have been working in groups since the days of prehistoric hunting bands, the emphasis on teamworking in management theory is relatively recent. It really began 'by accident', following research at the Hawthorne plant of the General Electric Company in the 1920s. Elton Mayo's researchers found that team dynamics influenced productivity more than any changes in working conditions. In recent decades – thanks to major issues such as labour flexibility, worker involvement and empowerment – teamworking has become a key aspect of work organisation and management.

In this chapter, we look at the ways in which groups form and operate, and how they can be 'built' and managed for effective working and member satisfaction.

1 Groups and teams in procurement and supply

1.1 Handy *(Understanding Organisations)* defines a group as 'any collection of people who perceive themselves to be a group'. The point of this definition is the distinction it implies between a random collection of individuals and a group of individuals who share a common sense of identity and belonging.

1.2 JC Coleman (*Psychology and Effective Behaviour*) suggests that, in many ways, groups behave in similar ways to individuals. 'Groups, like individuals, have structural and integrative characteristics and operate in physical and social settings. Like individuals, they strive to maintain themselves and resist disintegration and seek to grow and develop their potentials. Like individuals they may solve their problems in either task-oriented or defence-oriented ways, and if their problems are beyond their resources – or believed to be – they may show evidence of strain, de-compensation and pathology.'

1.3 However, people also behave differently in groups than they do as individuals, because of the dynamics of groups: patterns of communication, roles, relationships and influence within the group. This is why it is important to study group behaviour as part of the behaviour of people in organisations.

Reasons for the formation of groups

1.4 People in organisations are drawn together into groups by a number of factors.

- A preference for smaller units where closer relationships can develop, offering a source of companionship and support
- The need to belong (sense of identity and solidarity) and to make a contribution that will be noticed and appreciated
- Shared space, specialism, objectives and interests
- The attractiveness of a particular group activity or resources
- Access to power greater than individuals could muster on their own (eg by forming coalitions), to protect their interests
- Access to contribution, experience, expertise and other resources required to perform complex tasks (and, most simply, tasks requiring more than one person)

1.5 Groups may be formed more or less automatically by the division of labour (eg the grouping of tasks into sections or departments); by task technology (eg the grouping of operators on an assembly line); or by identification with particular shared characteristics (eg the perceived 'grouping' of people of similar status, occupational group, trade union affiliation and so on).

Formal and informal groups

1.6 Formal groups are deliberately and rationally designed and created by management to achieve objectives assigned to them by the organisation. They are characterised by:

- Membership and leadership appointed and approved by the organisation
- Compliance of the members with the organisation's goals and requirements
- Focus on performance of allocated tasks or functions
- Structured relationships of authority, responsibility, roles, task allocation and communication, within the formal organisation structure.

Formal groups are broadly concerned with the co-ordination of work activities.

1.7 Informal groups may spring up as a result of these formal arrangements (for example, if the members of a committee become a social network), and will invariably be present in any organisation. Informal groups include workplace networks of people who regularly get together to exchange information, groups of friends who socialise outside work, 'cliques' and political groupings and so on. Unlike formal groups, they have constantly fluctuating membership and structure, and leaders emerge usually through personal (rather than 'positional') power.

1.8 The purposes of informal groups are usually related to group and individual member satisfaction, rather than a particular task. However, S Stryker claims that the informal organisation is also a 'hidden operating structure that gets the work done'. It operates via mechanisms such as informal communication networks ('the grapevine'), 'short-cuts' and ways of doing things developed over time, and the influence of informal leaders (often by-passing communication and authority 'blockages' in the formal structure).

1.9 Kenneth Lysons suggests four main purposes for informal groups in an organisation.

- Maintenance of an informal 'culture': a set of values and behavioural norms which shape group behaviour and acceptance into the group
- Socialisation and social control: the use of group influence (eg by way of giving or withholding acceptance) to enforce conformity to the group culture, norms and values
- Development of informal communication networks: informal groups can supplement 'official' information sources and communication channels. This can be helpful for the organisation, if management can tap into the 'grapevine' to disseminate information and encourage knowledge sharing. However, it can also undermine formal communication programmes by disseminating inaccurate, distorted or subversive information (rumours, exaggerations and so on)
- Social satisfactions: informal groups can add interest, fun and the satisfaction of interpersonal relationships, to compensate for monotony or alienation in the work and formal work interactions

Groups and teams

1.10 A team has been defined as 'a small group of people with complementary skills who are committed to a common purpose, performance goals and approaches for which they hold themselves basically jointly accountable' (JR Katzenbach & DK Smith, *The Wisdom of Teams*).

1.11 Teams are groups – but groups are not necessarily teams. A group may be larger than a team, with a more fluctuating or random (unselected) membership than a team (typically small in size and with carefully selected members). A group may not have the defined goals or mutual accountability of a team, or the closely defined norms for member interaction. A large group is likely to be led by a sole leader, while a team may have shared or rotating leadership roles, and a greater emphasis on shared responsibility and contribution. A formal work group is more likely to operate as a team than an informal group.

1.12 There are a number of approaches to the organisation of teamworking in purchasing and supply. We will briefly outline some of the main ones here.

Multi-skilled teams

1.13 Multi-skilled teams bring together a number of individuals, each of whom can perform any of the group's tasks. Work can thus be allocated flexibly, according to who is best placed to do a given job when required. Multi-skilling is a cornerstone of team empowerment, since it cuts across the barriers of job descriptions and demarcations to enable teams to respond flexibly to internal and external customer demands and environmental changes. A commodity buying team within the purchasing function, for example, may be multi-skilled: any member can perform the range of tasks and responsibilities required.

Cross-functional teams and matrix structures

1.14   Multi-disciplinary or cross-functional teams bring together individuals with different skills and specialisms, so that their competencies and resources can be pooled or exchanged, and/or so that their (potentially divergent) goals and interests can be represented. An example might be a multi-functional procurement strategy team, or even a multi-organisational supply management team (involving representatives of all the stakeholders in the supply chain).

1.15   Ongoing cross-functional working is often organised as a matrix structure. This structural form emerged at American aerospace company Lockheed in the 1950s, when its customer (the US government) became frustrated at dealing separately with a number of functional specialists when negotiating defence contracts. The essence of matrix structure is dual authority: staff in different functions or regions are responsible both to their departmental managers, in regard to the activities of the department, and to a product, project or account manager, in regard to the activities of the department related to the given product, project or account.

1.16   A matrix structure in purchasing may be something like the following: Figure 6.1. The buyer represented by ● is responsible both to his line manager in the purchasing function (eg the head of Purchasing) and also to the project leader for Project B.

Figure 6.1   *A matrix structure for purchasing*

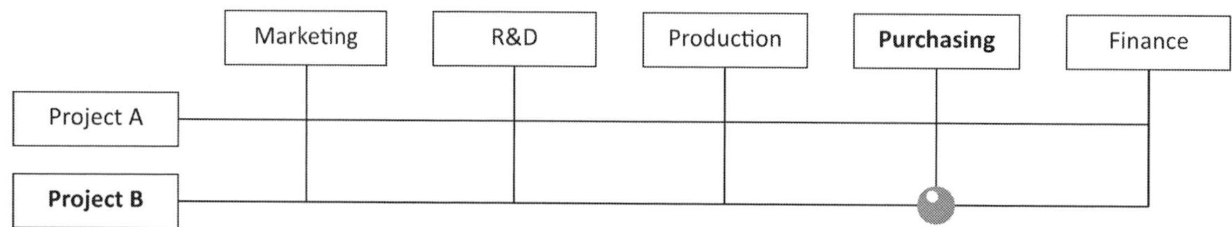

1.17   **Project teams** are typically cross-functional teams set up to handle specific strategic developments (such as the introduction of a just in time approach), tasks relating to particular processes (such as the computerisation of inventory control), tasks relating to particular 'cases' or accounts (such as co-ordination of traffic with a particular supplier) or special audit and investigation of procedures or improvement opportunities (such as a review of order parameters or supplier ethical codes). Project teams are examples of task force or problem-solving teams: they are often short-term in nature, and empowered to take action within the limited remit of the project specification and terms of reference.

The merits of cross-functional teams

1.18   Cross-functional teams are particularly valuable in increasing team members' awareness of the big picture of their tasks and decisions – and therefore dovetailing functional objectives with overall strategy.

1.19   They enable a wider pooling of viewpoints, expertise and resources, and represent a wider range of interests (which may both enhance the quality of the decision-making *and* minimise the potential for conflict and resistance at the implementation stage). This can help to generate innovative and integrative solutions to problems, and suggestions for performance or process improvements, by contributing more pieces of the overall puzzle. These qualities are particularly valuable for applications such as innovation and brainstorming groups, quality circles, employee representative committees, task forces and committees.

1.20   Tom Peters *(Thriving on Chaos)* used the term **horizontal structures** for forms which allow work and information to flow freely across functional boundaries, without the vertical barriers created by specialisation, departmental job demarcations and formal communication channels. Cross-functional teams are a key tool for co-ordination across organisational boundaries, since they typically involve representatives of different functional departments or units. This increases the flow of communication, informal (network) relationships and co-operation. It is an important element in aligning business processes, so that the flow of added value towards customers (and customers' experience of the organisation) is not impeded by vertical barriers.

1.21 Product development and innovation, partnering, networking and learning are all horizontal activities, requiring the free exchange of information across functional boundaries. Cross-functional teams contribute significantly to the flexibility and responsiveness of organisations in competitive and fast-changing environments. They support innovation through the pooling of different expertise and knowledge, and they enable swift decision-making by avoiding lengthy vertical channels of communication and authorisation.

Network structures and virtual teams

1.22 Another use of teams in developing the supply chain is multi-organisational teamworking: involving various interested parties (or stakeholders) in the supply chain, whose relationships and efforts need to be coordinated, in a team structure and atmosphere. Making suppliers 'part of the team' can be more than lip service to a supportive and mutually beneficial relationship. It can be reflected in regular meetings of stakeholders for the purposes of information-sharing, problem-solving, relationship-building and so on.

1.23 Supply chain networks may therefore take on the status of virtual teams: interconnected groups of people who may not be present in the same office or organisation (and may even be in different areas of the world) but who:

- Share information and tasks (eg technical support provided by a supplier)
- Make joint decisions (eg on quality assurance or staff training)
- Fulfil the collaborative functions of a team.

1.24 Information and communications technology (ICT) has facilitated this kind of collaboration, simulating teamworking via teleconferencing, video-conferencing, networked computers and the internet. Participants in the supply chain can use such technology to access and share up-to-date product, customer, stock and delivery information (eg using web-based databases and data tracking systems). Electronic meeting management systems allow virtual meeting participants to talk and listen to each other on teleconference lines, while sharing data and using electronic whiteboards on their PCs. On a more basic level, suppliers may simply offer technical support to production or sales teams, through telephone or online helplines.

Self-managed teams

1.25 Self-managed teamworking is the most highly developed form of teamworking. They are permanent teams in which members jointly decide all the key issues of their work: processes and schedules, allocation of tasks, selection of team members, distribution of team rewards and so on. The team leader is a team member, acting in the role of facilitator: this role may be rotated as appropriate to the task.

1.26 In self-managed teams, team members collaboratively share decision-making on all the major issues affecting their work and internal processes. Leadership roles may be shared or rotated, as appropriate. Weekly team meetings are typically used to identify, analyse and solve problems: reviewing teamworking and progress; getting team members to research and present issues and so on. Any external management input, once goals have been set for the group, is primarily supportive and facilitative (and only when needed).

1.27   Self-managed teams are said to offer advantages in: harnessing commitment (with gains in quality and productivity); reducing managerial costs, enhancing co-ordination and flexibility; and encouraging initiative (with gains for responsiveness and customer service). However, in a full-blown form, they are a comparatively new (and rare) phenomenon: they require skilled leadership and strong cultural support.

1.28   Self-managed teamworking requires a high level of competence on the part of team members – and a high degree of trust on the part of managers (to give the team discretion in planning, implementing and controlling tasks). There must also be clear objectives, role definitions and review milestones and measures, as a framework for team discretion. Communication and reporting mechanisms must be in place for co-ordination and control.

2   The value of teamworking

2.1   The basic work units of organisations have traditionally been specialised functional departments. In more recent times, organisations have adopted what Peters and Waterman *(In Search of Excellence)* called 'chunking': the breaking up of the organisation structure into small, flexible units, or teams.

2.2   From the organisation's standpoint, teams have a number of advantages.

- Teams facilitate the performance of tasks which require the collective skills, experience or knowledge of more than one person or discipline. Groups have been shown to produce better evaluated (though fewer) decisions than individuals working separately.
- Teams facilitate the co-ordination of the work of different individuals or groups, because they bring them together across organisational boundaries (eg disciplines or departments) with shared goals and structured communication.
- Teams facilitate interactive communication and interpersonal relationships, and are thus particularly well-adapted for:
  - Testing and ratifying decisions, because they offer multi-source feedback and may make the decision more acceptable (by taking account of a cross-section of stakeholder views). Acceptance of the decision by a group may be important if it affects them and their work (for example, if they are responsible for carrying it out).
  - Consulting, negotiating and conflict resolution, because they allow an interactive exchange of views and influence.
  - Generating ideas, because of their potential for 'bouncing' ideas off each other and getting multiple input.
  - Collecting and disseminating information, because of the multiple networks in which the members are involved.
- Teams can motivate individuals to devote more energy and effort to achieving the organisation's goals, since:
  - They offer rewards in the form of satisfying relationships.
  - Group influences may reinforce performance, as long as the group's aims are harmonised with those of the organisation.

2.3   From the individual's standpoint, teams also perform some important functions.

- They satisfy social needs for friendship and belonging, mutual encouragement and support.
- They help individuals to develop self-image and identity (as part of something larger than themselves).
- They enable individuals to share the burdens of work responsibility and achieve more than they could do themselves.
- They enable people to make noticeable individual contributions (which bolsters their self esteem) and at the same time to share responsibility and be part of something bigger than themselves (which bolsters their sense of security). Peters and Waterman *(In Search of Excellence)* suggested that these were the key dual needs of workers.

2.4   However, there are some **problems** in using teams.

- Group decision-making takes longer, especially if the group seeks to reach consensus by working through disagreements (as is the preferred style in Japan).
- Group working requires a certain amount of attention to group dynamics and group maintenance processes (as we will see a bit later): this can draw energy away from the task.
- Group decisions may partly be based on group norms and interests – the group's own agenda – rather than the needs of the task, or indeed of the organisation.
- Team decisions have been shown to be riskier than individual decisions. Shared responsibility blurs the individuals' sense of responsibility for the outcome of the decision. Very cohesive groups, in particular, tend to protect their consensus by ignoring 'outside' information and feedback: they become blinkered and over-confident. This effect is intensified by inter-group competition, which can result in dis-integration, lack of communication and conflict between different groups.
- Group norms of behaviour may restrict and inhibit individual contribution and may produce negative work results. Elton Mayo's studies at the Hawthorne plant (discussed in Chapter 5) showed that groups use their power for such aims as restricting output and 'freezing out' unpopular supervisors.

2.5   You should also be aware that while 'teamworking' is regarded as a positive value in itself, there is such a thing as an ineffective team. Teamworking involves complex dynamics, roles and relationships and it is not easy to get it right. Pedler, Burgoyne & Boydell *(A Manager's Guide to Leadership),* having outlined the ideal of teamworking, write as follows.

Dream on. In reality, teams that present a public face of cohesion often fall apart at the seams under pressure. They may be unsupportive to members or driven by internal conflicts and turf wars and talented individuals do not always make good team players.

The important thing is not just to have teams – but to have effective teams.

3   Team development

3.1   JC Coleman notes the complex social nature of groups. 'Groups have power structures, leadership structures, role structures, communication structures.… They develop norms and ideologies and characteristic atmospheres and degrees of cohesiveness and morale.' Teams are complex and dynamic: not static. They mature, develop and change over time. We will look at a number of team dynamics and processes, starting with team development.

Tuckman's stages of group development

3.2   Four stages in group development were identified by Bruce W Tuckman ('Developmental sequences in small groups': *Psychological Bulletin).*

- **Forming** is the first stage, in which members try to find out about each other and about how the group is going to work: its purpose, composition, leadership and organisation are still being established. There will probably be a wariness about introducing new ideas: members will 'toe the line' in order not to make themselves unacceptable to the group. This cautious introductory period is essential, but not conducive to task effectiveness.
- **Storming** is the second stage, in which members begin to assert themselves and test out roles, leadership, behavioural norms and ideas. There is more or less open conflict and competition around these areas – but this may also be a fruitful time, as more realistic targets are set, open communication develops and ideas are generated.
- **Norming** is the real settling-down stage, in which agreements are reached about work, sharing, individual requirements and output expectations. Group procedures and customs will be defined and adherence secured. The enthusiasm and brain-storming of the second stage may have died down, but methodical working can be introduced and maintained.

- **Performing** is the stage at which the group focuses on executing its task: the difficulties of group development no longer distract from performance.

3.3   Tuckman and MAC Jensen ('Stages of small group development revisited': *Group & Organisation Studies*) have added further stages to the original model.

- **Dorming**: the team has been performing successfully for some time and grown complacent. It goes into a semi-automatic mode of operation, with efforts devoted primarily to the maintenance of the team itself.
- **Mourning** or **adjourning**: The team sees itself as having fulfilled its purpose, and the group disbands – either physically (eg in the case of a temporary project team) or psychologically (as the team turns to new goals, renegotiates membership roles, and returns to the forming stage for its next phase).

3.4   A group may progress through these stages quickly or slowly, may overlap stages, or may get stuck at a given stage (particularly 'storming').

Schutz's FIRO model

3.5   William C Schutz (1958) proposed a theory of interpersonal orientation based on the belief that individuals actively seek to establish compatibility with others in their social interactions, because relationships fulfil certain basic human needs: the need for inclusion (ie belonging), the need for control (ie enjoying a balance of influence in relationships) and the need for affection. He developed a concept known as FIRO: **fundamental interpersonal relations orientation.**

3.6   To assess the relative importance placed on each of these needs by different individuals Schutz developed a questionnaire, comprising 54 questions. Each question invites the respondent to consider how often he performs particular behaviours. The responses are evaluated and the individual's personality orientation is determined.

3.7   The FIRO model suggests that a compatible group (ie a group of individuals with similar needs) will work together and perform better than groups composed of people with desires that clash.

3.8   Schutz's FIRO model can also be used to identify issues that arise for the group and need to be dealt with at each stage of its development. These issues may be repeated a number of times during the life of the group, but they follow broadly in sequence as the group develops.

- **Inclusion issues**: 'in or out'. ('Can I identify with group goals and feel I have sufficient in common with others in the group to choose to stay and be involved in group activity?')
- **Control issues**: 'top or bottom'. ('Can I also be different and have some say in the running of the group?')
- **Affection issues**: 'near or far'. ('Do I trust and value the group sufficiently to lower my defences, to share and commit to group goals?')

3.9   Unlike other models of group development (eg Tuckman and Jensen), Schutz doesn't deal specifically with a termination stage. However, he talks of the above stages reversing themselves as the group ends: members disengage emotionally, become pre-occupied with control issues again, and finally resolve the inclusion issue as the group disbands.

Team building

3.10   Teams are not generally left to develop by themselves. One of the tasks of a manager or team leader is the 'building' of the team: initiating or accelerating the stages of development, to support progress towards mature performance. So, for example, a leader may *not* act to stifle or prematurely resolve conflicts in a new team: these may be encouraged, and brought into the open, in order to progress the team healthily through the storming stage.

3.11 Team building poses a particular challenge for managers in loosely structured, physically dispersed and matrix-structured teams – including supply chain partnerships and virtual teams. (Additional challenges of such teams include the establishment of roles and shared goals, and the monitoring and control of work.)

3.12 We will look further at the issue of team building in the context of developing team cohesion, in Section 5 of this Chapter.

4 Team roles

Team size

4.1 The optimum size for group effectiveness has been variously estimated. Some authors put the optimum primary working group at 10–12 (comparable to primitive hunting bands), while others advocate groups as small as 5–7 people. Although smaller groups limit the synergy available from pooled skills and experience, larger groups involve more complex dynamics and processes (decision-making, communication, influence and so on). Larger groups – like larger organisations – may require greater formality of rules and procedures to ensure co-ordination and control, unless group leadership and norms are very strong. When a team becomes too large, it may split into smaller sub-groups, with the potential for dis-integration.

Team membership

4.2 Team membership may be dictated by existing arrangements, organisational appointment or election (in the case of a staff representative committee). Where a manager is able to select team members, a **mix** of attributes, competencies and resources should be secured to match the needs of the task. It may be argued that a homogeneous team (in which individual members broadly share the same attitudes, values and characteristics) is likely to be more cohesive. However, member diversity can offer complementary skills and viewpoints for enhanced creativity and decision-making.

4.3 Specialist skills and knowledge may be required (perhaps from different areas in the organisation); experience may be helpful (particularly to guide less experienced members of the team); organisational influence or access to resources (including information) may help to 'champion' the team in its competition for limited resources.

4.4 In addition to the specific requirements of its objectives (which may be called *content* roles), an effectively functioning team requires its members to adopt various task and team-maintenance (or *process*) roles. People management in all its aspects requires attention to both content (*what* is being done and said; task requirements and task performance) and process (*how* people are doing and saying things; how the team goes about the task). **Team processes** include the adoption of norms and roles, communicating, decision-making, team development and cohesion and so on.

Belbin's team roles

4.5 R Meredith Belbin *(Team Roles At Work)* researched business-game teams at Henley Management College in the UK and developed a model of the mix of roles in an effectively functioning team. Belbin's work suggests that an effective team is made up of people who, between them, fill nine roles (Table 6.1). He notes that 'strength of contribution in any one of the roles is commonly associated with particular weaknesses. These are called allowable weaknesses. Executives are seldom strong in all nine team roles.'

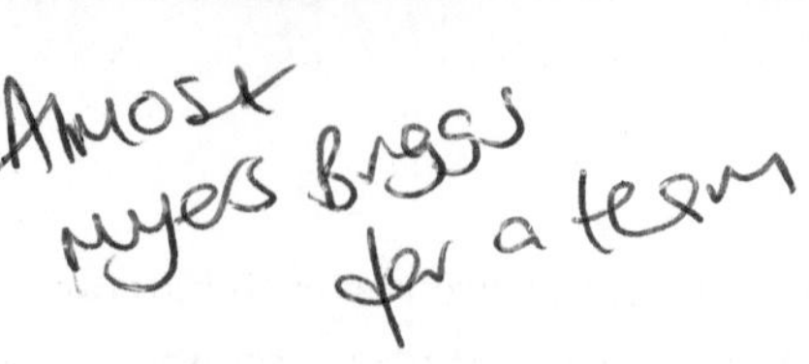

Table 6.1 *Belbin's team roles*

ROLE AND DESCRIPTION	CONTRIBUTION	ALLOWABLE WEAKNESSES
Plant Creative, imaginative, unorthodox	Solves difficult problems. Presents new ideas.	Ignores details. Too preoccupied to communicate effectively.
Resource investigator Extrovert, enthusiastic, communicative	Explores opportunities. Develops contacts.	Overoptimistic. Loses interest once initial enthusiasm has passed.
Coordinator (or chairman) Mature, confident, a good chairperson	Clarifies goals, promotes decision-making, delegates well	Can be seen as manipulative. Delegates personal work.
Shaper Challenging, dynamic, thrives on pressure	Has the drive and courage to overcome obstacles	Can provoke others. Hurts people's feelings.
Monitor evaluator Sober, strategic, discerning	Sees all options. Judges accurately.	Lacks drive and ability to inspire others. Overly critical.
Team worker Cooperative, mild, perceptive and diplomatic	Listens, builds, averts friction, calms the waters	Indecisive in crunch situations. Can be easily influenced.
Implementer (or company worker) Disciplined, reliable, conservative and efficient	Turns ideas into practical actions	Somewhat inflexible. Slow to respond to new possibilities.
Completer/finisher Painstaking, conscientious, anxious	Searches out errors and omissions. Ensures delivery on time.	Inclined to worry unduly. Reluctant to delegate. Can be a 'nitpicker'.
Specialist Single-minded, self-starting, dedicated	Provides knowledge and skills in rare supply	Contributes only on a narrow front. Dwells on technicalities. Overlooks the 'big picture'.

Source: *Team Roles at Work*, R Meredith Belbin

4.6 The team roles are not fixed within any given individual: team members can occupy more than one role, or switch roles according to need. Effective teamworking requires a healthy mix and balance of all the roles, which between them support task functions (such as ideas generation, problem-solving, implementation and follow up) *and* team maintenance functions (support, conflict management, leadership and so on).

5 Team dynamics and processes

Team values and norms

5.1 As we saw in Chapter 2, in our discussion of the Hawthorne Experiments, teams have been found to develop strong collective values and behavioural norms, and to use social pressures to bring members into line with them. And this is an important factor both in group behaviour *and* in broader organisational behaviour and performance.

5.2 A norm may be defined as: 'a standard of specific behaviour expected of and by the members of a social group'. A work group establishes behavioural norms and ideologies to which all members of the group are expected to conform. The Hawthorne Experiments (in the Bank Wiring Room phase) uncovered an informal 'code' in the group, which set norms for outputs (not out-performing others, but not shirking) and for relationships with authority (not 'squealing' to management, and not being 'officious' in the exercise of authority).

5.3 The general nature of group pressure is to require the individual to share in the group's own identity. Individuals may react to group norms and customs with compliance ('toeing the line' without real commitment), internalisation (full acceptance and identification) or resistance. Charles Handy (*Understanding Organisations*) suggests that the pressure to conform is greatest when the issue is not clear cut, the individual lacks support for his own attitude or behaviour, and when he is exposed to other members of the group for a length of time. Intelligent, independent and self-confident people are less likely to conform. Norms may be reinforced in various ways by the group.

- Positive reinforcement is provided by *identification*: a sense of belonging, prestige and acceptance as members of the group. Various badges, symbols, vocabulary, 'in jokes' and initiation rituals are used to promote identification and strengthen the boundaries between those who are 'in' and those who are 'outside'.
- Negative reinforcement is provided by *sanctions* of various kinds: a deviant member who has not responded to challenge or attempted correction may be threatened with ostracism ('the cold shoulder'), ridicule, reprimand, physical aggression (in cultures where this is tolerated) and – ultimately – expulsion from the group.

5.4 Group norms may be *functional* (supporting group identity and new member socialisation, reinforcing organisational values and goals, and providing standards of conduct) – but they may also be *dysfunctional* (if they diverge from or undermine organisational values and goals, discourage divergent viewpoints or resist change). They may become deeply ingrained over time. **Changing team norms** may require:

- Team consensus around the need for change (eg on the basis of crisis, new demands or recognition of dysfunction)
- The generation of support for change (eg by creating a strong change champion in the team, or providing incentives for change)
- Utilising systematic processes for attitude and cultural change, such as Lewin's 'unfreeze-change-refreeze' model. This involves challenging and disrupting dysfunctional behaviours and attitudes (strengthening the driving forces for change and weakening the resisting or restraining forces); communicating and implementing new norms and messages; and then stabilising and consolidating the new *status quo* (by repetition and positive reinforcement).

Team cohesion

5.5 In an experiment reported by Morton Deutsch, psychology students were given puzzles and human relations problems to work at in discussion groups. Some groups ('cooperative' ones) were told that the grade each individual got at the end of the course would depend on the performance of the group. Other groups ('competitive' ones) were told that each student would receive a grade according to his own contributions.

5.6 No significant differences were found between the two kinds of group in the amount of interest and involvement in the tasks, or in the amount of learning. But the cooperative groups, compared with the competitive ones, had greater productivity per unit time, better quality of product and discussion, greater coordination of effort and subdivision of activity, more diversity in the amount of contribution per member, more attentiveness to fellow members and more friendliness during discussion. This is a powerful argument for building cooperative, cohesive teams.

5.7 Cohesion is partly the result of positive factors such as communication, agreement and mutual trust – but in the face of a 'common enemy' (**competition or crisis**) cohesion and performance will be even stronger. Within each competing or crisis-facing group, members close ranks and submerge their differences: loyalty and conformity are highly motivated. The climate changes from informal and sociable to task-focused, and individual needs are put aside. The group may accept a much more authoritarian style of leadership than normal, to mobilise its resources more efficiently. Meanwhile, the polarised sense of 'us and them' further reinforces cohesion.

5.8 Cohesion is broadly regarded as desirable in order to create committed, cooperative working, mutual loyalty and accountability, and open information sharing, all of which may help to maximise the potential synergy of teamworking *and* individual social satisfaction. However, you should be aware that it is possible for groups to become *too* cohesive. Handy *(Understanding Organisations)* notes that 'ultra-cohesive groups can be dangerous because in the organisational context the group must serve the organisation, not itself'. If a group is completely absorbed with its own maintenance, members and priorities, it can divert energy and attention away from the task.

Groupthink

5.9 Ultra-cohesive groups can also become dangerously blinkered to outside information and feedback and may confidently forge ahead in a completely wrong direction IL Janis *(Victims of Groupthink)* described this as 'groupthink': 'the psychological drive for consensus at any cost, that suppresses dissent and appraisal of alternatives in cohesive decision-making groups'. The cosy consensus of the team prevents consideration of alternatives, constructive criticism or conflict.

5.10 Symptoms of groupthink include the following.

- A sense of invulnerability – blindness to the risk involved in 'pet' strategies
- Rationalisations for inconsistent information
- Moral blindness ('might is right')
- A tendency to stereotype all outsiders as 'enemies'
- Strong group pressure to quell dissent and 'rocking the boat'
- A perception of unanimity – filtering out or ignoring divergent views
- Mutual support and solidarity to guard the decision

5.11 Since by definition a group suffering from groupthink is highly resistant to criticism, recognition of failure and unpalatable information, it is not easy to break such a group out of its vicious circle. It must, however, be encouraged to exercise self-criticism, to welcome outside ideas and evaluations and to respond positively to conflicting evidence. A member may be appointed to the role of 'devil's advocate', to deliberately inject alternative viewpoints and energise conflict. It may help to rotate team roles (where possible), to encourage people to see the team's purpose and objectives from alternative viewpoints, and to reduce power imbalances that would stifle opposition or questioning. The *status quo* should continually be 'refreshed' in order to avoid complacency.

Building team cohesion

5.12 There are many different techniques of team building (creating cohesive groups), but team cohesion is often based on fostering the following elements.

- Team identity: the sense of being a team (sometimes called *esprit de corps* or team spirit). This may be done by naming the group; expressing the team's identity in slogans and mottos; building a team history in stories and jokes (especially heroic successes and failures); or giving the team distinctive 'badges' or symbols.
- Team solidarity: loyalty to the group, so that team members put in extra effort for the group and in support of its norms and values. This may be done by expressing solidarity ('one for all and all for one'); encouraging interpersonal relationships within the team; controlling intra-group conflict and competition in positive, affirming ways; and celebrating group (rather than individual) successes.
- Commitment to shared goals: cooperation in the interests of team objectives. These may initially be team maintenance goals, but if they can be integrated with task goals (by offering the team the satisfaction of achievement, recognition or reward) the cooperative drive can be turned to the organisation's advantage.
- Competition, crisis or emergency: members of a group will act in unison if the group's existence or patterns of behaviour are threatened from outside. Competition within groups erodes cohesion – but competition with other groups enhances it.

Team decision-making

5.13   Decision-making is a key team process. Team decisions may be arrived at in various ways.

- The application of authority by the leader, perhaps after taking members' views into account
- The use of power or influence, eg by a team specialist or charismatic member
- Majority rule: by voting or the leader's getting a 'sense' of the view supported by the majority of team members
- By consensus: a process whereby divergent views are examined and persuasive arguments used until there is broad agreement among all members. This takes longer, but is often more effective in implementation, as all members of the group are able to 'own' the decision.

5.14   In less effectively functioning teams, this may be a negative process, where decisions are taken without input from team members; by minority (eg a dominant clique within the team); or by default (eg if the leader has abdicated his responsibility).

5.15   As discussed earlier, group decision-making tends to take longer (especially through consensus-seeking), but decisions are often better evaluated and more representative (owing to the input of different viewpoints) and therefore implemented with more commitment. Perhaps the key task of the manager is to avoid the 'risky-shift' phenomenon, whereby groups tend to take greater risks than the same individuals on their own. As we have seen, this is aggravated in cohesive groups, because of groupthink, and must be combated by a rigorous insistence on hearing divergent viewpoints and evaluating options.

5.16   In an effectively functioning group, decision-making will become less leader-centred over time: processes for constructive problem-solving will be carried out with appropriate member involvement and information sharing (without degenerating into groupthink).

Team communication

5.17   Effectively functioning groups tend to move from a leader-centred, leader-initiated pattern of communication to one where interaction is multi-directional or 'all-channel': any member can communicate directly with any other member. Cliques and isolated individuals become included within this web of interaction over time.

5.18   Here are some features of effective group communication.

- Open, honest communication – including the ability to deal with conflicts, issues and criticism openly, directly and fairly (without personal animosity or grudge-holding)
- Task-relevant information sharing (no withholding on a 'need to know' or 'knowledge is power' basis)
- All-member participation in meetings, discussions and decision-making. Equitable participation does not mean that all members will share *equally*, but that all members can get a fair hearing when they have something to say
- Absence of artificial status barriers, so that senior and junior members communicate with ease
- Positive contributions (giving and seeking information, suggestions and opinions; encouraging and affirming others; being appropriately vulnerable; checking understanding; giving constructive feedback; summarising etc) outweigh negative contributions (attacking, being defensive, difficulty stating, fault finding, interrupting or overriding others and so on).

Team leadership

5.19   Contingency theory sees management effectiveness as being dependent on a number of variable or contingent factors. There is no 'one right way' to lead that will fit all situations; one must lead in a manner that is appropriate to a particular situation. According to Handy *(Understanding Organisations)*, the management situation consists of factors such as the following.

- The manager's power and influence in the organisation and with the work group, affecting the extent to which a command-and-control style is possible
- The nature of the task and technology, affecting the extent to which workers require close instruction and supervision
- The skills and motivation of the work group, affecting the extent to which workers will want or expect autonomy or involvement in decision-making
- The culture of the organisation and its management, affecting the style likely to be perceived as acceptable and effective.

Team maturity

5.20 As we mentioned in Chapter 5, Hersey and Blanchard propose an influential situational model of team leadership, in which a manager's style is a combination of directive and supportive behaviours. Directive behaviour involves: 'clearly telling people what to do, how to do it, when to do it, and then closely monitoring their performance'. Supportive behaviour involves: 'listening to people, providing support and encouragement for their efforts, and then facilitating their involvement in problem-solving and decision-making'.

5.21 The most appropriate managerial style for a given team depends on the readiness (or maturity) of the team members to perform a given task, in terms of their task ability (experience, knowledge and skills) and willingness (whether they have the confidence, commitment and motivation) to complete the task successfully. The model is depicted in Figure 6.2.

Figure 6.2 *Hersey and Blanchard's situational leadership model*

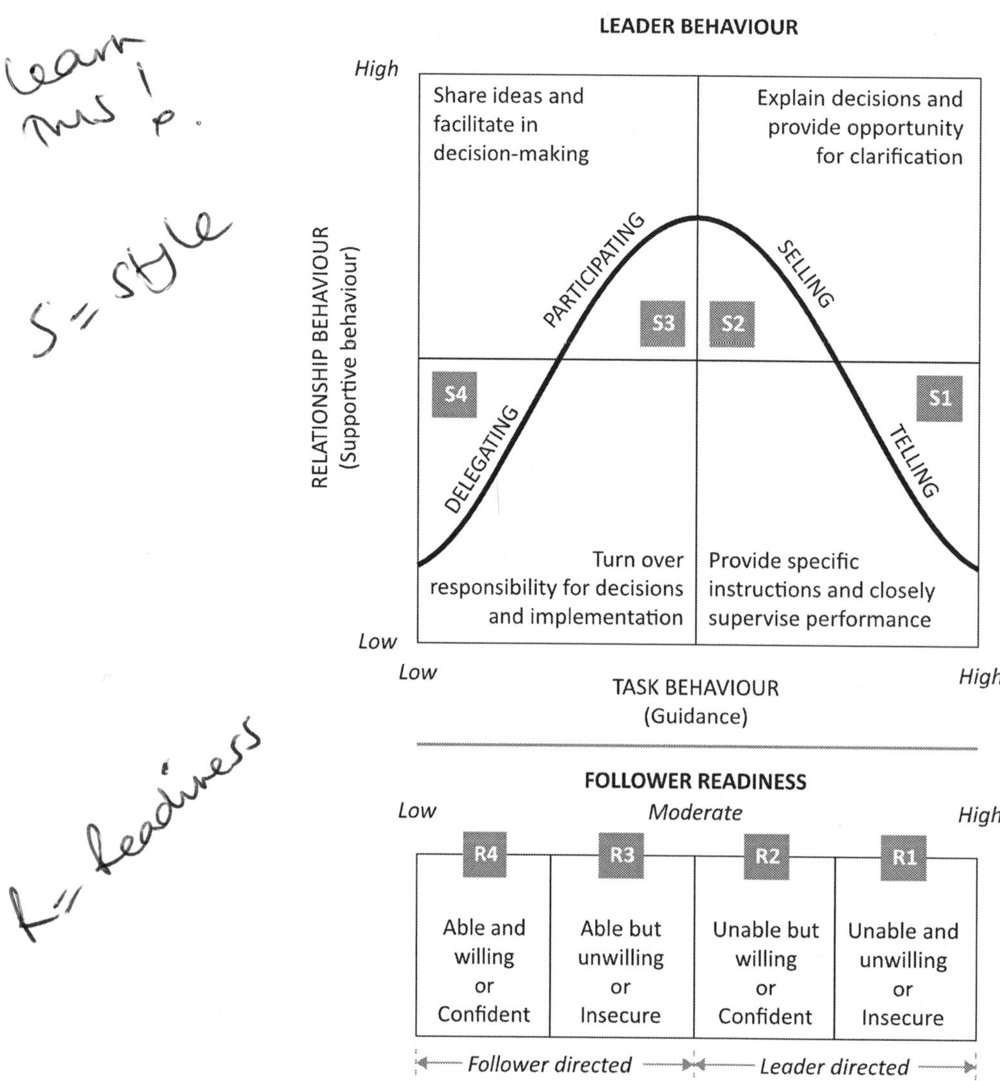

5.22   The four quadrants of the diagram describe four leadership 'styles' labelled S1, S2, S3, S4.

S1   Low-readiness teams (lacking ability and motivation or confidence) require more directive behaviours in order to secure an adequate level of task performance: the most appropriate leadership style may be a 'telling' style. An example might be where staff are new to the organisation or to particular technology or procedures.

S2   Low-moderate readiness teams (willing and confident, but lacking ability) require both directive and supportive behaviour to improve their task performance without damaging morale: the most appropriate leadership style may be a 'selling' style. An example might be more experienced members of staff taking on new responsibilities for the first time.

S3   High-moderate readiness teams (able, but unwilling or insecure) are competent, but require supportive behaviour to build morale: the most appropriate leadership style may be a consults or 'participating' style. An example might be a team member returning from training to apply newly-learned skills; or teams going through a period of low morale or resistance to organisational changes.

S4   High-readiness teams (able and willing and/or confident) do not need directive or supportive leadership: the most appropriate leadership style may be a joins or 'delegating' style. An example would be any mature and effectively functioning team which is capable of getting on with performing, only needing to appeal to the leader for guidance in the event of unforeseen problems or new situations.

6   Building effective teams

What makes a team successful?

6.1   The task of the team leader is to build a 'successful' or 'effective' team. The criteria for team effectiveness, however, are both:

- Fulfilment of task and organisational goals (quality and productivity) *and*
- Satisfaction of team members (especially the fulfilment of their high-level needs for growth and development).

6.2   According to the human relations school of management the one is not, in fact, possible without the other: satisfied team members are more likely to work in a committed and cooperative fashion towards task objectives – and the successful achievement of task objectives, in turn, actively promotes satisfaction. Meanwhile, team processes (decision-making, leadership, communication, role allocation and so on) must be balanced, dynamic, functional and mature in order to support both achievement and satisfaction.

What does an effective team look like?

6.3   There are a number of factors, both quantitative and qualitative, that might be assessed in order to decide whether or how far a team is operating effectively. Some factors cannot be taken as evidence on their own, but may suggest underlying problems in the team: accident rates, labour turnover and absenteeism, for example. In an effective team, you may observe both quantifiable and qualitative factors.

Quantifiable factors
- Low rate of labour turnover, accidents and/or absenteeism
- High output or productivity
- High quality output or low wastage and error rates
- Achievement of specific individual and team targets and standards
- Infrequent disruptions of work for problems, conflicts and so on

Qualitative factors
- High commitment to the achievement of targets and goals
- Clear understanding of team goals, and of the team's role in organisational or supply chain activity (particularly customer care or quality)

- Clear understanding of the role of each member within the team
- Trust between members, reflected in free and open communication and the willingness to share tasks (trusting others to 'do their part')
- New ideas generation, sharing of ideas and welcoming of divergent views
- Mutual support and facilitation by members of each other's work
- Open confrontation and investigation of problems by the group, with commitment to finding mutually satisfactory solutions
- Active interest and involvement in work decisions
- Seeking of opportunities for individual challenge, responsibility and development
- Ability and motivation to keep functioning in the temporary absence of the group leader.

Diagnosing poor-functioning teams

6.4   We have focused on the attributes and dynamics of effectively functioning teams. You should be able to use the *opposite* factors to describe an ineffective or dysfunctional team. Drawing together all that we've said, the following is a brief checklist of some of the reasons identified for poor team performance.

- Lack of support, information or resources from management to fulfil the task (including lack of genuine decision-making authority and accountability)
- Unclear or unrealistic individual or team objectives
- Inappropriate team size or composition (gaps or lack of balance in team roles)
- Conflicts of interest, interpersonal hostility or status barriers blocking team development, co-operation and information-sharing
- Under-performing or under-motivated individuals holding back the team, and causing mistrust and resentment
- Poor team leadership, creating power conflicts and imbalances, lack of communication and uncertainty
- Unchecked team cohesion, diverting attention from the task and creating 'groupthink'
- Lack of leadership and teamworking skills to maintain team development and guide team processes (role allocation, decision-making, communication) in helpful ways
- Group norms undermining performance (eg restricting output, resisting leadership)

You can no doubt think of other factors – perhaps even from your own experience...

Factors in effective teamworking

6.5   There are many different models of the factors required for effective teamworking. AG Sheard and AP Kakabadse ('From loose groups to effective teams': *Journal of Management Development)* suggest nine essential factors: clearly defined goals; aligned priorities; agreed roles and responsibilities; individual self-awareness; facilitative leadership; open group dynamics; open communication; task content over which the team has some discretion; and a supportive organisational infrastructure.

6.6   Mike Woodcock *(Team Development Manual)* similarly suggests ten 'building blocks' for effective teamworking.

- Leadership: adopting a leadership style that fits the task, team and situation (if there is a designated leader) or ensuring that leadership roles and functions are fairly distributed or rotated to those best able to exercise them (and to develop others)
- Membership: ensuring a suitable mix of competencies and member roles
- Climate/culture: creating a cooperative atmosphere and style, based on trust
- Objectives: clarifying and articulating specific, meaningful and achievable goals which can be shared by the whole team
- Achievement: creating opportunities to learn and celebrating improvement
- Work methods: developing workable procedures for task and group functioning

- Communication: facilitating openness and honesty, information sharing, ideas generation and constructive feedback, often via team briefings
- Interpersonal relations: controlling conflict and facilitating trust and co-operation
- Individual development needs: giving team members opportunities to grow and develop within the team
- Review and control: regularly evaluating and feeding back on team performance and improvement needs

6.7 The opposite of these building blocks (inappropriate leadership style, inadequate mix of competencies, poor communication etc) are referred to in Woodcock's model as 'blockages'. You should be able to work out what the ineffective version of each building block is – and the effect they would have on team functioning.

6.8 Mullins summarises the factors contributing to effective teamworking (many of which we have already discussed): see Table 6.2.

Table 6.2 *Mullins's factors in group cohesion and performance*

Membership	• *The size of the group*: not too large for cohesion • *Compatibility of members*: balance of homogeneity (for cohesion) and diversity (for contribution and avoidance of groupthink) • *Permanence of membership*: sufficient member retention to allow group development over time
Work environment	• *Nature of the task*: the extent to which cohesion is supported by — Shared tasks and problems — The need to interact and communicate regularly (even in virtual teams) • *Physical setting*: balancing physical proximity and/or isolation from other groups (for cohesion) and privacy (for focused performance) • *Communications*: freedom of open, multi-directional communication (for cohesion), supported by task organisation, physical conditions (eg noise), technology (communication systems) and leadership (allowing or facilitating interaction) • Technology, eg: — The extent to which technology fosters a sense of identity (eg craft or skill-based) for cohesion — The extent to which technology allows or restricts social interaction for cohesion (eg in assembly lines) — The extent to which technology facilitates task performance (eg freeing workers for other tasks; supporting knowledge-sharing; reinforcing best practice procedures)
Organisational context	• *Management and leadership*: supporting cohesion and performance (through facilitative behaviour, opportunities for participation, conflict resolution, team building and motivation, effective delegation, information sharing and so on) • *HR policies and procedures*: equitable policies; team values reinforced by recruitment, appraisal, rewards and training and development • *Success*: creating cohesion and satisfaction; supported by feedback and recognition of good team results • *External threat*: expression of a shared threat (external business threat, competition, change etc) enhancing cohesion and motivation
Group development and maturity	• *Stage of development for cohesion and performance*: forming, storming, norming, performing or adjourning (Tuckman/Jensen)

A contingency approach to team effectiveness

6.9 No two groups of people are the same, and no group of people stays the same over time – even if they are doing the same type of work in the same organisational setup. Charles Handy suggests one contingency approach to team effectiveness. In any team situation, there are certain 'givens' which cannot be varied much in the short term: they represent the raw materials with which the team leader has to work. Other factors, however, may be regarded as 'intervening' variables, which are within the influence of the team leader, and therefore need to be managed in such a way as to maximise the 'outcomes' of teamworking (in terms of productivity and member satisfaction) for effectiveness.

6.10   The 'givens' in the team management situation are as follows.

- The group – including factors such as team members' skills, attitudes, goals and personalities
- The task – including the complexity, structure, technology and timescales of the work the team has to do
- The environment – including the team's physical surroundings, other groups and organisation culture.

6.11   The intervening factors, which the manager can (to an extent) manipulate are as follows.

- The motivation of the group
- The leadership style of the manager
- Processes and procedures: methods of working, group learning, feedback, communication, group decision-making, conflict handling and so on.

7   Managing diverse teams

Benefits of cultural diversity in teams

7.1   As we saw in Chapter 3, diversity is an issue of productivity and team effectiveness, because heterogeneous (diverse, multicultural) teams have been shown to out-perform homogeneous (non-diverse) teams in the long term. As Belbin's role model suggests, successful teamworking depends on a mix and balance of different task and team roles and contributions. Diverse – and even divergent – styles, viewpoints, personality types and backgrounds are a positive asset in teamworking, if they have any of the following effects.

- Widening the range of ideas and information which is taken into account in decision-making and problem-solving. This may enhance the quality and creativity of solutions, and their acceptability (where required) to a wider constituency.
- Demonstrating willingness to formulate solutions which take into account the views and concerns of a diverse organisation, supply chain or customer base.
- Controlling the risk of blinkered and complacent thinking, by challenging and testing dominant or unquestioned viewpoints.
- Opening processes and methods to fresh scrutiny, questioning and criticism – as the basis for learning and continuous improvement
- Creating a group climate in which ideas and feelings can be safely expressed, and differences are welcomed and respected. (This may be essential to support the contribution of all members.)

Managing virtual or 'remote working' teams

7.2   As we noted in Section 1 of this chapter, the globalisation of business has increasingly led to the formation of 'virtual' organisations and teams, supported by developments in ICT. This presents various challenges for team management.

- **Team building and co-ordination.** Virtual teams imply that team members are working in remote or dispersed locations – potentially worldwide. This limits many opportunities for team cohesion-building and interpersonal interactions, which must be replaced by management. This may involve: creating opportunities for personal interactions where possible (eg annual conferences); regular virtual meetings and briefings; data sharing (eg using email or extranet and intranet facilities); opportunities for informal networking (eg using social media); and strong expressions of team and corporate identity and solidarity.
- **Team communication.** In addition to ICT-enabled communication systems and mechanisms for regular communication, the organisation may have to give attention to the training of remote team members, and their leaders, in communication skills: rapport building (over audio and/or audio-visual links); facilitative communication styles and so on. Remote communication lacks the richness of face-to-face interaction (even when audio-visual): careful attention will have to be given to the accuracy of

communication; checking understanding; and avoiding misunderstanding due to lack of visual cues and/or the distancing effect of technology (eg the tendency to sound more abrupt in emails).

- **Leadership and supervision**. 'Position power' may have little meaning in virtual working, and virtual teams are by their nature more or less self-managing. Team leaders or co-ordinators will have to develop management styles appropriate to this situation: developing mutual trust; delegating effectively (while maintaining availability for guidance where required); and adopting the role and style of a facilitative coach and resource mobiliser. It may be difficult to 'supervise' work in any conventional sense: the leader will have to focus on monitoring and measuring outcomes and results – rather than attempting to control work patterns or time management.
- **Cultural diversity.** Team members may live and work in widely different geographical regions and countries, giving rise to challenges of cultural diversity. Francesco and Gold (*International Organisational Behaviour)* argue that: 'Cultural diversity, which will be increasingly common, adds to the complexity of managing virtual teams because different values, customs and traditions require leadership – under conditions that reduce the ability to use direct leadership.'
- **Infrastructure and 'logistical' issues**. In addition, globalised virtual teamworking creates a range of challenges in regard to: different time zones and working hours; different availability of infrastructure (eg access to broadband internet or mobile telecommunications networks); different legal regimes and jurisdictions (as the context for employment contracts, as well as supply and business contracts); and so on.

Building and managing a culturally diverse team

7.3   An effective culturally diverse team requires leadership in the following areas.

- Acknowledging cultural conflicts when they arise (without attributing all conflicts to cultural differences) and encouraging mutual learning about assumptions, values and culture-based behaviours
- Identifying and focusing on shared values and common ground
- Clarifying expectations and gaining commitment to the group's shared goals and objectives
- Identifying individual interests, strengths and preferences, and showing appreciation and respect for different cultural contributions
- Flexibly exploring culturally appropriate ways of team building and rewarding excellence (in the process developing a shared group culture)
- Being sensitive to power imbalances (such as a dominant language which may not be the first language of all members, or culture-based reluctance to contribute to a meeting or contradict a leader) and supporting all-member contribution
- Facilitating communication and feedback processes, so that people are encouraged to learn, develop sensitivity and behavioural flexibility, and confront potential conflicts and power imbalances before they become dysfunctional.

Chapter summary

- Formal groups are created by management to achieve organisational objectives. Organisations are also home to informal groups.
- Cross-functional teamwork has increasingly been recognised as vital in modern organisations.
- Teamworking has many advantages in improving organisational performance and in satisfying the needs of team members.
- Tuckman identified typical stages in the development of teams: forming, storming, norming and performing. He later added dorming and mourning.
- Belbin identified the typical roles carried out by team members.
- Team cohesion is an important aid to effective performance, but there is a danger that excessive cohesion may lead to groupthink.
- There are many quantitative and qualitative measures by which we can diagnose an effective or ineffective team.

Self-test questions

Numbers in brackets refer to the paragraphs where you can check your answers.

1 List reasons why work teams are formed. (1.4)

2 Explain the benefits of cross-functional teams. (1.18–1.21)

3 What are the advantages of work teams from the organisation's point of view? (2.2)

4 Describe the stages in group development identified by Tuckman. (3.2, 3.3)

5 According to the FIRO model, what are the three issues that need to be dealt with at each stage of a group's development? (3.8)

6 List the team roles identified by Belbin. (Table 6.1)

7 Explain what is meant by groupthink. (5.9)

8 List ways by which teams may arrive at decisions. (5.13)

9 List quantifiable and qualitative factors that indicate effectiveness of a work team. (6.3)

10 What is meant by 'givens' and 'intervening factors' in Handy's theory of team effectiveness? (6.9–6.11)

11 What are the particular challenges associated with management of virtual teams? (7.2)

CHAPTER 7

Co-operation and Conflict

Assessment criteria and indicative content

 **3.4** Analyse the nature of role relationships in work groups or teams in the procurement and supply function

- The stakeholders of a procurement and supply function
- Role congruence and incongruence
- Intra-group/team cohesion and conflict
- Positive and negative outcomes from conflict
- Behaviours to reduce conflict
- Developing effective groups/teams

Section headings

1   Roles in procurement and supply
2   Stakeholders in procurement and supply
3   The nature of conflict
4   Causes of conflict
5   Managing conflict in work teams

Introduction

One of the key roles of management is to develop and maintain co-operative working in the organisation (and supply chain).

In an interpersonal sense, this involves a complex, ongoing process of managing diversity and difference. 'Diversity', because the organisation is made up of individuals and groups with potentially very different personalities, goals, attitudes, backgrounds and so on. 'Difference', because those areas of diversity will inevitably, from time to time, cause misunderstandings, disagreements, competition and perhaps hostility. This is the kind of difference we generally call 'conflict' – although conflict itself is a complex term which can be seen from a number of different points of view.

In this chapter we discuss what conflict might mean in a work team, and whether it is a good or bad thing. We outline common causes (why conflict arises) and symptoms (how you can know it when you see it) and how it can be prevented, controlled and resolved.

1 Roles in procurement and supply

What are roles?

1.1 Role theory suggests that people behave in any situation according to other people's expectations of how they should behave in that situation in relation to other people. A role may be seen as a part you play: people sometimes refer to wearing 'different hats' in different situations or groups of people. Mullins defines a role in the context of organisations as: 'the expected pattern of behaviours associated with members occupying a particular position within the structure of the organisation [and] how they perceive their own situation.'

1.2 A *role set* is a group of people who respond to a person in a given role. Staff in the procurement and supply function will relate to the purchasing manager in his role as professional and superior authority – rather than as a parent or partner (within the role set of the family), a friend (within the role set of non-work peers) and so on. Individuals need to be aware of which role set they are operating in, in order to behave appropriately for their role.

1.3 *Role signs* indicate what role people are in at a given moment, so that others relate to them in that role without ambiguity or confusion. Role signs have traditionally included matters such as styles of dress and address (use of first names or terms of respect, say) in the office, to establish professionalism and relative status. These may now be perceived as artificial barriers to be broken down, but you should notice other behaviours taking their place as role signs: think about how you might behave differently towards a work colleague in a meeting with suppliers and in a bar after work, for example.

1.4 Role definition, differentiation and behaviours are important, as we saw in Chapter 6, to group team processes, structures and relationships. The relationship between functions in the organisation can also be seen in terms of roles: for example, the role of Procurement and Supply as a business partner, service provider or internal consultant to other departments.

Role congruence and incongruence

1.5 **Role incongruence** is a situation in which an individual's roles are not 'congruent': that is where two or more sets of expectations about a role do not 'match'. Different stakeholders may have different expectations about what an individual's role or status is – which may also differ from the individual's own role expectations. A manager may have high status or responsibility, but lack power or authority to back this up in some contexts (eg in a cross-functional team). A procurement officer may be relatively junior in authority to a senior production manager, but may be in a position of having to 'enforce' procurement policies or challenge materials requisitions.

1.6 **Role conflict** is a situation in which poor role definition and divergent role expectations lead an individual to behave inconsistently with the pattern of behaviour expected in their role.

- *Role ambiguity* arises when the individual (and/or members of his role set) is not sure what the role requires. This may arise from uncertainty about the scope, authority or responsibilities of the job (eg because of changing job descriptions or lack of job descriptions); or uncertainty about other people's expectations and lack of clarity about how performance in a role will be evaluated. For example, a procurement manager may be unsure whether his role is primarily cost reduction, or whether he is expected to contribute strategic value as a business partner. A procurement member of a cross-functional project team may similarly be unsure of his role in the team.
- *Role incompatibility* arises where two sets of divergent expectations mean that the individual cannot behave 'appropriately' in a role from both points of view. A manager who has positioned himself as a 'friend' to team members, for example, may find himself unable to meet their expectations of support and consideration at the same time as discharging his responsibilities to exact discipline or make

staff cuts. Role incompatibility often occurs in matrix structures (including devolved procurement structures) and cross-functional project teams, where individuals 'have a foot in two camps': the user department or project on the one hand, and the procurement and supply function on the other.

- *Role overload* arises where an individual is expected to perform too many roles, or where a role carries too many different sets of expectations. This creates conflicting priorities and stress. Again, it can easily occur in matrix and project structures, with competing demands.
- *Role underload* arises when an individual's allocated or perceived role falls short of their expectations: for example, if a job or team role is insufficiently challenging for an individual who believes he has the capacity to discharge a larger or more varied role or roles.

1.7 Role conflict is often a source of conflict in groups, teams and organisations. It is important to distinguish between:

- Role conflict – arising from inadequate or inappropriate role definition
- Personality clash – arising from the incompatibility of two individuals (even though their roles may be defined clearly and understood fully).

The roles of procurement and supply

1.8 It is common to distinguish three kinds of authority in organisations.

- **Line** authority is the direct flow of authority down the vertical chain (or line) of command: for example, the authority a manager has over a subordinate. This confers the right to set objectives, make decisions and issue instructions and expect to see them carried out.
- **Staff** authority is the authority one manager or department may have to give specialist advice or guidance to others. This does not include the right to make or influence decisions. Whether the advice is taken depends on how much power the department has – and this in turn depends on its credibility, the persuasive quality of its advice, and the perceptions of other departments that its expertise is valuable and necessary.
- **Functional** authority is a mix of line and staff authority, whereby a manager or department has the authority, in certain circumstances, to direct, design or control the activities or procedures of another department.

1.9 A manager in the purchasing and supply function therefore has direct line authority over his own staff, and over any subordinate departments or sections within the function.

1.10 In relation to other departments in the organisation, the purchasing manager may exercise functional authority in some areas: from day-to-day purchase requisition and authorisation procedures to policy guidelines on environmental and ethical sourcing or quality management. In other areas, his role may be purely advisory: recommending suppliers, prices or order quantities to project purchasing officers, say, or advising product designers on materials, specifications and quality issues.

1.11 Areas of ambiguity can become a cause of conflict. It is common for 'strategic' functions (such as production or finance) to resist what may be perceived as ignorance, interference or empire building by 'support' functions. Where support functions are excluded from any strategic role, they tend to become preoccupied with their own specialisms and status – so that their priorities may genuinely diverge from (or be irrelevant to) the strategic objectives of the organisation.

1.12 These issues of lack of integration and negative perception within the organisation must be addressed by purchasing and supply managers. They place a high premium on a manager's networking, relationship-building and negotiation skills.

2   Stakeholders in procurement and supply

2.1   Stakeholders are individuals and groups who have a legitimate interest or 'stake' in an organisation, process, project or decision. They may have invested money in it, or contributed to it, or they may be affected by its activities and outcomes.

2.2   The stakeholders of an organisation include internal, connected and external groups, whose **interest** in the organisation can be summarised as follows.

- **Internal stakeholders**. The directors, managers and employees who operate within the organisation's boundaries have a key stake in the organisation's survival and growth (for continued employment and prosperity); the fulfilment of task goals (as a measure of their competence and success); and the fulfilment of their personal goals (for income, security, career, status and so on).
- **Connected stakeholders**. These include shareholders, who have a key stake, as owners, in the financial performance of the organisation. They also include:
  - Financiers, such as banks (*interest:* security of loans, return on investment).
  - Customers and consumers (*interest:* satisfaction of complex expectations and motives for purchasing a product or service; ethical business dealings; helpful service and support; accurate information).
  - Suppliers (*interest:* efficient information flow; payment as agreed; mutually beneficial long-term relationship; feedback and support to enhance service).
  - Distributors (*interest:* reliable supply; quality and added value; marketing support; earnings through discount margins or commissions; mutually beneficial long-term relationship).
- **External stakeholders**. These include:
  - Government regulatory bodies (*interest:* economic activity; tax revenue; compliance with legislation; reports and returns; social responsibility).
  - Pressure and interest groups (*interest:* awareness of a particular cause or issue, eg environmental impacts; protection of the rights and interests of the group, eg disabled workers).
  - Professional bodies, trade unions and other representative groups (*interest:* protecting the interests of members; promoting professional standards and ethics).
  - The local community (*interest:* employment; provision of goods and services; social responsibility and involvement).

2.3   Stakeholder groups can apply pressure to **influence** organisations in different ways and to different degrees.

- Managers exercise direct influence (formal authority or power) over planning, organisation and control. They may also exercise informal power through leadership or charisma, influencing skills (eg in negotiation), or the exercise of discretion when implementing strategy.
- Staff members may have power through control over the labour resource or through specialist knowledge or skills (expert power) to influence human resource management policy and task performance.
- Customers are (in a 'marketing oriented' business) the focus of all organisational planning and activity.
- Supply chain partners have the ability to influence supply, quality, value addition, costs and pricing decisions, efficient flow-to-market, and therefore competitive advantage. They have power through control of strategic resources, expertise (eg subcontractors), influence on strategy implementation – and perhaps interpersonal influence with managers.
- Government has the power to constrain organisational activity by legislation and regulation – and so on.

2.4   All these influences may impact on the structure, systems, policies and values of the organisation – and individual functions such as purchasing and supply. The more influence a stakeholder has, the more likely it is that managers will have to take that stakeholder's needs and wants into account.

Stakeholders in procurement and supply

2.5   In addition to organisational stakeholders in general, each function, unit and project of an organisation may be said to have stakeholders, whose needs and influence must be taken into account. For any given purchasing activity or decision, it should be possible to identify stakeholders with similar interests and influence to those listed above.

- The owner or sponsor of the project or activity, who puts authority behind it, initiates it, and sets its objectives
- Customers and users of the activity or its outputs: departments who receive purchasing advice or assistance, or end users of the purchased resources and services
- Participating staff, who may be drawn from the purchasing department or from other functions, whether through cross-functional work- and information-flow, or in dedicated cross-functional project teams (depending on the activity and its organisation)
- Suppliers, who have a key stake in any purchasing activity or project, and are the subject of purchasers' key social responsibilities
- External collaborators, such as outsourced-service providers (project management, logistics etc), research consultants, legal advisers and so on
- Secondary stakeholders not commercially connected to, but impacted by, the project: for example, the communities from which supplier labour is drawn; those affected by environmental and economic impacts of the project; interest groups concerned with the environment, trading practices, consumer rights and so on.

2.6   The **internal customer concept** implies that any unit of the organisation whose task contributes to the task of other units (whether as part of a process, or in a staff or service relationship) can be regarded as a supplier of goods and services like any other supplier: each link in the value chain is a customer of the one before. The task of each unit thus becomes the efficient and effective identification and satisfaction of the needs and wants of its internal customers. This helps to integrate the objectives of units throughout the value chain – and makes each unit look at what added value it is able to offer.

2.7   The internal customers of the purchasing function include: senior management and shareholders, who expect their strategic objectives to be met through supply chain management; related functions such as finance, manufacturing, warehousing and logistics which depend on efficient co-ordination with purchasing; and line managers in other functions, who expect timely supply of the right quality and quantity of resources to meet their own objectives.

Stakeholder management

2.8   Stakeholder management recognises the need to take stakeholders into account when formulating strategies and plans. For a purchasing manager, it may be helpful in several ways. It enables you to gain expert input from stakeholders at the planning stage of a project, to improve the quality of your decisions. Stakeholders are more likely to 'own' and support plans to which they have had input: this will make ongoing collaboration easier. Gaining the support of powerful stakeholders may, in turn, mobilise power and resources within the organisation in support of your plans. At the very least, sources of resistance to your plans (from stakeholders whose goals are different from or incompatible with yours) can be anticipated and planned for.

2.9   A proactive systematic approach to managing stakeholders is shown in Figure 7.1.

Figure 7.1 *Managing stakeholders*

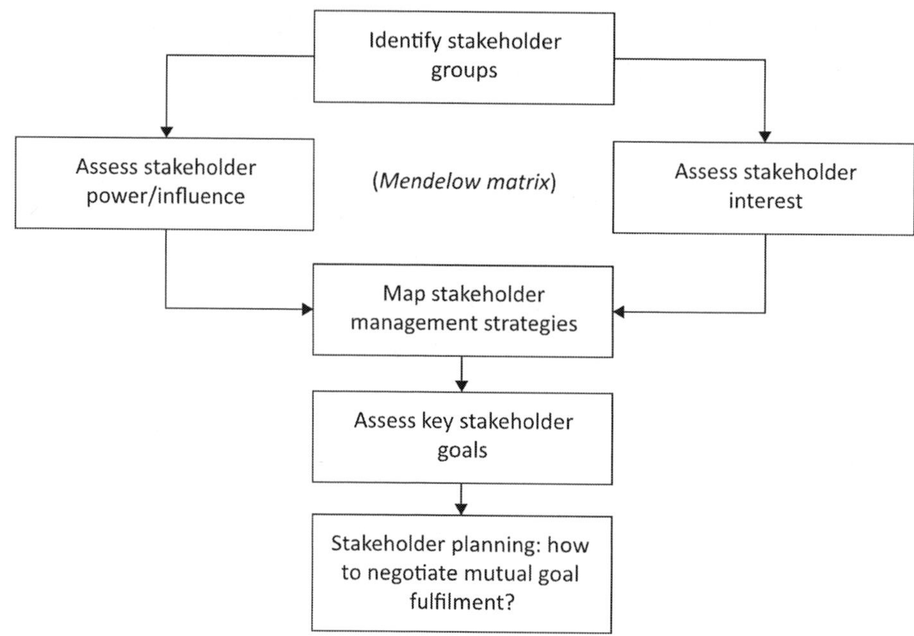

2.10 *Mendelow's* power/interest matrix is a useful tool for mapping stakeholders according to their power to influence organisational activity and the likelihood of their showing an interest in it: Figure 7.2.

Figure 7.2 *Mendelow's power/interest matrix*

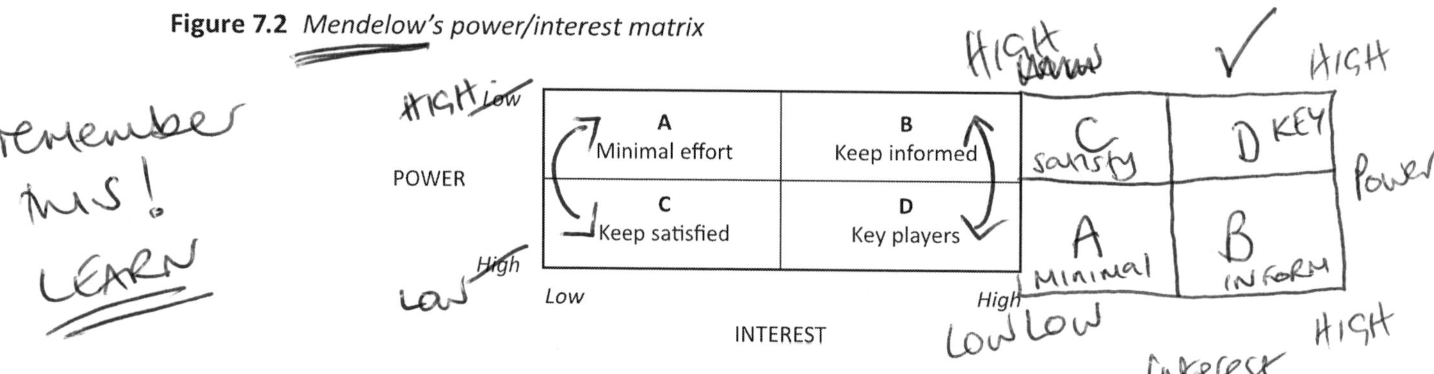

2.11 Working through each of the segments in Figure 7.2:

- Stakeholders who have neither interest nor influence in organisational activity (A) are a low-priority group: resources will not be wasted taking their goals into account, and they are likely simply to accept outcomes and directives.
- Stakeholders in Segment B are important because of their high interest: they may have low direct influence, but unless they are kept 'in the loop' and understand the need for a strategy, they may seek additional power by lobbying or banding together against it. (Community and employee groups may be in this category.) The recommended strategy is to keep them informed of strategies and outcomes, through stakeholder marketing, communication and education.
- Stakeholders in Segment C are important because of their high influence: they currently have low interest, but if dissatisfied or concerned, their interest may be aroused. (A large institutional shareholder or regulatory body may be in this category.) The recommended strategy is to keep these stakeholders satisfied.
- Stakeholders in Segment D are known as 'key players': they have influence and are motivated to use it in their own interests. (Senior internal customers and key suppliers may be in this category.) The recommended strategy is one of early involvement and participation, so that stakeholder goals can be integrated with organisational goals as far as possible.

2.12 Once key stakeholders have been identified, it is possible to plan a management strategy for each. You might use a standard process, such as the following.

- Goal analysis. What motivates these stakeholders? What are their goals or desired outcomes from your plans? What fears or issues might your plans raise for them? Where might they support you – and where might they oppose you?
- Desired outcomes. What do you want or need from these stakeholders? What levels of support do you want from them? What role(s) would you want them to play in your project or plans?
- Stakeholder marketing. What messages will you need to convey to these stakeholders? How can you 'sell' them the benefits of what you are proposing or doing? How can you confront and overcome any resistance?
- Relationship management. How will you manage communication to, and input from, each of these stakeholders? How will you keep your key supporters motivated? How will you win over or neutralise resistance? How will you engage the interest of potential supporters?
- Issues management. How will you raise potential issues and problems, where stakeholders' goals may differ from yours? How will you gain stakeholders' early involvement, and collaborate with them in minimising or managing the impacts?

2.13 In regard to supply chain relationships, *Baily, Farmer, Jessop and Jones* distinguish between transactional relationships, in which there is a simple exchange between supplier and buyer, and mutual relationships, in which 'the benefits of doing business together arise from ideas of sharing as well as exchanging'. Other areas of your CIPS studies will emphasise the process of building and maintaining supplier relations. However, you should be aware of the extent to which effective stakeholder communications are crucial for managers in general, in terms of:

- Customer care and customer relations management (including internal customers)
- Team building and cooperative, satisfying teamworking
- Facilitating communication, and minimising barriers caused by conflict and difference
- Motivation of team members (given people's social needs) and management of team briefings
- Managerial roles in liaison, ambassadorship and culture creation
- Influencing (applying power in a way that does not alienate others, but gains their willing compliance and even commitment).

3 The nature of conflict

3.1 There are different ideological perspectives on conflict in organisations.

- The **happy family view** (or **unitary perspective**) assumes that organisations are basically co-operative structures, in which there are no systemic conflicts of interest. Conflicts are unnatural and exceptional, caused by lack of leadership, poor communication or inflexibility on the part of individuals or interest groups. Strong culture, good communication, co-operative values and motivational leadership should be able to eliminate conflict.
- The **conflict view** (or **pluralist perspective**) assumes that organisations are natural arenas for conflict, as members compete for limited resources, status and rewards, and pursue different goals and professional values. Individual and organisational interests cannot always coincide – but a mutual survival strategy, involving the control of conflict through compromise, can be made acceptable in varying degrees to all concerned.
- The **evolutionary view (or interactionist perspective)** regards conflict as a force for gradual, evolutionary change: it maintains the *status quo* (by balancing competing interests) while also keeping the organisation sensitive to the need for change. (This is in contrast to a radical perspective, based on the ideas of thinkers such as Karl Marx, which sees conflict as inevitable and necessary as a force for the destruction of an oppressive social system, in order to introduce revolutionary change.)

Positive and negative outcomes from conflict

3.2   Conflict can be highly desirable. It can energise relationships and clarify issues. John Hunt *(Managing People in Organisations)* suggests that conflict is **constructive**, when its effect is to:

- Introduce different solutions to problems
- Define power relationships more clearly
- Encourage creativity and the testing of ideas
- Focus attention on individual contributions
- Bring emotions out into the open
- Provide opportunity for catharsis (the release of hostile feelings that might otherwise be repressed).

3.3   Conflict can also be **destructive,** negative and damaging to social systems (which the radical perspective still regards as positive and desirable). Hunt suggests that conflict of this kind may act in a group of individuals to:

- Distract attention from the task
- Polarise views and 'dislocate' the group
- Subvert objectives in favour of secondary goals
- Encourage defensive or 'spoiling' behaviour
- Result in disintegration of the group
- Stimulate emotional, win-lose conflicts, or hostility (damaging communication).

3.4   Stephen P Robbins *(Managing Organisational Conflict: a Non-Traditional Approach)* suggests that a contemporary approach to conflict:

- Recognises the inevitability (even necessity) of conflict
- Explicitly encourages opposition and challenge to ideas and the *status quo*
- Defines conflict management to include stimulation as well as resolution of conflict
- Considers the management of conflict as a major responsibility of all managers.

4   Causes of conflict

4.1   Gary Dessler *(Human Resource Management)* classifies four major sources of organisational conflict.

- *Interdependence and shared resources.* Conflict is most likely to occur where groups are dependent on each other to achieve their goals and use shared resources in pursuit of these goals.
- *Differences in goals, values and perceptions.* Groups are distinctive social units and will have special interests, particular views of what is important and what is not, and will tend to see the world in a way which supports the maintenance and success of the group. (Overlapping membership – eg if a team member is also a trade-union member – may cause conflict within the individual, as well as within the group.)
- *Authority imbalance.* Where a group has too little authority compared to its responsibilities or prestige, it will aggressively seek more (in competition with other groups). If it has too much, it will be a target of others who attempt to enhance their own authority or prestige. If group contributions are equivalent or substitutable, political conflict may escalate as groups by-pass or replace one another.
- *Ambiguity.* Where a group's responsibilities are ambiguous or unclear, power vacuums arise: competition to fill the vacuum ensues. Similarly, uncertainty about *other* groups' purposes or motives leads to mistrust and political game-playing.

4.2   Mullins summarises the potential sources of organisational conflict: see Table 7.1.

Table 7.1 *Mullins's causes of conflict*

Differences in perception	Different people attach different meanings to the same objects or events: different attitudes and value judgements can then become a source of interpersonal conflict
Limited resources	Individuals and groups often have to compete for a share of limited (or scarce) resources, such as budget, staff, space and so on.
Specialisation	Division of labour on the basis of specialisation leads to functional departmentation. Functional departments may have different goals, priorities, methods and culture – creating potential for a 'silo' mentality and self-interested (sub-optimal) behaviour. This can lead to conflict especially where departments need to work together in a co-ordinated manner.
The nature of work activities	Where the task of one person or group is dependent on another, as part of a process, there is potential for conflict due to failure to meet the internal customer's needs (failure to meet agreed schedules or meet output targets, say) – especially if the customer department feels that it is being unfairly judged on results which were 'sabotaged' by the other party.
Role conflict	As discussed earlier, the failure of people to behave as they are expected to, or to live up to the requirements of their role in the eyes of stakeholders.
Inequitable treatment	Conflict may arise if a person or group feels they have been treated unjustly or unfairly, especially in relation to another person or group (as discussed in Chapter 5 in connection with the equity theory of motivation)
Violation of territory	People tend to be 'territorial' and 'possessive' in regard to resources and responsibilities perceived to be 'theirs'. They may feel resentful or threatened if others 'invade' or 'encroach' on their territory: usurping power, taking over clients, sharing their workspace and so on.
Environmental change	Environmental change can be a catalyst for any of the above sources of conflict: eg economic recession causing intensified competition for scarce resources, or employment legislation causing conflicts of interest between workers and management.

Inter-group conflict

4.3   Various forms of inter-group conflict are common in organisations.

- Institutionalised conflict, such as that between trade unions and management.
- Hierarchy-based conflict, caused by inequalities of positional power.
- Functional conflict, caused by clashing goals and competition for power and resources between different organisational functions.
- Line/staff conflict, such as that between production and sales functions and 'advisory' functions such as the HR department, Accounts and so on: the power of staff functions is often resented and resisted by line managers as interference, and staff functions have to reassert their authority (often by negative means, such as red-tape and rule enforcement).
- Formal/informal conflict, where the unwritten rules, communication channels and power structures of the informal organisation clash with those of the formal organisation.
- Status conflict, where groups compete for status and prestige.
- Resource conflict, where groups compete for finance, staff, space and other resources. This is often the basis of adversarial negotiations: 'win/lose' competition where one party can gain only at another's expense.
- Political conflict, where individuals or interest groups exercise whatever power they can amass to influence the goals, criteria or processes used in organisational decision-making to advance their own interests.

Intra-group conflict

4.4   In addition, conflict may arise within a team because of everyday factors such as the following.

- Disagreement about needs, goals, values, priorities and interests (since individuals may have different 'agendas' – or different perceptions about the team's goals and purposes). This will be made worse by:

- Lack of direction (from the organisation or team leader) as to what the team's purpose and goals are.
- Lack of clarity in the roles assigned to team members, leading to stressful role ambiguity (where individuals don't know clearly what they are expected to contribute) and/or frustration and loss of co-ordination, as roles are duplicated or left vacant.
- Poor communication, which is a cause (as well as a symptom) of conflict. The less people communicate, the more potential there is for negative assumptions, stereotypes and misunderstandings. Withholding of information may also escalate conflict, as it is perceived to be a hostile political 'game'.
- Competition for scarce resources, which also operates at the team level. Individuals may compete for power, office space, team-based rewards, the manager's recognition and attention, machine time (or other resources) and so on.
- Interpersonal issues, such as 'personality clashes', aggression or domination by strong individuals, argumentative or manipulative communication styles and so on.
- 'Hygiene' issues (in the technical sense used by Herzberg): dissatisfactions with the leadership, working conditions or pay, say, which can cause grievance against the organisation (or leader) and/or spill over into interpersonal conflict in the team (eg if some members feel others are being paid more).

Organisational politics

4.5 The interests of different individuals or groups in organisations may include the acquisition of individual power or influence, 'empire building', career advancement, or favourable allocation of organisational resources.

4.6 The techniques for achieving these objectives (referred to as 'games' by Mintzberg and others) include the enhancement of individual power by forming networks, alliances and coalitions, and exercising power to undermine and control others (eg by withholding information, creating red tape and so on).

4.7 Here are some other power strategies.

- *Contracting:* negotiating a *quid pro quo* agreement between groups, making concessions to make gains (eg in collective bargaining)
- *Co-opting:* short-circuiting opposition and criticism by getting potential critics to share responsibility for the decision
- *Forming networks and coalitions:* combining the information and power of individuals or groups by making strategic alliances
- *Influencing decision criteria:* 'moving the goal posts', changing the criteria by which success and failure are judged, to make yourself look good or others bad
- *Controlling information:* selectively giving, withholding or distorting information to strengthen your position ('knowledge is power') or undermine that of others
- *Coercion and pressure tactics:* threatening or applying negative power (eg withdrawal of labour in industrial action)
- *Rule making:* imposing rules, procedures, restrictions or official requirements on other groups in order to bolster one's own importance

Conflict behaviours

4.8 According to Handy *(Understanding Organisations)*, the observable symptoms of conflict in an organisation will be as follows.

- Intra-personal struggles or frustration, where an individual has conflicting goals within himself
- Poor communication (upward, downward and/or lateral)
- Interpersonal friction

- Inter-group rivalry and jealousy
- Low morale and frustration
- The proliferation of rules, norms and myths (to protect different positions)
- Widespread use of arbitration, appeals to higher authority and grievances
- Inflexible attitudes towards change
- Poor co-ordination between hostile, non-communicating groups, resulting in work delays (and possibly customer complaints).

5 Managing conflict in work teams

5.1 There are many approaches to the management of conflict and the suitability of any given approach must be judged according to its relevance to a particular situation. There is no 'right way'. In some situations, the best outcome may be achieved by compromise; in others, imposition of a win-lose solution may be required; in others, the process of seeking a win-win solution, whatever the eventual outcome, may be helpful.

5.2 The term **conflict resolution** may be used to refer to what Handy calls 'regulation strategies': resolving disputes or conflicts once they emerge. Such strategies include: establishing detailed rules and procedures for conduct; appointing liaison or co-ordination officers to manage areas of conflict; using confrontation and negotiation meetings to hammer out differences and reach compromise; providing mechanisms for third-party intervention (eg by mediation, conciliation or arbitration); or separating conflicting individuals.

5.3 The term **conflict management** may be used to refer to a more proactive process, involving what Handy calls 'ecological' strategies: creating conditions in which individuals and groups may be better able to interact co-operatively with each other, and in which issues and potential conflicts can be openly discussed with a view to mutual understanding (if not always agreement).

5.4 Such strategies are wide-ranging and ongoing, including measures such as: agreeing shared objectives and values; reinforcing the group or team nature of organisational life via cultural mechanisms and supportive leadership; training people in group process skills; setting up mechanisms for multi-directional communication, employee relations and involvement; clarifying territorial and role ambiguities; eliminating unnecessary status barriers and inequalities; distributing resources fairly and with transparency; setting ground rules for group discussion and issues management; and so on.

Conflict resolution approaches

5.5 Robbins provides the following classification of possible strategies for resolving conflict.

- Problem-solving: the parties are brought together to find a solution to the particular issue
- Superordinate goals: the parties are encouraged to see the bigger picture and identify shared goals that override their differences
- Expansion of resources: resources are freed and mobilised to meet both parties' needs, eliminating the need for competition
- Avoidance: one or both parties withdraws from the conflict or denies or conceals the incompatibility
- Smoothing: one or both parties plays down the differences and 'papers over the cracks'
- Compromise: bargaining, negotiating and conciliating, so that each party makes some concessions in order to obtain some gains
- Authoritative command: an arbitrator with authority over both parties makes a decisive judgement
- Altering the human variable: effort is made to change the attitudes, beliefs and perceptions underlying the conflict
- Altering the structural variable: effort is made to re-organise work relationships in order to minimise the potential for conflict

5.6   Mullins summarises the range of strategies as follows.

- Clarification of goals and objectives, role definitions and performance standards, in order to avoid conflict based on misunderstandings
- Resource distribution: increasing the share of resources, mobilising new resources, or allocating resources in such a way as to maximise perceived fairness and utility
- The use of non-monetary rewards, where financial resources are limited
- Just and equitable human resource management policies and procedures: fair rewards, grievance and disciplinary procedures; positive employee relations; and training managers in coaching and negotiation skills; and so on
- Development of interpersonal and group process skills, to foster self-awareness and self-control, conflict management and problem-solving
- Group selection and development: eg careful selection of members for cross-functional teams; using formal and informal mechanisms to encourage cross-functional communication
- Leadership and management. Mullins suggests that 'a more participative and supportive style of leadership and managerial behaviour is likely to assist in conflict management' (eg fostering interpersonal respect, team values and so on) – but you might also note that more directive styles may be necessary to resolve conflict
- Organisational processes: removing unnecessary stressors from authority structures (eg status barriers); communication channels; decision-making processes; and bureaucratic 'red tape'
- Socio-technical approach: as discussed in Chapter 2, attending to the psycho-social factors of work and organisation, alongside technical and structural requirements.

A model of conflict styles

5.7   Kenneth W Thomas ('Conflict & Conflict Management': *Handbook of Industrial and Organisational Psychology*) suggested that individuals' conflict-handling styles could be mapped on two dimensions, according to the intentions of the parties involved: their assertiveness (the extent to which they try to satisfy their own concerns) and their co-operativeness (the extent to which they try to satisfy the other party's concerns).

5.8   The five extreme points on this map are shown in Figure 7.3.

Figure 7.3 *Model of conflict-handling styles*

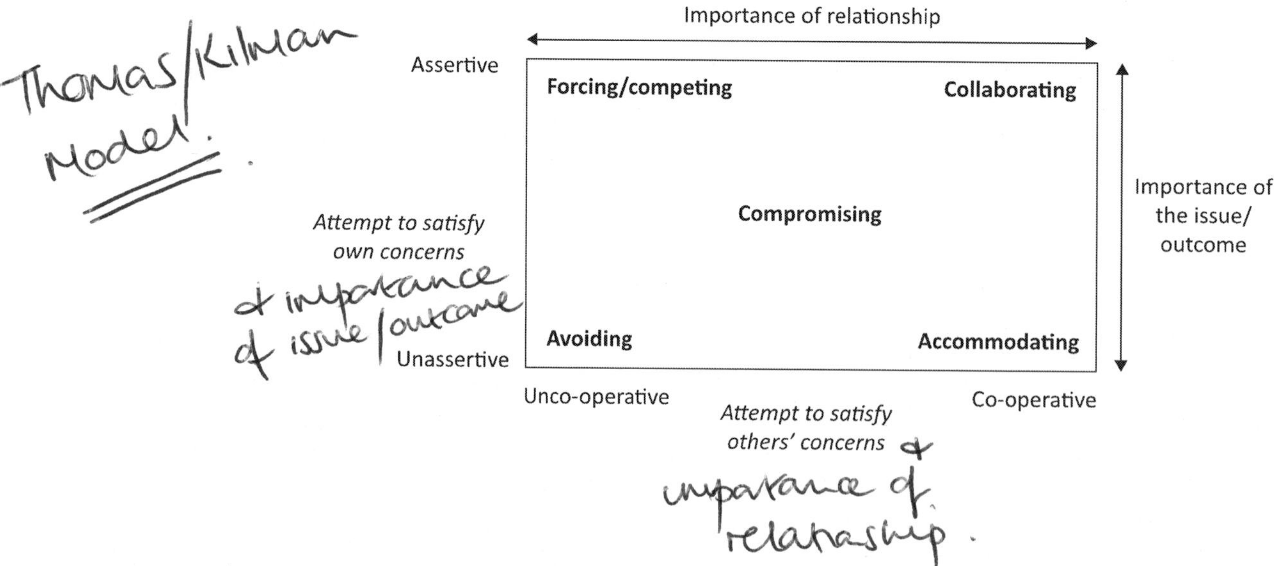

5.9 The five styles can be compared as follows.

- **Avoiding**: you withdraw from the conflict or attempt to sweep it under the carpet. This allows you to avoid dealing with conflict, and avoids immediate tensions: it may be appropriate if the issue is genuinely trivial, or you need a 'cooling off' period, or someone else is better placed to deal with the conflict. However, underlying problems don't get resolved: long-term frustrations and resentments may emerge in other ways.
- **Forcing/competing**: you impose your solution on the problem. This allows you to get your way, and may be appropriate for issues that need winning: breaking down the inflexibility of others or implementing unpopular measures quickly in a crisis, say. However, the other party is likely to feel defeated and demeaned, and this can damage ongoing collaboration and trust.
- **Accommodating**: you concede the issue without a fight, to preserve harmony. This avoids upsetting people, and may be appropriate where maintaining the relationship is more important than the issue (or if you realise you are wrong!). However, you are giving permission for the other person to take advantage of the situation, and your authority may be undermined.
- **Compromising**: you use bargaining or negotiation, so that each party trades some concessions for some gains. This reaches an agreement that both parties can live with, and enables you to get on with work. It may be necessary where power is evenly balanced and there is genuine conflict of interest. However, the solution is often more expedient than effective, and may leave both parties unsatisfied.
- **Collaborating**: you work together to try and find an outcome which meets the clearly stated needs of both parties as far as possible: a problem-solving or 'win-win' approach. This assumes that both positions are important, even if they are not necessarily equally valid. It takes time, but at the end of the process, both parties should be committed to the solution and satisfied that they have been treated fairly. This facilitates learning, generates more creative options and encourages trust. (We examine the 'win-win' approach in more detail below.)

Note that there is still no 'one best' style: managers need behavioural flexibility.

5.10 Thomas suggests that research backs collaboration as the best way to settle conflict. However, it may also be argued that:

- Competition is a valid response to a different set of assumptions than those underlying collaboration. It may be necessary for solving ideological disputes, obtaining flexibility, avoiding vulnerability and establishing autonomy: in other words, sometimes you just have to 'stick to your guns'.
- Collaboration is a useful way to resolve conflict when there is at least a moderate amount of interdependence among the parties (so that a win-lose situation would damage both); a perceived equality of power exists between the two parties (so that both can afford to be as open as collaboration requires); there are mutual advantages to collaboration that can be seen by both parties; and the collaborative process is supported by the organisation.

The win-win approach to conflict resolution

5.11 Another useful model for conflict resolution is 'win-win'. Helena Cornelius and Shoshana Faire *(Everyone Can Win)* suggest that there are three basic ways in which a conflict or disagreement can be worked out.

- Win-lose: one party gets what he wants at the expense of the other party. However well justified such a solution is, there is often lingering resentment on the part of the 'losing' party, which may begin to damage working relationships.
- Lose-lose: neither party gets what he really wants. Compromise comes into this category. However logical such a solution is, there is often resentment and dissatisfaction on both sides: even positive compromises only result in half-satisfied needs.
- Win-win: both parties get as close as possible to what they really want. Whether or not the outcome is possible, the approach generates more options, more creative problem-solving, more open communication, and enhanced cooperation, as well as preserving working relationships.

5.12   Cornelius and Faire outline a win-win approach as follows.

> **Step 1**   Find out why each party needs what they say they want. Getting to the other party's fears and needs in the situation facilitates meaningful problem-solving. It also encourages communication, supports other people's values, and separates the problem from the personalities involved.
>
> **Step 2**   Find out where the differences dovetail. Diverging needs may seem like the cause of conflict – but they also offer potential for problem-solving, since the different needs may not be mutually exclusive, but may dovetail at some point.
>
> **Step 3**   Design new options, where everyone gets more of what they need. Techniques include: brainstorming; chunking (breaking a big problem down into manageable chunks and seeking solutions to those); and devising usable 'currencies' (suggestions and concessions which are easy or low-cost for both parties, and can be traded). The aim is mutual gain.
>
> **Step 4**   Co-operate. Treat the other person as a partner, not an opponent.

5.13   The example given is of two men fighting over an orange. The win-win approach would ask each man why he needs the orange. One may want to make orange juice, while the other wants the skin of the orange to make candied peel: the conflict disappears. If they both want the juice, other options will be explored: sharing the juice; getting more oranges; diluting the juice; buying one man some bottled orange juice and so on. Even if compromise is settled on, the outcome will be a win-win, because both parties will have been fully assertive and willingly cooperative, enhancing the relationship between them (which adds to the 'win' outcome).

Formal conflict resolution mechanisms

5.14   Formal mechanisms are often set up in organisations to prevent or resolve conflict.

- **Disciplinary procedures:** reflecting the attempt of the organisation to enforce its rules and standards of acceptable behaviour. Many enterprises base their disciplinary procedures on the idea of progressive discipline: sanctions of increasing severity for each repetition or exacerbation of an offence. A typical progression might be from informal talk to oral warning to formal written warning; and thence to disciplinary sanctions of escalating severity (eg demotion, loss of pay, lay-off or suspension); with the 'last resort' sanction of dismissal.

- **Grievance procedures:** reflecting the attempt of the organisation to investigate and resolve claims by employees to have been unfairly or wrongly treated, victimised, discriminated against, harassed and so on. Some grievances may require informal conflict resolution between the individuals concerned, mediated by their manager. However, there may be situations where the grievance is more serious, or where the manager himself is the subject of the complaint. In such circumstances, it is important to have systematic formal grievance procedures in place, allowing for escalation to higher authorities where required.

- **Consultation mechanisms**: a form of 'issues' management, in which potential causes of conflict are discussed, and stakeholders have an opportunity to give their input, before the problem arises (or as soon as possible, once it has arisen). Informal consultation may take place in team briefings, discussion forums – and day-to-day team communication.

- **Negotiatory mechanisms.** Negotiation is a useful approach to conflict resolution at any level.
  - As a style of communication, it may be used by managers or teams to resolve issues between them. Each party puts forward its position persuasively, and then seeks constructive compromise, through bargaining (trade-offs) or common ground (as seen in the 'win-win' approach above), so that both parties come to a solution they can agree to.
  - As an official mechanism, it is often used in industrial relations: the resolution of collective disputes (between employees and their employer), the negotiation of pay agreements and so on. *Collective bargaining* is the process whereby employers and employee representatives negotiate agreements by which terms and conditions of employment (and related matters) are determined for groups of represented employees. This is generally carried out at a series of formal meetings, specifically convened for the purpose.

- **Dispute resolution**: formal mechanisms for resolving individual and collective disputes.
  - *Conciliation* is a process where conflicts or grievances are aired in a discussion facilitated by an impartial conciliator. The conciliator's role is to provide information, to manage the process (eg by laying down ground rules and keeping participants to them) and to make constructive suggestions: *not* to make judgements for one side.
  - *Mediation* may follow conciliation, if a voluntary settlement has not been reached. It involves the appointment of an independent person (or panel) who will consider the case of both sides (set out in writing); hear evidence and arguments at a mediation hearing; and make a formal proposal or recommendation (not binding on either party) as a basis for settlement of the dispute.
  - *Arbitration* may follow unsuccessful mediation, if both parties agree (or if organisational policy requires it). It involves the appointment of an independent person (or panel) who will follow a similar procedure to mediation – except that, at the end of the process, the arbitrator delivers a decision or judgement which is binding on both parties.

The importance of teamwork

5.15 Mullins emphasises that: 'How people behave and perform as members of a group is as important as their behaviour or performance as individuals. Harmonious working relationships and good teamwork help make for a high level of staff morale and work performance. Effective teamwork is an essential element of modern management practices such as empowerment, quality circles and total quality management, and how groups manage change. Teamwork is important in any organisation, but may be especially significant in service industries, such as hospitality organisations where there is a direct effect on customer satisfaction.'

5.16 Guirdham (*Interactive Behaviour at Work*) argues that: 'More and more tasks of contemporary organisations, particularly those in high technology and service businesses, require teamwork. Taskforces, project teams and committees are key elements in the modern workplace. Teamwork depends not just on technical competence of the individuals composing the team, but on their ability to "gel". To work well together, the team members must have more than just team spirit. They also need *collaborative skills:* they must be able to support one another and to handle conflict in such a way that it becomes constructive rather than destructive.'

Developing effective groups and teams

5.17 As we mentioned in Chapter 6, team-building strategies encourage commitment to shared work objectives and to the cooperative working required to achieve them. This is likely to be a key tool for building virtual or multi-organisational supply chain teams, as well as conventional in-house teams. It will involve the following activities.

- Clear articulation of the team's task objectives and their place in the organisation's (or supply chain's) activity as a whole
- Involving the team in setting specific targets and standards and agreeing methods of organising work. (This may also include a broader consensus on how the team wishes to work together: members' expectations of each other; and ground rules for group processes such as role allocation, information-sharing, decision-making, leadership and so on.)
- Ensuring that, as far as possible, all interests and perspectives have been heard and acknowledged, so that consensus is genuine (rather than false, because a 'group' decision has been imposed)
- Providing the resources the team requires to fulfil its objectives
- Giving regular feedback on progress and results via team briefings
- Continually inviting input, feedback and suggestions from team members (depending on leadership and operating style), so that they can influence work methods and drive improvements
- Positively reinforcing behaviour that demonstrates commitment to the task (through rewards, recognition and celebration)

5.18 Cloke & Goldsmith *(The End of Management and the Rise of Organisational Democracy)* outline the ten skills team members need to develop, in order to support effective self-managed teamworking.

- Self-management: ownership, responsibility, commitment and efficiency
- Communication: effective listening, empathy, information-sharing, openness and issue framing and definition
- Leadership: organising, planning, co-ordinating, collaborating, facilitating and coaching
- Responsibility: both personal and shared
- Supportive diversity: overcoming biases and prejudices; valuing diversity and contribution
- Feedback and evaluation: welcoming, acknowledging and rewarding negative (constructive, developmental) feedback and evaluation of processes and results, for learning and improvement
- Strategic planning: identifying environmental threats and opportunities, and focusing on long-term, proactive solution-seeking and opportunity-exploitation
- Shaping successful meetings: making meetings shorter, more productive, more participative and consensus-seeking
- Resolving conflicts: problem-solving, integrative negotiation, difficult behaviour handling and conflict resolution
- Enjoyment: the ability to derive pleasure from challenges, achievement and collaborative work processes.

Chapter summary

- Role theory suggests that people behave in any situation according to other people's expectations.
- Stakeholders in an organisation may be classified as internal, connected and external.
- Mendelow's matrix is an influential tool used in planning the management of stakeholder groups.
- Conflict within organisations can be destructive, but in some circumstances it may have beneficial effects.
- Dessler identifies four major sources of organisational conflict: interdependence; differences in goals; authority imbalance; and ambiguity.
- Both Robbins and Thomas have suggested influential approaches to the management and resolution of conflict.

Self-test questions

Numbers in brackets refer to the paragraphs where you can check your answers.

1   What is meant by a role set? (1.2)

2   Distinguish between line, staff and functional authority. (1.8)

3   Give examples of internal, connected and external stakeholders of an organisation. (2.2)

4   Give examples of stakeholders in procurement and supply. (2.5)

5   Sketch Mendelow's matrix. (Figure 7.2)

6   In what circumstances may organisational conflict be constructive? (3.2)

7   List factors that may give rise to conflict within a work group. (4.4)

8   List strategies identified by Robbins for the resolution of conflict. (5.5)

9   Describe the five conflict resolution strategies identified by Thomas. (5.9)

10   List formal mechanisms for the resolution of conflict. (5.14)

CHAPTER 8

Human Resource Management

Assessment criteria and indicative content

4.1 Explain the importance of human resource management in the procurement and supply function

- Definitions of human resource management (HRM)
- HRM policies, activities and functions
- HRM as a shared organisational responsibility

4.2 Identify the skills and knowledge requirements for personnel in the procurement and supply function

- Human capital management

Section headings

1. What is human resource management?
2. HRM and organisational performance
3. HRM functions and policies
4. Shared responsibility for HRM

Introduction

Organisations are made up of people – as are the markets from which they source labour and supplies and to which they offer products and services. Most organisational functions depend on human knowledge, relationships, decisions or activity. Human beings are therefore, arguably, one of the key resources of any organisation.

Like other resources, labour must be managed. It needs to be sourced, controlled, utilised and developed with a view to key strategic objectives such as added value, distinctive competencies, organisational learning and flexibility, and competitive advantage. This is what human resource management (HRM) is all about: a systematic approach to ensuring that the organisation has the right human resources available in the right place at the right time, behaving in the right way to support organisational objectives.

In this chapter we will look at the nature of human resource management, and its importance in supporting organisational performance – and effective purchasing and supply management. We will also emphasise the key role of purchasing and supply managers (at the departmental level) in delivering HRM outcomes.

In following chapters we will look at systematic approaches to some of the key HRM tasks – recruitment and selection, and training and development – and why they are important.

1   What is human resource management?

The development and importance of HRM

1.1   As we noted in our introduction to this chapter, organisations are made up of people. The day-to-day management of people involves a number of task- and teamwork-related roles and functions: articulating goals, giving instructions, controlling conflict and so on. We have discussed many of these aspects of management in this Course Book.

1.2   However, there is another aspect to the management of people, arising from the broader relationship between an employer and its employees, and the 'employment lifecycle' from recruitment to exit. People are sought by the organisation; they enter into a contractual relationship with it; they are required to function within it according to certain policies and procedures; they are deployed, appraised, trained, developed, disciplined and rewarded in such a way as to meet their own changing needs and those of the organisation; and (sooner or later) they leave.

1.3   *Someone* in an organisation will have to be responsible for these matters. Traditionally, that has meant a specialised **personnel function**. However, 'personnel management' may also refer to those aspects of a line manager's job – in any department – which deal with the management of the employment relationship and lifecycle.

1.4   One of the cornerstones of the managerial concept is that productivity is not gained solely through programmes and activities, but through people: people add value to material, financial, informational and other resources. Why do we need people to work effectively? Why do we need to help them develop their skills and contributions? Because that is the source of competitive advantage and added value in an ever-changing, networked, knowledge-based, customer-focused business environment.

1.5   Personnel practitioners have long argued that people are the key to an organisation's success, added value and the bottom line. Peters and Waterman *(In Search of Excellence)* argued that it was a key characteristic of 'excellent' companies, such as IBM, McKinsey and 3M: they called it simply 'success through people'. Research findings appear to back this up. 'The acquisition and development of skills (via selection, induction, training and appraisal) and job design are significant predictors of changes in both profitability and productivity. More broadly, the study concludes that – compared with, say, research and development, quality, technology and strategy – by far the most powerful indicators of future business performance are [personnel] practices.' (*People Management*, 1998)

1.6   Employees are increasingly being regarded not as a cost to be controlled, but as an asset to be nurtured, developed and empowered over time, in order to maximise their contribution and commitment to the organisation's objectives.

1.7   At the same time, the growing complexity of the social and business environment has placed HR issues at the centre of organisational objectives and concerns: quality; social responsibility; the management of change; workforce diversity; the need for flexibility; the expectations of an increasingly sophisticated marketplace. HR issues have had to be more closely integrated into the strategic plans of the organisation.

1.8   People are the key resource of businesses in an age where value is added through knowledge, creativity and interpersonal relations. ICL (*The ICL Way*) affirm that: 'Our attitude to people is created by the fact that we are in a knowledge industry. Our business success will therefore be led by people first and products second. We are no longer mainly selling boxes of computer equipment. We are selling creative solutions to business problems. If we are to be successful, to excel in all we do, to win rather than merely compete, then the full capabilities of all ICL people must be realised and released into action. That is the business of our managers, who are expected to cultivate employees' skills continuously and systematically.'

1.9 This is the cornerstone of what has come to be known as a **human resource management (HRM)** orientation to management and leadership.

- Michael Armstrong *(Strategic Human Resource Management)* has defined HRM as: 'a strategic and coherent approach to the management of an organisation's most valued assets: the people working there who individually and collectively contribute to the achievement of its objectives.'
- John Bratton & Jeff Gold (*Human Resource Management: Theory and Practice*) define it as: 'A strategic approach to managing employment relations which emphasises that leveraging people's capabilities is critical to achieving sustainable competitive advantage.'
- The Chartered Institute of Personnel & Development (CIPD) defines it as: 'The design, implementation and maintenance of strategies to manage people for optimum business performance, including the development of policies and processes to support these strategies and the evaluation of the contribution of people to the business.'

1.10 HRM tends to focus on managing people for key strategic aims such as quality, innovation, organisational flexibility and learning, and employee commitment. It tends to be associated with managerial approaches such as: replacing rules and controls with cultural values, goals and customer focus; open communication and employee involvement; collaborative employee relations; empowered teamworking; a facilitative (rather than directive) style of leadership; and continuous learning and development.

Key features of an HRM approach

1.11 The main features of an HRM orientation may be summarised as follows (Armstrong, *Strategic Human Resource Management*).

- The attempt to integrate HR and corporate planning, with HR policy formulated at a strategic level and directly related to the organisation's strategic objectives
- The development of coherent and mutually-supporting HR policies and practices: in other words, horizontal integration across functions
- An orientation towards 'commitment' rather than compliance: securing employee identification with the goals and values of the organisation, rather than mere compliance with directives. As we saw in earlier chapters, this is often associated with management practices such as team building, empowerment, involvement, employee development and the creation of organisation culture.
- The treatment of people as assets (or 'human capital') rather than costs: regarding employees as a strategic resource and source of value and competitive advantage. This is often associated with a managerial emphasis on delivering customer and shareholder value; on rewarding performance, competence and contribution; and on support for employee development.
- The responsibility of line managers (rather than specialised HR departments) for the delivery of people-based objectives and outcomes.

Human capital management

1.12 As we have suggested, the cornerstone of HRM is the recognition that people are crucial to organisational performance. Bratton & Gold *(Human Resource Management: Theory & Practice)* suggest that: 'Human beings... become **human capital** by virtue of the roles they assume in the work organisation.. In management terms, 'human capital' or 'human resources' refers to the traits that people bring to the workplace – intelligence, aptitude, commitment, tacit knowledge and skills, and ability to learn.'

1.13 The Chartered Institute of Personnel & Development (*Human Capital: Factsheet*) has emphasised that people form an important part of the **intellectual capital** or intellectual assets of an organisation, which comprises:

- **Human capital:** the knowledge, skills, abilities and capacity to develop and innovate brought to the organisation by its people

- **Social capital**: 'the structures, networks and procedures that enable those people to acquire and develop intellectual capital, represented by stocks and flows of *knowledge* derived from relationships within and outside the organisation'
- **Organisational capital**: 'institutionalised knowledge possessed by an organisation, which is stored in databases, manuals etc'

1.14 Some writers have questioned the validity of the view of human beings as 'capital' or 'resources', feeling that this is a cold, impersonal approach which dehumanises people and implies manipulation and control. However, the impact of the term has generally been to *elevate* the status of people in organisations, as a key factor in organisational performance and value creation, and as a resource to be nurtured and developed. Even so, managers must remember that human beings cannot be manipulated and controlled or 'managed' in the same way as non-human resources: either practically (since they are unique, complex and unpredictable) or ethically.

Different perspectives on HRM

1.15 It is generally recognised that the role of HRM is twofold – and perhaps somewhat ambiguous: both business-oriented (focused on the improvement of organisational performance and value) and people-oriented (focused on the motivation, development and working life of employees). Key writers on HRM have identified two 'versions' of HRM, often characterised as 'hard' and 'soft'. (You may recognise this terminology from other models which distinguish a focus on quantitative and qualitative aspects.) Essentially, hard HRM focuses on human resources as 'resources', while soft HRM focuses on human resources as 'human'.

1.16 **Hard HRM** emphasises 'the close integration of HR policies with business strategy, which regards employees as a resource to be managed in the same rational way as any other resource being exploited for maximum return' (Karen Legge, 'The morality of HRM'; *Strategic Human Resource Management)*. Key features of the hard HRM model include:

- Close integration of the strategic objectives of HRM with business strategy
- Emphasis on business-case justification of investment in people (eg in training and development)
- An emphasis on the need for performance management and other forms of managerial control (rather than employee empowerment, for example).

1.17 **Soft HRM** emphasises employees as 'valued assets and as a source of competitive advantage through their commitment, adaptability and high levels of skills and performance' (Legge). It is based on management approaches (such as the human relations school, discussed in Chapter 2) emphasising the influence of psycho-social factors (relationships, attitudes, motivation, leadership, communication, learning and so on) on work behaviour. Key features of the soft HRM model include:

- Focus on the human relations aspects of people management, such as learning and development, communication, involvement, motivation and job satisfaction
- Emphasis on gaining the trust and commitment of employees, in order to tap their potential for contribution, initiative, flexibility and high levels of performance.

2 HRM and organisational performance

The people and performance model

2.1 As we saw in Chapter 4, two of the core questions of people management are: (a) how do you get individuals to put forth extra effort and energy, and make extra contribution to team and organisational success, and (b) does this in fact influence the performance of the organisation?

2.2 Research by Purcell, Hutchinson, Kinnie, Rayton & Swart (*Understanding the people and performance link*) attempted to explain the link between HRM and improved organisational performance, in their 'People and Performance' model: Table 8.1.

Table 8.1 *The people and performance model*

HR POLICIES/PRACTICES ➤	KEY WORK DIMENSIONS ➤	OUTCOMES
Recruitment Training and development Performance appraisal	Ability and skill	Positive psychological contract (commitment; job satisfaction) *Leading to* Discretionary behaviour (beyond the requirements of the job description)
Rewards (pay satisfaction and job challenge)	Motivation/incentive	
Team working Involvement Communication	Opportunity to participate	*Leading to* Performance outcomes

2.3 This model was based on the earlier AMO model (E Applebaum *et al*) which argued that if employees are to engage in the kind of discretionary work behaviour that impacts on performance, they must be equipped with the necessary **A**bilities (skills, experience, knowledge and competences); be **M**otivated to work and contribute to the best of their abilities; and be given the **O**pportunity to contribute and make a difference (both to their own job performance and to the organisation's success).

The Michigan model 

2.4 The Michigan Model (Fombrun, Tichy & Devanna, *Strategic Human Resource Management*) is a 'hard HRM' model focused on the proposition that HR systems should be managed in such a way as to 'match' or align with the business strategy of the organisation. If aligned effectively, the basic functions of the 'human resource cycle' (the progression of human resources within the organisation over time) can drive business performance. These basic functions include the following.

- **Selection:** matching available human resources to the roles, skills and attributes required by organisational strategy
- **Performance management and appraisal:** matching performance to agreed objectives and standards, in support of organisational strategy
- **Rewards:** matching rewards to the achievements and attributes which need to be reinforced in order to support organisational strategy
- **Development:** matching skills, knowledge and competencies to the identified requirements of organisational strategy.

2.5 The Michigan model is useful in emphasising the need for HR strategies and policies (such as procurement and other functional strategies) to be aligned with organisational objectives. However, you might notice that it considers a limited range of variables in organisational performance: as we have seen, there may be other performance barriers and drivers in variables such as leadership style, wider motivational issues (beyond financial rewards), employee relations, work systems and methods, or technology. Moreover, as Huczynski & Buchanan note, for this model to work in practice 'an organisation's strategy has to be

relatively stable and well understood. That is not always the case, particularly in today's rapidly changing competitive environment.'

The Harvard model

2.6 The Harvard Model (Beer, Spector, Laurence, Quinn Mills & Walton, *Managing Human Assets)* is a 'soft HRM' model, emphasising the human dimensions of performance. The Harvard 'map of the HRM territory' may be depicted as follows: Figure 8.1.

Figure 8.1 *Map of the HR territory*

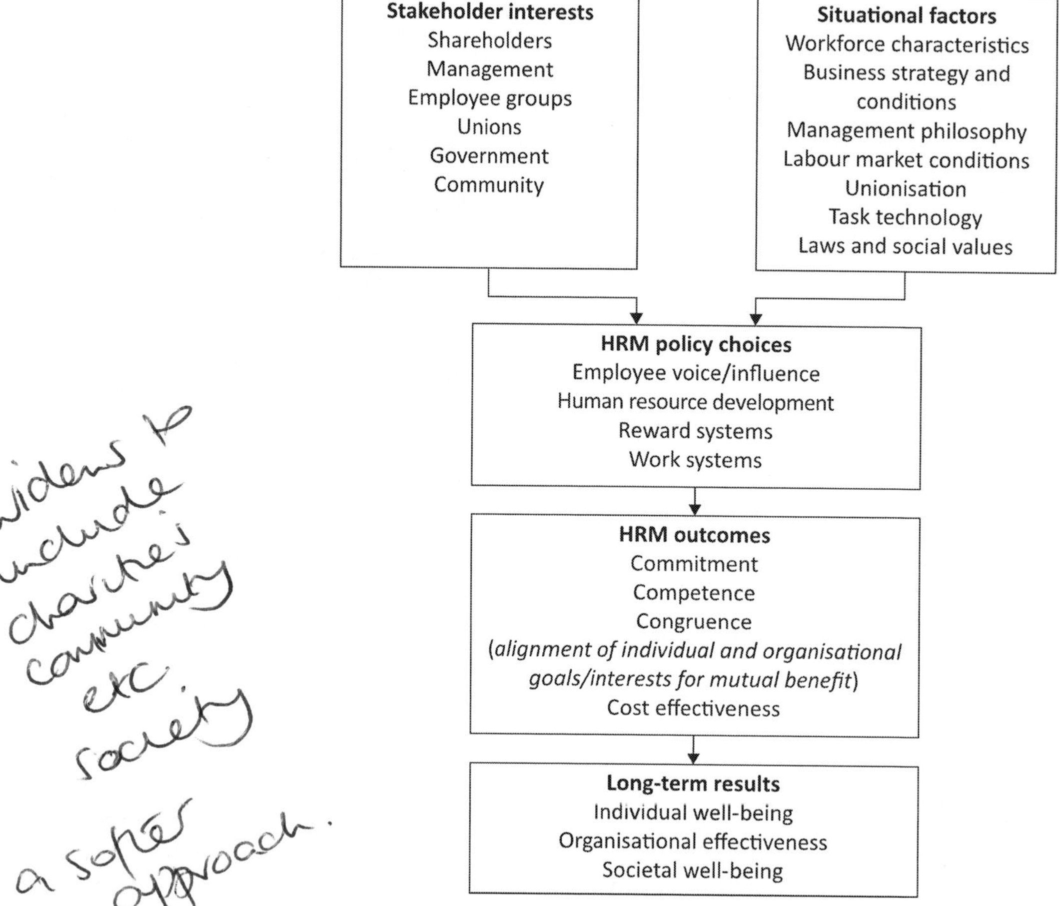

Advantages of a strategic/systematic approach to HRM

2.7 The general benefits of a systematic approach to HRM, based on well-defined policies and procedures, are as follows.

- It ensures **compliance** with employment legislation and regulation – on equal opportunity, health and safety, employment protection, employee involvement and so on.
- It also supports **ethical values** such as fairness and equity in dealing with people: ensuring (as far as possible) objectivity, impersonality and equal treatment in matters such as selection, pay awards and discipline and grievance handling.
- It communicates and supports the desired **culture** of the organisation. Consistent, integrated HR systems can be used to bring suitable values and attributes into the organisation (through selection), and to reinforce them (through appraisal, training and reward).
- It enables the organisation to meet its **human resource needs**, both currently and in the future – in the light of its own plans, and forecast changes and challenges in its environment. The role of human

resource planning (HRP) is to ensure that the organisation has plans in place to source (from outside) and/or develop and retain (from within) the skills it needs to pursue its objectives.

- It supports the **motivation, commitment and retention** of staff, offering structured opportunities for recognition and reward (through appraisal), job satisfaction (through job design) and personal growth (through training and development). It also minimises 'hygiene' factors, which might otherwise cause dissatisfaction: ensuring fair treatment (through grievance and disciplinary procedures), fair pay (through job evaluation) and so on.
- Its core purpose is to **improve the performance** of individuals, teams and the organisation as a whole, by:
  — Acquiring or developing high-calibre, job-relevant skills and competencies
  — Ensuring that employees are informed, involved and empowered to pursue team and organisational objectives
  — Encouraging labour flexibility and versatility
  — Facilitating continuous organisational learning and development, for innovation and adaptability in response to changing demands.

Evaluating HRM

2.8	The Harvard Model (discussed earlier) suggested that the effectiveness of HRM outcomes should be evaluated under four headings, identified as The Four Cs.

- **Commitment**: employees' identification with the organisation and its goals, loyalty and work motivation, and the application of discretionary behaviour (above and beyond what is defined by the job description) to add value at work. This may be assessed through methods such as attitude surveys and analysis of other variables (such as absenteeism and labour turnover).
- **Competence**: employees' skills and abilities, role competence, learning needs, and potential for performance improvement and career development. This may be assessed through competence assessments, performance management and appraisal processes, skill audits and results monitoring.
- **Congruence**: the harmonisation or alignment of employees' goals, values and efforts with those of management (or at least the *perception* by employees that there is shared purpose and mutual benefit). This may be assessed by the incidence of grievance and disciplinary actions, conflicts, the openness of communication and so on.
- **Cost-effectiveness**: benefits obtained from HRM outcomes at an acceptable input cost: whether costs are justified by equal or greater (qualitative and quantitative) benefits; whether costs and/or benefits are increasing or decreasing over time; and how costs and/or benefits compare to those of benchmark organisations or competitors.

2.9	You should be able to see how each of these potential outcomes would be relevant to the performance of a purchasing and supply function – as well as the organisation as a whole. They may, indeed be particularly important where purchasing functions are devolved to 'part-time' buyers in user or budget-holder departments. In the absence of direct line authority over part-time buyers, the procurement function will benefit from the indirect direction and control offered by goal congruence, commitment and competence (including best practice procurement disciplines).

# 3	HRM functions and policies

Overview of HRM functions

3.1	We will be looking at the key HRM functions highlighted by the syllabus – including recruitment and selection, and training and development (with which we also include the related process of performance management) in Chapters 9 and 10 of this Course Book. The range of functions commonly carried out by HR practitioners, however, is broader than this: see Table 8.2.

Table 8.2 *Human resource management functions*

Organisational design and development	• *Organisational design*: optimising organisational structure and process design • *Organisational development*: interventions in the organisation's social processes (eg structural change, team building, process consultancy, role negotiation and interpersonal skill development) to facilitate change and improved performance • *Job and role design*: structuring the scope and content of work roles; analysing and defining tasks and competence requirements (eg for recruitment, appraisal, reward and development); and planning and implementing flexible structures and work methods to maximise adaptability, efficiency and work-life balance
HR planning (HRP) and resourcing	• *Human resource planning*: forecasting the organisation's current and future capability requirements; analysing the organisation's current capabilities; conducting gap analysis; and planning to fill gaps through plans for recruitment, deployment, retention and development of staff • *Recruitment* (engaging the labour market) and selection (assessing and selecting suitable recruits to meet the requirements of the HR plan • *Retention*: monitoring and managing levels of labour turnover; identifying 'talent' that should be retained within the organisation; and applying retention policies to create incentives and rewards for loyalty • *Exit management*: managing the termination of contracts (eg through retirement, resignation, dismissal or redundancy) within legal and ethical frameworks
Performance management	• *Setting performance objectives and standards*: developing and agreeing frameworks of organisational, team and individual performance goals (and related competence requirements) • *Performance assessment*: monitoring and periodic appraisal of performance against agreed objectives and standards (with a view to improvement and development planning, intervention and/or – often as a separate exercise – reward planning) • *Performance gap analysis* and identification of learning and development needs • *Performance management interventions*, including: discipline handling; grievance handling; motivation and reward; learning, training and development; employee counselling and support.
Reward management	• *Pay systems*: developing and managing wage and salary structures that are equitable and motivational; managing performance-related pay systems and benefit schemes (employee entitlements and indirect pay or 'fringe' benefits)
Human resource development	• *Learning, training and development*: planning and managing learning activities, programmes and interventions to meet identified competence gaps; facilitating individual learning and personal development planning • *Career management*: succession and promotion planning; individual mentoring and career planning; identifying promotable 'talent' and development paths to retain, motivate and leverage available talent • *Management development*: facilitating education, training and experiential opportunities to develop managerial competencies and plan management succession • *Learning organisation*: creating a supportive climate and systems to enable individual and organisational learning, knowledge creation and sharing (as discussed in Chapter 4)
Employee relations	• *Industrial relations*: managing formal collective relationships with employee representatives (eg trade unions); collective bargaining on terms and conditions; the resolution of collective disputes; and implementing formal consultative and partnership agreements • *Employee communications*: informing employees about matters of concern to them; managing the communication 'climate' to encourage multi-directional, open, constructive communication; encouraging upward communication (eg feedback, suggestion schemes); and managing 'internal marketing' (corporate 'good news' swapping, image management and issues management) • *Employee voice and involvement*: involving employees in decision-making, through both formal mechanisms (eg joint consultative committees) and informal mechanisms (eg participative management style)
Occupational health, safety and welfare	• *Health and safety*: monitoring and managing work environments, practices, training and culture to identify and reduce risks to health and safety; complying with relevant legislation; and, where possible, actively promoting health and wellbeing (eg through work-life balance) • *Welfare services*: providing services such as employee assistance programmes (counselling and support) and support for employees impacted by illness, domestic difficulties, and forthcoming retirement or redundancy (eg outplacement services)
HR services	• Developing and administering HR policies and procedures; developing and operating HR information systems ('personnel records'); managing employment contracts; and managing compliance with relevant law and regulation (as discussed in Chapter 11).

The role of HR policy

3.2   HR policies may be specifically formulated to comply with *employment legislation* and regulation, for example on equal opportunities or health and safety. They may also, however, be based on the organisation's *values and beliefs* about how people should be treated. Some organisations, for example, introduced policies banning age discrimination in recruitment, or smoking in the workplace, well *before* legislation on ageism or passive smoking was implemented.

3.3   The organisation must also take into account the needs and expectations of employees, and potential employees in the labour pool, in order to *attract and retain* the kind of employees it wants. Positive equal opportunities policies, for example, may help an organisation recruit women and people from ethnic minorities at a time when more traditional sources of skills are drying up. Meanwhile, other policies – on multi-skilling or flexible working, say – will be aimed at ensuring the efficient utilisation of available *labour resources*.

3.4   Functional managers, such as purchasing managers, should remember that HR policies are not merely 'red tape' designed to enforce the HR function's power in the organisation (although they have often been seen that way). They are there to *help line managers do their job*, enabling them to 'do the right thing' – treat employees fairly and consistently – without having to wade through legal and strategic complexities every time an issue comes up.

4   Shared responsibility for HRM

4.1   The arguments for personnel management activities to be centralised (in an HR or Personnel Department) or decentralised (to line managers) boil down to the need for specialist expertise and 'big picture' thinking on the one hand, and the need to support line authority on the other.

4.2   There are constant developments (and related compliance issues) in the field of HRM. These may arise from any of the following factors.

- Changes in the social environment and labour market (for example: fluctuating availability and market value of skills; the ageing workforce; increasing globalisation of the labour market and so on)
- Developments in the behavioural sciences (for example: new research on methods of motivation, the causes of stress or the effects of leadership style)
- Ongoing legislation and regulation (for example: the implementation of EU directives in areas such as discrimination, health and safety, employment protection and so on)
- Increasing awareness and advocacy of employment rights (for example: consumer-led pressures for corporate social responsibility; legal requirements for employee consultation and involvement; and the role of trade unions, Employment Tribunals and advisory bodies).

4.3   There is therefore a need for line managers to access *specialist advice* on HR matters (so that the organisation is aware of all the above) and for *well defined policies* (so that HR management practice is both compliant and consistent throughout the organisation).

4.4   However, as Mullins points out ('The personnel function: a shared responsibility'), line managers 'have both the right and the duty to be concerned with the effective operation of their own department, including the management and well-being of their staff.' In *Management and Organisational Behaviour*, Mullins argues further that: 'The HRM function is part of the generality of management and the responsibility of all managers and supervisors.'

The role of the HR function

4.5 So how can responsibility for HRM be divided between the HR function and departmental line managers such as purchasing managers? Traditionally, according to Anne Crichton (*Personnel Management in Context*), it has been a matter of the HR department's 'collecting together such odd jobs from management as they are prepared to give up'. With increasing awareness of the importance of employees as the human resources of the organisation, however, the role of a specialist, centralised HR function has become more strategically integrated at the **organisational level**. It now often involves the following key processes.

- Planning HR-related activity at the strategic level: organisational change programmes, human resource planning, reward system development, HR auditing and so on.
- Implementing organisation-wide HR programmes: employee communications, involvement schemes and collective bargaining, for example.
- Developing a coherent framework of personnel policies (eg on discrimination), plans (eg for recruitment), systems (eg for appraisal) and rules (where necessary to ensure compliance with legislation) to guide line managers.
- Providing specialist services and consultancy (business partnering) to line managers, where required: advice on new legislation and compliance, delivery of training programmes, arbitration of grievances and so on.

4.6 A dedicated HR function may therefore – much like a purchasing and supply function – occupy a number of different roles in relation to line departments, depending on its status and organisational context.

- **Service provider**: providing administrative services (eg payroll administration, record keeping, reports and returns); specialist advice and guidance; and delivery of HRM programmes (eg training or recruitment) and employee services (eg welfare, counselling) to a range of internal customers
- **Management reporting and auditing role**: eg human resource forecasting and planning, employee attitude surveys, analysing HR indices (such as wage costs or labour turnover), benchmarking, capability reviews, and compliance audits (eg in regard to health and safety or equal opportunity)
- **Internal consultancy**: working alongside line managers to analyse business processes, diagnose performance problems and recommend solutions that the internal client can own and implement
- **Business partnering**: sharing strategic responsibility with senior and line management for the performance of the enterprise, through identifying and exploiting opportunities, seeking competitive advantage, and adding value; influencing strategic planning by highlighting the human resource implications of objectives and strategies; and supporting corporate objectives through strategic management of the human resource.

The role of line managers

4.7 Within the coordinating and controlling framework of centrally-formulated HR policies and procedures, people management functions are increasingly being devolved to line managers – in much the same way that non-strategic purchasing activities are increasingly devolved to user-department buyers and budget holders. At the **departmental level,** therefore line managers may have responsibility for a range of operational HR matters.

- Organising and allocating tasks (an aspect of job design)
- Setting, monitoring and maintaining standards of performance
- Requisitioning, recruiting and selecting team members
- Providing and/or requisitioning team member induction and training
- Establishing and maintaining teamworking
- Day-to-day employee communication, consultation and involvement
- Day-to-day employee relations, including individual discipline and grievance handling
- Maintaining a safe and healthy workplace

- Maintaining day-to-day personnel records
- Complying with HR policies, plans and rules (where applicable) on all of the above
- Consulting and/or liaising with the HR function (where required).

4.8 In effect, a manager of people in purchasing and supply is an *internal customer* of the HR function. Mullins suggests that: 'It is the job of [the HR function] to provide specialist knowledge and services to line managers, and to support them in the performance of their jobs.... It is the line managers who have authority and control over staff in their departments and who have the immediate responsibility for personnel activities, although there will be times when they need specialist help and advice. If the HRM function is to be effective, there has to be good teamwork, co-operation and consultation between line managers and the HR manager.'

The role of senior management

4.9 A third major stakeholder in HRM is therefore top management, which has an important role in:

- Formulating and communicating the philosophy, attitudes, values, culture and general 'orientation' of the enterprise towards its people and people management
- Formulating key HRM strategies and policies (eg in regard to organisational structure and design, performance management and reward systems, equal opportunity and diversity, and human resource development)
- Formulating agreed terms of reference for the HR function, and the extent to which HRM responsibilities will be devolved to line management
- Creation of the organisational climate, and management of overarching direction and leadership, which will shape perceptions of the status of 'support' functions like HR (and purchasing), the co-operation between support and line functions, and the extent to which concepts such as 'business partnering' are taken seriously (with HR – and purchasing – integrated into management at the strategic level).

Chapter summary

- HRM is a strategic approach to the management of an organisation's most valued assets: the people working there. The development of HRM approaches reflects the increasing importance placed by managers on the skills and commitment of their staff.
- Research by Purcell suggests that such an approach pays dividends: they conclude that effective HRM policies and practices lead to improved performance.
- The effectiveness of HRM outcomes can be evaluated in light of The Four Cs: commitment, competence, congruence, and cost-effectiveness.
- HRM policies must be formulated to comply with legislation and regulation, but this is only the minimum required. Managers must also consider what is needed to attract and retain the kind of employees they need.
- HRM is a responsibility shared between line managers, a dedicated HR function, and the senior management team.

Self-test questions

Numbers in brackets refer to the paragraphs where you can check your answers.

1   Give definitions of HRM that emphasise its strategic nature. (1.9)

2   What are the key features of a strategic HRM orientation, according to Armstrong? (1.11)

3   Distinguish between hard and soft HRM. (1.16, 1.17)

4   List the basic functions of the human resource cycle, as identified in the Michigan Model. (2.4)

5   List advantages of a strategic approach to HRM. (2.7)

6   List the main organisational functions comprised in the term HRM. (Table 8.2)

7   What factors typically give rise to the constant change in the field of HRM? (4.2)

8   List some of the HR responsibilities of line managers. (4.7)

CHAPTER 9

Recruitment and Selection

Assessment criteria and indicative content

4.2 Identify the skills and knowledge requirements for personnel in the procurement and supply function

- Job analysis and job skills
- Identifying knowledge and skills for roles

4.3 Develop a recruitment and selection plan to meet the skills and knowledge needs of the procurement and supply function

- Drafting job descriptions
- Screening and assessing candidates to meet requirements
- The interview process
- The use of IT software solutions in recruitment

Section headings

1. Systematic resourcing
2. Analysing skill and knowledge requirements
3. Recruitment processes
4. Selection processes
5. Induction

Introduction

Recruitment and selection are two different (though closely related) processes.

Recruitment is the process by which an employer reaches out to the labour market in order to inform potential employees of opportunities in the organisation, with a view to generating interest and/or applications. It is a vital avenue – not just for filling specific labour requirements – but for corporate communication with the outside world: a public relations exercise and the creation of an 'employer brand' in the labour marketplace.

Selection is the process by which an employer chooses between applicants, weeding out those who are unlikely to suit the job or organisation (or _vice versa_) and evaluating potentially suitable candidates in order to fulfil the required criteria. Its purposes are broadly twofold: to fulfil the relevant labour requirements of the organisation, and to treat potential candidates fairly and courteously as part of the organisation's corporate identity and employer brand.

In this chapter we first consider how an organisation determines its human resource requirements (through human resource planning) – and how it describes them (as the basis of recruitment and selection decisions). You should recognise parallels in this process with the procurement cycle (identifying and defining needs).

We then explore a systematic approach to recruitment and selection.

1 Systematic resourcing

Human resource planning (HRP)

1.1 The aim of human resource planning is to ensure the availability of the right quantity of the right skills at the right price and at the right time to meet the organisation's requirements. It has been defined as: 'a strategy for the acquisition, utilisation, improvement and retention of the human resources required by the enterprise in pursuit of its objectives'.

1.2 You may think this sounds unnecessarily complicated, particularly for a small or medium-sized organisation, or for an individual department such as purchasing. After all, if someone leaves – creating a 'vacancy' – you replace him. If you find you have a staff shortage, or new skill requirements arise (from the introduction of technology or legislation, say) you hire or train someone to do the job. In fact, though, the process is rarely so simple, particularly at the level of the organisation.

1.3 Bryan Livy *(Corporate Personnel Management)* suggested that 'Human resource planning has maintained its imperative for several reasons: (i) a growing awareness of the need to look into the future; (ii) a desire to exercise control over as many variables as possible which influence business success or failure; and (iii) the development of techniques which make such planning possible'.

1.4 Human resource planning can be seen as a form of supply management. As with any other resource, the flow of people into and through the organisation must be planned and controlled so as to meet requirements efficiently and effectively.

1.5 The scarcity of the labour resource (particularly in terms of specific skill shortages) is one of the strongest arguments for proactive HR planning. Forecasting labour requirements gives the organisation the lead time it needs to acquire skills from the labour pool (by recruitment) or to retain and develop them internally (by motivation, training, redeployment or promotion). Likewise, if skill requirements are declining (because of new technology or business contraction, say), proactive HR planning allows the organisation the lead time it needs to retrain and redeploy people, to shed surplus labour by voluntary means (natural wastage, including retirement and staff turnover) or to give adequate notice of redundancies, as required by law and the organisation's desired image as a socially responsible employer.

1.6 The advance planning of labour supply and demand has never been an exact science – and it is, arguably, becoming increasingly difficult. HR planners' assumptions are constantly undermined by changes affecting labour turnover (such as the rise of temporary, part-time and freelance working), changes in the sources of labour (such as the expansion of the European labour market) and changes affecting skill requirements (such as the emergence of new technologies and markets).

1.7 According to MW Cuming *(Theory & Practice of Personnel Management)*, these are not reasons to abandon HR planning, but to perform it flexibly. 'The environment, then, is uncertain, and so are the people whose activities are being planned. HR plans must therefore be accepted as being continuous, under constant review and ever-changing.'

A systematic approach to HRP

1.8 The process of HRP may be outlined as follows.

- Forecast the likely **demand** for labour (staff skills and competencies, grades, numbers). This will take into account factors such as: the objectives of the organisation; proposed expansion, contraction or diversification; current labour utilisation (ie productivity); and environmental influences which will affect demand (technology, economic recession, competition and so on).
- Forecast the likely **supply** of labour. This will take into account factors such as: the actual and potential

skills and productivity of the existing workforce; likely changes in the structure and size of the existing workforce due to labour turnover (by resignation or retirement), promotion or transfer; the flexibility of the existing workforce; and the likely supply of relevant skilled labour in the external labour market (given competitor activity, demographic changes, educational trends, market rates of pay and so on).

- Prepare plans to **close the gap between demand and supply** by meeting a labour shortfall (eg by recruitment, training, retention, redeployment, productivity or outsourcing) or reducing a labour surplus (eg by freezing recruitment, supporting labour turnover, banning overtime, redeployment or redundancy).

1.9   The outcome of human resource planning will – naturally enough – be a **human resource plan**. This should include integrated tactical plans for recruitment, training, flexible working, promotion (or management succession), productivity, employee retention, natural wastage (as an alternative to non-voluntary redundancies) and so on.

1.10   Human resource decisions at the departmental level, taken within the constraints and guidelines of these plans, will therefore support the strategic requirements of the organisation as a whole. A purchasing manager will not, for example, be advertising exciting new career opportunities in his department at a time when the organisation is planning to downsize. Or watching half the department retire just as the organisation is taking on a new project. Or training staff in technology and methods which will be unsuited to organisational requirements within three years.

A systematic approach to recruitment and selection

1.11   A systematic approach to this process would include the following stages.

- Human resource planning, defining the organisation's human resource requirements
- Job analysis, so that for any given job there is a job description (a concise statement of the tasks, duties, objectives and conditions of the job) and a person specification (a reworking of the job description in terms of the kind of person needed to perform the job competently)
- The identification of vacancies (from the requirements of the HR plan, the need to replace an outgoing team member, or the emergence of new task requirements)
- The authorisation and initiation of recruitment activity (perhaps using a job requisition form)
- The evaluation of alternative sources of labour: the internal and/or external labour markets; standard and/or non-standard contract labour (part-time, temporary, freelance and so on)
- The evaluation of alternative media and methods for advertising vacancies: recruitment consultancies and agencies; advertising at source (eg in schools); media advertising; the internet; informal word-of-mouth networks and so on
- Job advertisement: preparing and issuing information about vacancies and inviting applications
- The processing of applications: screening responses at the end of the application period, notifying candidates of the initial result or progress of their application, planning the selection process
- The assessment of candidates: shortlisting potential candidates, conducting interviews and/or various forms of selection testing, checking references
- Follow-up: the offer of employment, notification of unsuccessful shortlisted candidates, planning the induction of new recruits
- Evaluation of the whole process, to ascertain whether it has been effective (resulting in the employment of the right people and the fostering of the desired employer brand) and efficient (in a timely and cost-effective manner).

2 Analysing skill and knowledge requirements

Determining the need for recruitment

2.1   Recruitment may be identified as necessary where:

- The *human resource plan* sets out specific requirements for the recruitment of a given number and type of people (or skills) within a given timeframe.
- *Labour or skills* have been lost (or are expected to be lost) through retirement, resignation, temporary absence, promotion or transfer – *and* the fulfilment of departmental objectives and the HR plan requires that they be replaced.
- *Task requirements* have changed (or are expected to change) in such a way as to require a new job or job skills: for example, the organisation introduces an e-procurement platform, or plans to implement category management – or needs to respond to new regulations on sustainable procurement.

In each case, note that the requirements of departmental objectives and the HR plan should be observed: not every departing team member will automatically create a 'vacancy', for example.

2.2   There may also be alternative sources for the required skills, and these should be evaluated according to their relative benefits and costs, as well as relevant organisational policy. For example, if the required skills are available (or potentially available) in the existing workforce, internal transfer, training and/ or promotion may be preferred, where possible, to external recruitment. (A purchasing vacancy may, for example, be opened to part-time buyers in user departments, who can be developed into the role, before external recruitment.) Organisational flexibility may, on the other hand, give priority to the use of temporary, freelance or agency staff (or even outsourcing) over the recruitment of permanent labour: for example, sourcing purchasing staff for peak periods.

2.3   Departmental managers should expect to justify their decision to fill a vacancy by external recruitment with a sound business case. They may have to complete a *job requisition*, setting out the need and criteria for recruitment: the vacancy can then be approved or authorised. This process ensures that other options are considered where appropriate and that the decision to recruit is in line with the human resource plan.

2.4   Whether internal or external recruitment is used, the vacancy will have to be closely defined, in terms of: what the job involves; and what kind of person the job (and organisation) requires.

Job analysis

2.5   The British Standards Institution describes job analysis (also known as job appraisal) as 'the determination of the essential characteristics of a job'. These essential characteristics may include the responsibilities of the job, its key tasks and priorities, the physical and social environment and conditions in which it is performed, the demands it makes on the job holder and so on.

2.6   The analysis may be carried out in different ways, depending on the nature of the job. For routine or repetitive tasks, observation of work in progress and documentary evidence of various kinds may be used to determine basic facts such as the job title, duties and tasks, reporting relationships, targets and standards applied, working conditions and so on.

2.7   For less programmed jobs, especially those which involve 'invisible' work (such as planning, people management, ideas generation, relationship-building and so on), more complex methods will be required. Interviews, questionnaires, diaries or logs may be used to gather information from job holders' managers or supervisors and/or the job holders themselves. They allow analysts to ascertain what the job entails in practice *and* how it is *perceived*, covering such qualitative issues as the difficulty of the job, discretion allowed, social skills required, the value or importance of the job and its different components and so on.

2.8 There are difficulties in carrying out job analysis. Workers may be suspicious about the purpose of the exercise, fearing that it will be used to impose higher standards, cut rates or rationalise staffing. There will be differences in perception between job holders and management as to the nature of the job. Many of the findings will be subjective to a greater or lesser degree, particularly in the case of un-programmed work. In some contexts, the 'job' itself is a thing of the past, with flexible, multi-skilled staff performing whatever roles the team's goals require at a given time.

2.9 Nevertheless, job analysis is a useful exercise. When jobs fall vacant, it should be regarded as an opportunity to review and revise existing job information.

Job description

2.10 A job description is a broad statement of the purpose, scope, duties and responsibilities of a particular job. It is one of the products of job analysis.

2.11 The precise content of a job description will vary from organisation to organisation and job to job, but might typically include the following information.

- The title of the job
- The business unit or department
- A summary of the job: its overall purpose, main functions, position in the organisation structure
- Job content: a list of the job's main tasks, including factors such as frequency, importance, difficulty, responsibility
- Key accountabilities: what the job holder is expected to achieve in key areas
- Reporting relationships: superior and subordinate positions; collaboration with other team members or departments
- Working conditions: location, special demands (health hazards, physical conditions, potential stressors, social conditions)
- Employment conditions: working hours, basis of pay and entitlements, development opportunities and so on

2.12 Figure 9.1 shows an example of a basic job description for a buyer in a retail environment.

Figure 9.1 *Job description*

JOB DESCRIPTION

Job title   Buyer I

Department   Books

Job summary   Operating under close supervision, (a) participates in the selection of new titles from wholesale and publisher catalogues and (b) negotiates purchase and promotion agreements with suppliers. Administers core replacement and purchase order processing.

Job content (general nature and level of duties performed

1. Reviews wholesale and publisher catalogues and promotion plans, and recommends new title purchases to the bookshop manager.
2. Participates in negotiations of purchase and promotional agreements with suppliers.
3. Issues and coordinates purchase orders.
4. Processes incoming stock; coordinates release of stock and promotional materials for agreed dates; coordinates processing of discrepant supplied items; issues replacement purchase orders as required on returned items.
5. Ensures all requirements and special terms and conditions are met.
6. Approves supplier invoices for payment by the accounts department.
7. Processes returns and credits under sale-or-return agreements.
8. Actions individual customer orders, liaising with customer service staff.
9. Monitors and maintains levels of core stock titles.
10. Monitors and analyses sales of new titles to support buying and promotion decisions, and prepares report summaries for the bookshop manager.
11. Attends relevant book fairs and trade conferences.
12. Liaises with appropriate personnel in accounts, warehousing, despatch, customer services and other departments as required.

The above statements are not intended to be an exhaustive or definitive list of the responsibilities of the job holder; flexibility in responding to marketing opportunities and customer requirements is essential.

Reports to   The bookshop manager. Close supervision is required in the areas of new title selection and negotiation of purchase/promotion agreements.

Supervises work of   N/A.

Special conditions   Some lifting may occasionally be required.

Experience/education   One to three years retail purchasing experience (ideally in book trade). Minimum of two A-levels (or equivalent).

Training provided   Initial on-the-job training offered as required. Opportunities for vocational certification after one year.

Terms and conditions   38 hours per week. Salary: see separate grading structure.

Prepared by   Personnel Dept.

Date   10 August 201X

2.13 Job descriptions provide information for:

- Recruitment and selection (indicating the requirements of the job)
- Appraisal (indicating the criteria for assessment)
- Training and development (indicating areas for improvement)
- Pay-setting (indicating job components and their value)
- Performance improvement (indicating problems in work conditions, the necessity of jobs, their relationship to each other and so on).

2.14 However, it has been argued that job descriptions are of limited usefulness and, at worst, counterproductive. They are only able to give an accurate and meaningful description of certain types of job, where the work is observable, programmed and repetitive. If a job involves variety, discretion and adaptability (as managerial jobs do), a job description will be unrealistic and constantly out of date. Job descriptions are, at best, a limited and static 'snapshot' of a job at a particular moment in time.

2.15 If job descriptions are rigidly adhered to, they can become a straitjacket: demarcation disputes may arise where people adhere strictly to the scope and territory of their job description rather than responding flexibly to customer requirements, opportunities for quality improvement or a problem which needs solving.

2.16 Organisational flexibility is a hot issue in human resource management. Jobs are being redesigned to allow adaptability and responsiveness to changing task requirements, through multi-skilling, multi-disciplinary teamworking, flexible working hours and so on. Indeed, commentators such as William Bridges *(Job Shift)* have suggested that the 'job' itself is a thing of the past: tasks and teams must be constantly redefined by customer and environmental demands.

Competence analysis and definition

2.17 Competence profiles, based on key success factors in a given business or sector, offer a flexible, menu-driven alternative to traditional job descriptions (and person specifications, covered below). Competence may be defined as: 'The ability to perform activities within an occupation to the standards expected in employment. The concept also embodies the ability to transfer skills and knowledge to new situations within the occupational area and beyond, to related occupations.'

2.18 Competence definitions typically identify the key roles of a given occupation and break them down into areas ('units') of competence. These in turn are formulated as statements describing what a competent person should be able to do at different levels, including:

- The specific activities concerned (elements of competence)
- To what standard (performance criteria)
- In what contexts (range statement)
- With what underpinning knowledge and understanding.

2.19 Competence definitions for purchasing and supply professionals have been developed by CIPS, under the direction of the Institute of Leadership and Management, to establish what specific outcomes purchasing staff should be able to achieve.

2.20 The advantages claimed for competence-based profiles include the following.

- They can be linked directly to the strategic objectives of the organisation and to best practice in the relevant occupation or profession (such as purchasing and supply).
- They are more readily adaptable to changing circumstances and requirements, since they are non-prescriptive about job specifics.
- They can be made applicable to employees at all levels of the organisation hierarchy (although the specific behaviours expected will vary), which also helps to create consistent organisational values and practices.

Role analysis and definition

2.21   Role analysis (like job analysis) collects information relating to the work people do. But while job analysis focuses on tasks to be performed (a 'job'), role analysis focuses on the part that people play in carrying out their jobs, by working competently and flexibly. 'The concept of a role... emphasises the need for flexibility and is concerned with what people do and how they do it rather than concentrating narrowly on job content.' (Armstrong: *A Handbook of Human Resource Management Practice*).

2.22   A role profile or definition will therefore specify: the overall purpose of the role; what role holders are expected to achieve (key result areas) and what they will be held to account for (accountabilities); and the behavioural and technical competencies required to achieve acceptable levels of contribution and performance.

Person specification

2.23   It may sound obvious, but it is worth being clear: a 'job description' describes the job. A description of the type of person required to do the job is called a 'personnel specification' or 'person specification'.

2.24   A person specification identifies the type of person the organisation should be trying to recruit for a given job: the education, training, experience, personal attributes and competencies a job holder will need to perform the job satisfactorily.

2.25   A systematic approach was formulated by Alec Rodger *(The Seven Point Plan)*, a pioneer of recruitment and selection systems in the UK. He suggested that 'if matching the demands of the job and the person who is to perform it is to be done satisfactorily, the requirements of an occupation (or job) must be described in the same terms as the aptitudes of the people who are being considered for it.'

2.26   Rodger's **Seven Point Plan** draws attention to seven points about the job holder or selection candidate.

- Physical attributes (such as neat appearance or strength)
- Attainments (including educational and vocational qualifications)
- General intelligence (usually defined in terms of mental dexterity and verbal fluency)
- Special aptitudes (such as numerical proficiency or computer literacy)
- Interests (demonstrating practical abilities and social competence)
- Disposition (or manner: friendly or helpful, say)
- Background circumstances (place of residence, family situation and so on)

2.27   An alternative structure was put forward by J Munro Fraser *(Employment Interviewing)*, whose **Five Point Pattern of Personality** draws attention to the candidate's:

- Impact on others (including physical attributes, force of personality and interpersonal skills)
- Acquired knowledge or qualifications (including education, training and work experience)
- Innate ability (including intelligence and particular aptitudes: numerical, mechanical, artistic, linguistic and so on)
- Motivation (the ability to select and pursue appropriate behaviours to attain personal goals)
- Adjustment (emotional stability, tolerance of stress, social skills)

2.28   Whichever outline is used, the person specification should classify each feature listed as essential, desirable or contra-indicated (undesirable) for competent performance in the job. For the job of purchase expediter, for example, organisational ability might be considered essential; social skills, desirable, given the need to liaise with suppliers; and inability to work under pressure, contra-indicated.

2.29   Figure 9.2 shows a person specification for the book buyer's job described in Figure 9.1, based on the Seven Point Plan.

Figure 9.2 *Person specification*

<table>
<tr><td colspan="4">PERSON SPECIFICATION</td></tr>
<tr><td>Job title</td><td colspan="3">Buyer I</td></tr>
<tr><td>Department</td><td colspan="3">Books</td></tr>
<tr><td>Job description</td><td colspan="3">Ref 01234</td></tr>
<tr><td></td><td>Essential</td><td>Desirable</td><td>Contra-indicated</td></tr>
<tr><td>Physical attributes</td><td>• Clear speech
• Well groomed</td><td>• Age 22–40
• Strength (lifting)</td><td>• Age under 22
• Chronic ill health</td></tr>
<tr><td>Attainments</td><td>• Two A-levels
• One to three years retail purchasing experience</td><td>• Purchasing experience gained in book trade
• Vocational certificate (purchasing/book trade)</td><td>• No experience of purchasing or book trade</td></tr>
<tr><td>Intelligence</td><td>Above average</td><td></td><td>Low flexibility</td></tr>
<tr><td>Aptitudes</td><td>• Appreciation of market potential of new titles
• Organisational ability</td><td>• Understanding of IT/POS systems
• Eye for promotional opportunities
• Attention to detail
• Negotiation skills
• Analysis and preparation of management information
• Network skills</td><td>Poor problem-solving</td></tr>
<tr><td>Interests</td><td>Reading (wide range)</td><td>Team-based or methodical activities</td><td>'Solo' interests only</td></tr>
<tr><td>Disposition</td><td>• Team player
• Tolerant of pressure
• Patient/methodical</td><td>Assertive</td><td>• Low tolerance of supervision
• Antisocial</td></tr>
<tr><td>Background circumstances</td><td>Able to work late</td><td>Within one hour of workplace (where necessary)</td><td></td></tr>
</table>

2.30 A wide range of variables may be used in a person specification, including both capacities (what the job holder should be able to do) and inclinations (what the job holder should be willing to do). However, in the same way that a job description must be revised often and used flexibly, a person specification may also lose its relevance if it fails to evolve as job requirements change.

2.31 In addition, there are particular problems to avoid when developing a job description into a person specification. 'Physical attributes' and 'background circumstances', for example, may suggest criteria which may nowadays be interpreted as discriminatory: to the disabled (in the case of a speech impairment, say) or to women (for example, the contra-indication of family responsibilities or intended pregnancy) or to workers of a particular age.

2.32 You should also be aware of the assumptions behind other criteria. (This is one of the reasons why you are required to study some of the behavioural science concepts underpinning human resource management.) The category of 'general intelligence', for example, has traditionally been measured as 'IQ' or mental dexterity, but it is now generally accepted that there are many kinds of intelligence, including emotional intelligence, practical intelligence, spatial intelligence and interpersonal intelligence – all of which might come in handy in purchasing and supply.

Attributes of effective purchasing staff

2.33 Purchasing staff require both general and particular attributes. Some of the most relevant general qualities are listed in Table 9.1.

Table 9.1 *General qualities required in purchasing staff*

QUALITY	REMARKS
Honesty	Obviously – just think of the large sums of money that purchasing staff are responsible for.
Hard work	This is essential to cope with the rigours of the job at the same time as obtaining and maintaining professional expertise.
Reliability	Purchasing interfaces with many other functions. Failure in purchasing can lead to expensive disruption elsewhere.
Initiative and imagination	Purchasing tasks are rarely routine. Ability to tackle new and unexpected problems is essential.
Enthusiasm	In particular, purchasing staff require an energetic and inquiring approach to their jobs.
Interpersonal skills, including communication	Much of the effectiveness of purchasing depends on links with other functions, as well as links between purchasing personnel themselves.
Numeracy	Quantitative aspects of purchasing problems, and particularly financial aspects, cannot be overlooked.
Information gathering, processing and decision-making	A major component of purchasing effectiveness is the ability to pick out essential elements, ascertain and analyse relevant information, and arrive at logical decisions.

2.34 In addition to these general qualities, purchasing staff require particular skills, in order to perform the specialist tasks involved in the job. This is a dynamic area. Changes in the perception and activities of the purchasing function have led to a need for qualities which would have been less important at earlier stages in the development of the profession. In particular, the requirement to manage partnership relations with suppliers, and to participate in strategic planning processes, makes demands on purchasing staff which were absent in an earlier era of short-term transactional relationships.

2.35 These skills can only be applied on a foundation of detailed relevant knowledge. *Malcolm Saunders* suggests that relevant knowledge can be divided into three main areas.

- General knowledge of business and management, including strategic management
- Specific knowledge relating to purchasing and supply management
- Technical knowledge relating to products and processes of particular businesses

3   Recruitment processes

3.1 The objectives of recruitment are basically fivefold.

- To identify, target and engage the market in which the relevant labour resources can be found
- To attract interest in the organisation and the job, in the form of enquiries or applications
- To provide sufficient and relevant information about the organisation and the job to aid applicants in the decision of whether and how to apply
- To project a positive image of the organisation to the outside world
- To achieve all of the above effectively and cost-efficiently.

(You might see this as directly analogous to the sourcing or procurement process for materials and other inputs – and indeed, its objectives are very similar.)

Recruitment policy and procedure

3.2   Detailed procedures for recruitment should be devised and implemented within the context of a coherent *policy* or code of conduct which guides managerial decision-making.

3.3   Recruitment policies will be influenced by a number of considerations. The human resource plan will set out skill requirements and preferred sources of labour for the organisation as a whole. Legislation and regulation may affect recruitment methods and criteria in areas such as equal opportunities, discrimination and terms and conditions specified (minimum wage, working hours, flexible working arrangements and so on). The organisation's cultural values will be reflected in the type of people it aims to recruit and the way in which it treats candidates. In addition, the organisation's desired employer brand (its image in the labour market, which enables it to attract and retain quality staff) should influence its approach to labour market relations.

3.4   A typical recruitment policy might deal with matters such as the following.

- The authorisation of vacancies and job advertisements
- The internal advertisement of vacancies prior to (or in addition to) external recruitment
- The swift, efficient and courteous processing of all job applications
- The provision of fair and accurate information to all potential applicants
- The confidentiality of all applications and personal information provided by applicants
- The selection of candidates on the basis of suitability for the job, without discrimination on any grounds

Engaging the market

3.5   There are a number of methods through which organisations can contact potential job candidates.

3.6   Unsolicited enquiries and the use of existing contacts or networks are an inexpensive form of recruitment, and have the advantage of pre-selection: the organisation may know something about the candidate (if only that they show initiative). There is, however, a danger of perpetuating the existing characteristics of the workforce, instead of systematically fitting candidates to job requirements. This may not only hamper organisational change, but may be construed as indirectly discriminatory: if the workforce is overwhelmingly male, for example, recruiting through employee networks may perpetuate the tendency.

3.7   Other recruitment methods offer the organisation access to registers of job-seekers, often pre-screened and with the option of further selection help and advice if required. Here are some examples.

- Referrals: registers of members seeking employment kept by trade unions, business associations and professional bodies (including CIPS)
- Government-sponsored employment registers: registers of job seekers and employment opportunities offered through a network of local agencies
- Private-sector employment agencies, often specialising by occupation (accounts staff, media and advertising etc) or contract type (temporary, casual etc)
- The careers services of schools, universities and training institutions
- Web-based employment databases and job-search tools

3.8   More systematic recruitment, screening and selection services are offered by consultancies of various types. Recruitment consultants may perform a range of job advertising and applicant screening procedures on behalf of the organisation. Outplacement consultants specialise in finding new positions for employees being made redundant or facing early retirement. Search consultants (sometimes called 'head hunters') proactively approach (or 'poach') specialist or executive staff in one organisation on behalf of another.

3.9   The advantage of using external consultancies is that they have extensive contacts and specialist recruitment and selection skills and resources: they can enable overhead cost savings and give expert advice to support selection decisions. However, there are also disadvantages: consultancies may lack in-depth awareness of the organisation's cultural values and other selection criteria (unless there is detailed briefing or relationship-building); they exclude internal applicants (and the internal labour market may be important to the organisation); and they lack accountability for the outcome of selection decisions. There is also, of course, a cost involved.

3.10   The most common approaches to recruitment require the organisation to prepare and disseminate information about employment opportunities and specific vacancies: in other words, **job advertising**. There are a number of media through which the target audience can be reached, depending on the size of the target audience, their location, their special interests – and the cost of contacting them.

3.11   The relevance of the target audience should also be taken into account. Internal recruitment may be targeted most efficiently by using in-house magazines, noticeboards or intranet sites, for example. In the external labour market, specific skills may be targeted through relevant sections or issues of newspapers and magazines, or through relevant trade, technical or professional websites and journals – such as *Supply Management* for purchasing and supply chain professionals.

3.12   The **internet** is increasingly used as a medium for matching job-seekers and vacancies.

- Its global penetration offers a larger audience than other advertising media – although with a corresponding downside in the cost of handling huge responses.
- Job advertisements can be linked to recruitment databases for regular updating and interactivity, allowing relevant information search by recruiters and applicants (job and employer details, downloadable application forms, etc) and immediate contact by e-mail.
- It is low cost: most businesses can develop a basic web presence, with vacancy information posted on a 'Careers' page. More interactive tools allow online application and electronic screening (filtering applications using pre-set essential and desirable criteria), without the cost of human intervention.
- It allows the effectiveness of recruitment to be electronically monitored (counting 'hits' on the site, applications submitted, application forms downloaded but not submitted and so on).
- It 'pre-screens' applicants for familiarity with the technology, which may or may not be essential for a given vacancy.
- It allows the impact of multi-media presentation but with the wide reach and low cost of print media – with the added advantage of interactivity.

3.13   Note that job advertisements are, in a way, already part of the *selection* process. They should be placed where suitable people are likely to see them, immediately pre-selecting those people. Similarly, advertisements should contain information that will help the target population to narrow itself down.

3.14   The advertisement should be based on information set out in the job description and person specification for the vacancy; the organisation's recruitment policy (in regard to equal opportunities, for example); and any corporate identity requirements (use of logos, general mission and culture statements and so on). Typical content of a job advertisement might include the following basic elements.

- The organisation's name and field of business (at least: perhaps also a brief statement of its mission and culture)
- The title, department and location of the job
- The main duties and responsibilities of the job
- Special factors or conditions affecting the job (if any)
- Essential and desirable qualifications, experience, skills or attributes required
- Rewards and opportunities (negotiable, if appropriate)
- Application details: how to apply, to whom, by what date
- Statements or logos to indicate that the organisation is an 'equal opportunities employer' or is certified as an Investor in People (where applicable)

Screening applications

3.15   Applications may be invited (or received) in a number of forms.

- By letter, e-mail or 'walk-in' (usually enquiring about unadvertised vacancies or general employment opportunities). Details are usually put on file, or – if a suitable vacancy exists – enquirers are invited to apply by more orthodox means, such as one of the following.
- By curriculum vitae (CV) or resumé, usually accompanied by a covering letter drawing the recruiter's attention to points in the CV or resumé of particular relevance to the job.
- By application form (hard-copy or online).

3.16   CVs and application forms are used to screen applicants at the initial stages of selection, in order to weed out applicants who are clearly unsuitable for the job or organisation, and to identify those who might be worth interviewing or testing further. The information given at this stage is usually also a starting point for later interview discussion.

3.17   A CV or resumé is basically a summary of the candidate's education, qualifications, work experience and whatever other information he or she considers relevant to the application. It generally also includes the contact details of one or more individuals (referees) who would be willing and able to confirm that information and vouch for the candidate's employability. CVs are a flexible self-marketing tool, from the point of view of the applicant, allowing him or her to highlight strengths and minimise weaknesses. This may, however, be regarded as a disadvantage from the point of view of the recruiter.

3.18   An application form is typically used for large-scale recruitment of staff in lower-level, relatively standardised jobs. It ensures that information is gathered in a specific and consistent way, enabling selectors to locate items of information rapidly and aiding objective comparison between different candidates within a given intake (or between different intakes over time).

3.19   For managerial and specialist jobs, a more complex application package may be used to elicit more complex responses and evidence of problem-solving (such as psychological questionnaires, or response to case study scenarios). Competence-based questions may also be used to guide applicants in describing their job experience or critical incidents, focusing on the demonstration of a specific competence relevant to the job.

3.20   Applications received should be set against key criteria in the job advertisement, job description and/or person specification. Initial screening can then be carried out to sort applications into three groups.

- *Unsuitable applicants* will be sent standard letters, informing them briefly and tactfully that their application has not been successful.
- *Potentially suitable applicants* will be earmarked for closer scrutiny, with a view to shortlisting candidates for interview or other selection procedures.
- *Marginals* will be kept in reserve for closer examination in the event that no more suitable candidates emerge.

3.21   Selectors usually draw up a *shortlist* of the best candidates and invite them for interview. Despite their limited ability to predict whether candidates will actually perform well in the job, interviews are by far the most commonly used selection technique. They may be reinforced with some appropriate form of selection testing. We will discuss both of these options in detail below.

3.22   If candidates are identified as suitable, and their references confirm their suitability, an offer of employment may be made. Note that this is not necessarily the end of the process: offers of employment do get rejected. High-quality applicants may well have received other offers. They may not be sufficiently attracted by a closer view of the organisation, the job or the rewards offered. They may only have applied to test the job market or to practise their job-seeking skills. A small number of alternative candidates should be kept in reserve.

3.23 Even after the offer of employment has been made and accepted, the recruiter may wish to maintain contact with other eligible, but narrowly unsuccessful, candidates, for future recruitment drives. Such candidates should be sent a variation on the standard 'rejection' letter which suggests (for example): 'We will keep your details on file in case any suitable vacancy arises in future.'

4 Selection processes

4.1 Effective selection procedures have three main benefits for organisations.

- They make it more likely that the organisation will obtain the right skills, experience, values and attributes for the job or role.
- They increase the likelihood that employees will stay in the job (retention) because they find a good 'fit' with job requirements and organisational culture.
- They ensure that all potential candidates are treated fairly and courteously, in line with equal opportunity law, the organisation's ethical values and its desired 'employer brand' (or reputation in the labour market).

Selection interviews

4.2 Interviews give the organisation an opportunity to learn more about job candidates, not just by asking questions to elicit and test information, but by observing the candidate's interpersonal and problem-solving skills and other attributes at first hand. At the same time, this is a two-way process: the candidate will be looking to gather information and impressions of the organisation, the job and the potential superior.

4.3 Interviews may be variously structured and conducted, depending on the kind of effect the selectors wish to create and the type of information they need to gather.

- **Individual or one-to-one interviews** offer the advantages of direct face-to-face communication and potential rapport between the candidate and interviewer. They can, if the selector wishes, be fairly informal, minimising the effects of stress and the unnaturalness of the context on the behaviour of the candidate. The drawback is that a single interviewer may be biased in his or her judgement, or may lack the knowledge to assess or challenge a candidate in particular areas.
- **Panel interviews**, in which two or three people interview the candidate together, address the disadvantages of one-to-one interviews. They allow HR and relevant technical specialists to gain a well-rounded picture of the candidate and to cross-check their impressions, while cutting down on the information swapping required by the equivalent sequence of one-to-one interviews. Panels may, however, be more daunting to candidates. Their behaviour in a formal, artificial and stressful situation may not reflect their ability to handle workplace tasks and pressures.

4.4 Whichever structure is used, the preparation and conduct of selection interviews should be intentionally designed to elicit the required information, while creating the desired impression of the employer *and* allowing candidates to feel that they have been fairly treated. These aims leave room for a range of specific strategies.

- Some interviewers will wish to test candidates' behaviour under pressure, by creating a confrontational or inquisitional atmosphere ('stress' interviewing), while others will wish to put candidates at their ease in order to encourage self-expression and more natural interpersonal behaviours.
- Some interviews may be *structured*: directing questions to the application form or personnel specification; using a case study and 'what would you do?' question style to test the candidate's problem-solving skills ('situational' interviewing); or asking the candidate to describe his or her handling of work challenges in the past ('behavioural' interviewing). Structured interviews maximise the relevant information gained in the time available and facilitate comparison of candidates using consistent criteria. However, they can be limiting in the type of information that can be obtained.

- *Unstructured* interviews, on the other hand, encourage the candidate to talk freely, where self-expression is considered relevant. An unstructured period may be used at the beginning or end of a structured interview to put candidates at ease, or to elicit further information that the candidate may feel is relevant.

4.5 The interview process should be seen to be efficiently and fairly conducted. Arrangements should have been made to welcome and direct candidates to appropriate facilities. Interview rooms should be private and free from distractions and interruptions. Interviewers should be professional – however deliberately confrontational – in tone and manner. They should also be adequately prepared, so that time is not wasted on irrelevant questions.

4.6 An interviewer must be skilled in using different question types.

- *Open questions*, to encourage interviewees to respond in their own words
- *Probing questions*, to challenge a shallow, unfocused or possibly dishonest response
- *Closed questions*, allowing one-word, yes/no or either/or answers, to pin down a definite response
- *Problem-solving questions*, asking for a candidate's response to a hypothetical situation
- *Leading questions*, drawing interviewees towards a desired response.

4.7 An interviewer must also be able to listen actively and critically to what the interviewee is saying, trying to say, or trying *not* to say, using both verbal and non-verbal cues (body language, appearance, facial expressions and so on).

4.8 The interview may be based around preliminary information provided by the candidate in an application form or CV, as well as information about the organisation's requirements drawn from the job description, person specification and/or job advertisement. These sources will suggest areas in which the interviewer will need to confirm, challenge or seek additional information. Candidates must also be given the opportunity to gather information about the job and the organisation, the terms and conditions of employment (subject to negotiation), the next step in the selection process (if any) and so on.

4.9 Interviews are by far the most popular selection method used by organisations. They offer some significant advantages.

- They are highly interactive, allowing flexible question-and-answer interaction. This allows candidates opportunities to ask questions (eg about the job and organisation), as well as the interviewers. It allows questions and responses to be adapted to the direction and style of the interview.
- They offer opportunities to use non-verbal communication, which might confirm or undermine spoken answers (eg a candidate looking hesitant or embarrassed when making competence claims). This is particularly helpful to interviewers when challenging or probing in relation to inconsistencies or gaps in a candidate's application or answers.
- They offer opportunities to witness the candidate's personal appearance (relevant in areas such as grooming and conformity with social norms), interpersonal and communication skills.
- They offer initial opportunities to evaluate rapport between the candidate and his or her potential colleagues and bosses.

4.10 Despite their widespread popularity, however, research studies show that interviews have a poor record when it comes to predicting successful candidates' performance in the job. In a survey by M Smith and M Abrahamsen, interviews were the most popular selection method (94% of the surveyed organisations used them), but scored only 0.17 for 'predictive validity', on a scale ranging from 1 (the technique unfailingly predicts candidates' subsequent job performance) to 0 (the technique is no better than random chance at predicting candidates' subsequent job performance). In other words, interviews are not very much better than rolling dice when it comes to selecting staff.

4.11 Interviews have a number of limitations in practice.

- They are limited in scope. Interviews are too brief to gain a sufficiently full or complex knowledge of candidates' abilities and motivations to enable an employer to predict their behaviour in the variety of situations that may arise at work.
- They are artificial situations. Interviews do not necessarily bring out the kind of attributes and behaviours (good and bad) that candidates would display in the real work context.
- They are subject to manipulation by candidates. Interview behaviour is subject to coaching and practice effects, allowing candidates to develop 'interview technique' which may disguise their true attributes and behaviours.
- They are subject to errors of judgement by interviewers. The assessment of candidates may be distorted by various forms of prejudice, bias, stereotyping, unchecked assumptions, cultural incompatibility, ineffective listening and other perceptual or logical weaknesses on the part of unskilled interviewers. Examples include:
  - *Halo effect*, where interviewers allow an initial general judgement about a person, based on a single obvious attribute (such as appearance or verbal fluency), to colour their later perceptions of other attributes, positively or negatively.
  - *Stereotyping,* where interviewers attribute certain characteristics to 'groups' of people and then assume that each individual member of the supposed group will possess that trait.
- They are subject to poor interpersonal and communication skills on the part of either or both parties. The responsibility lies primarily with the interviewer to direct and control the discussion and elicit the required responses from the candidate.

Selection testing

4.12 Selection interviewing may be supplemented by some form of testing in areas considered relevant to the requirements of the job.

- Proficiency and attainment tests measure an individual's demonstrated competence in particular job-related tasks.
- Psychometric testing measures such psychological factors as aptitude, intelligence and personality.

4.13 **Proficiency tests** are designed to measure an individual's current ability to perform particular tasks or operations relevant to the job. **Attainment tests** are a similar measurement of the standard an individual has reached at a particular skill. There is a wide range of proficiency testing material available, including 'in-tray' exercises (simulating work tasks) on paper and via interactive computer programs. **Work sampling** (such as proficiency tests and portfolios of work) gained the highest score for predictive validity in Smith and Abrahamsen's study, at 0.57.

4.14 **Aptitude tests** are designed to predict an individual's potential for performing a job or learning new skills. There are a number of commonly recognised areas of aptitude which can be measured: reasoning (verbal, numerical and abstract or visual problem-solving); visuo-spatial ability (practical and creative intelligence); perceptual speed and accuracy; and 'psycho-motor' ability (the hand-eye coordination, fine muscle control and other responses involved in mechanical, manual, musical or athletic performance). Some of these areas of aptitude may be particularly relevant to a job: verbal and numerical reasoning in formulating and negotiating supply agreements, or perceptual speed and accuracy in reconciling purchase orders and delivery notes, say.

4.15 **Intelligence tests** (or 'cognitive ability' tests) are designed to measure an individual's memory, perceptual speed, verbal fluency, logical reasoning and problem-solving skills. Such elements are commonly identified as 'IQ'. Such a measure does not reflect the range of human intelligence (particularly, for example, what Daniel Goleman has popularised as 'emotional intelligence'. It is particularly difficult to exclude bias from such tests, to give a fair chance to candidates from different educational and social backgrounds (and particularly those for whom the test language is not their first language). Cognitive tests scored well on predictive validity (0.54) in Smith and Abrahamsen's study.

4.16   **Personality profiling** is designed to measure a variety of traits and tendencies in an individual's personality, in order to suggest how he or she is likely to behave in general, in particular work contexts, in response to particular managerial styles and so on. Examples include the 16PF, Myers-Briggs Type Indicator and DISC four quadrant behavioural assessments (discussed earlier) and the Minnesota Multiphasic Personality Inventory (MMPI). If selected for relevance to the job, and if used and interpreted properly, such tests may be able to predict job performance to an extent (with a 0.40 score for predictive validity, according to Smith and Abrahamsen). However, there is continuing debate about the relevance of personality factors, the accuracy with which traits can be measured and the difficulty of eliminating cultural and gender bias in designing and interpreting tests.

4.17   Most forms of testing share the limitations of selection interviewing. Attention must be given to the relevance of the criteria being tested, and to the expertise and objectivity of the designers and interpreters of the tests. Most forms of testing are subject to bias, in the form of culturally-specific assumptions. Most are also subject to manipulation by candidates: it is often possible to guess which response is 'correct' or desirable from an employer's point of view, to develop an effective test technique through coaching or practice and even to memorise specific answers.

4.18   Several trends have been identified in the use of selection testing, including a growing diversity of test producers and sources, expanded packages of tests (including workbooks, computer software and 'apps', and online test resources) and a growing focus on the elimination of bias and unfairness from tests.

Assessment centres

4.19   Assessment centres or **group selection methods** may be used as the final stage of a selection process for managerial roles. They consist of a series of tests, interviews and group exercises undertaken by a group of six to eight candidates over a period of two days, and assessed by a qualified team of assessors.

4.20   As well as individual interviews and tests, assessment centres typically use tools such as: group role-play exercises simulating interpersonal situations (conflict, negotiation or team-building, say); case study analysis and problem-solving; in-tray exercises simulating workload management as well as task performance; individual and team presentations; and leaderless discussion groups (LDGs) to assess candidates' communication and decision-making skills, assertiveness and potential for leadership.

4.21   Assessment centres are particularly useful for the recruitment of potential managerial staff, as they give selectors a longer, broader and (if only in simulation) more real-world assessment of candidates. They allow the organisation to assess interpersonal factors such as communication, negotiation, co-operation, leadership, persuasion and conflict resolution, which are important managerial skills. They demonstrate a candidate's attributes and attitudes not just in abstract, but as they affect other people (in the simulated team) and the candidate's own performance (in simulated tasks). They also allow direct comparison between potential candidates.

4.22   Such assessment does, however, require an investment of expertise, time and facilities, which is why it is usually only used at managerial or managerial trainee level. In addition it is still only a simulation, not a predictor of job performance in its real-organisation context – particularly since group exercises can create a kind of hype or 'euphoria' which may distort candidates' usual behaviours. And of course they only assess matters which can be staged away from the workplace, so they are necessarily partial.

Other selection methods

4.23   Interviews, testing and group selection methods are the most generally popular selection methods, but you may encounter others, such as the following.

*   **Background and reference checks** are aimed at verifying candidates' claims about their educational qualifications and previous employment experience. This is an essential support to other selection

methods, although references in themselves scored only 0.13 on Smith and Abrahamsen's predictive validity scale.

- **Physical or medical testing.** Some organisations require medical checks as a final stage in the selection process, usually to ensure fitness for physically demanding jobs, to determine any pre-existing conditions that might disqualify future compensation or insurance claims, and (in the case of genetic screening) to identify potential health and safety risks. There may be policy or legislative constraints on testing, for example for HIV/AIDS or drug and alcohol abuse. Strict relevance will have to be demonstrated, discrimination avoided and privacy assured.
- **Biodata analysis.** Biodata (biographical data) may be gathered via multiple choice questionnaires on family background, personal attitudes and so on: the individual's profile is compared against the 'ideal' profile for the given job (based on statistical correlations with successful job performance). Biodata scored a predictive validity of 0.40.

Equal opportunity in recruitment and selection

4.24 Recruitment and selection are areas of particular sensitivity for equal opportunity, or the avoidance of discrimination. There is always a risk that a disappointed job applicant, for example, will attribute lack of success to discrimination, especially if the recruiting organisation's workforce is conspicuously lacking in representatives of the same ethnic minority, sex or other group.

4.25 The legal framework on equal opportunity will be discussed in Chapter 11, but the recruiter will need to give attention to areas such as: developing clear, objective, job-related and justifiable selection criteria; job advertising (not implying or stating any intention to discriminate, and placing ads where minority groups have equal access to them); avoiding asking non-work-related questions of some groups and not others in interviews, application forms and selection tests (for example, asking only women about plans to start a family); interviewing at least one representative of all minority groups applying; and keeping detailed records of interviews and reasons for selection decisions.

Evaluating recruiting and selection

4.26 Stephen Connock (*HR Vision*) suggests that auditing of the recruitment process should occur at various levels.

- **Performance indicators** should be established for each stage of the process. KPIs might include: numbers of applications received; percentage of applicants interviewed; percentage of interviewees made an offer; time taken to process applications (or per application); percentage of applicants in monitored categories (women, minority, disabled); percentage of recruits subsequently appraised as competent in the job; percentage of starters still employed after one/two years; and cost per applicant or position filled.
- The **cost-effectiveness** of the recruitment and selection methods used should be measured, in terms of cost per application or per qualified (shortlisted) applicant.
- The **make-up of the workforce** and of each intake of new recruits should be monitored as part of an equal opportunities policy, to identify areas in which monitored groups are under-represented, and whether recruitment media or selection methods may be responsible.
- The **attitudes of recruits** should be surveyed, to find out how they perceived and experienced the various stages of recruitment and selection: the accuracy of information given, the organisation's speed in turning round applications, the image conveyed during interviews and so on. This can be done through staff attitude surveys, or interviews during the induction process.
- Areas where **practice deviates from planned standards and policy goals** will need to be investigated, and appropriate remedial action initiated. Long turnaround times for processing applications, for example, are said to be one of the main demotivators of job candidates. If selection interview and test results do not correspond to candidates' subsequent job performance, interviewer training or alteration of testing mechanisms may be considered.

5   Induction

5.1   Induction is the process whereby a person is formally introduced and integrated into an organisation or system. Induction training is designed for the following purposes.

- To help new recruits to find their bearings
- To begin to socialise them into the culture of the organisation
- To support initial performance
- To identify ongoing training and development needs
- To minimise labour turnover due to initial teething problems and difficulties of adjustment in the first year of work (known as 'induction crisis')

5.2   The advantages of formal induction training are listed in Table 9.2.

Table 9.2 *Advantages of induction*

BENEFITS FOR THE ORGANISATION	BENEFITS FOR THE INDIVIDUAL
Reduces risk of recruits leaving due to post-induction crisis, associated with difficulties settling in (see below)	Minimises disorientation, insecurity and stress of starting in an unfamiliar setting
Speeds adjustment, networking and competence development, to support initial work performance and conformity to behavioural norms and standards	Connects new recruits with supportive social and information networks
Fosters employee morale for retention and commitment	Gives new recruits positive (reassuring) experience of the organisation
Enhances the employer brand in the labour market	Helps recruits adjust to values and behavioural norms, so they 'fit in'
Begins an ongoing process of development planning	

The employment lifecycle and induction crises

5.3   The employment lifecycle shows a number of decision points at which employees experience a crisis in their relationship with the organisation: these are the points at which labour turnover is most likely. Stages in the employment lifecycle are as follows.

- *First induction crisis:* a decision point shortly after joining, when things are still new and perhaps difficult, and loyalty is insufficient to overcome the frustrations. Crisis triggers may include difficulties in establishing working relationships (eg breaking into cohesive groups or networks); a clash of culture (norms, management style) with what the recruit has previously experienced; or disappointed expectations (perhaps because of unrealistic claims made during recruitment). This is a point of high labour turnover in many organisations.
- *Differential transit period:* a period of mutual accommodation and adjustment between employer and employee. Areas of conflict are settled, and there may be additional labour turnover as a result of this process.
- *Second induction crisis:* both parties have to come to terms with the new *status quo*, creating a similar (though less significant) problem of adjustment to the original induction crisis.
- *Settled connection period:* mutual adjustment and loyalty have been established, and the likelihood of leaving is much less.

Induction training

5.4   A typical general format for an induction programme would be as follows.

- A general welcome and briefing on the geography, structure and culture of the organisation.
- An introductory tour of the work facility, both for an overview of the work process and to orient the recruit to relevant amenities.
- Briefing by the HR manager on HR policies and procedures: conditions of employment, pay and benefits, training and development opportunities, procedures for sickness and absence, holiday planning and so on. (Guidance in completing any initial employment paperwork may be given at this stage.)
- Introduction to co-workers and other key figures (managers, health and safety officers, union representatives and so on): ideally, appointing a co-worker (by agreement) as coach or mentor to integrate and develop the recruit on an ongoing basis
- Briefing on relevant company policies and procedures: discipline and grievance procedures; health and safety rules, provisions and officers; time-keeping and flexitime procedures and so on.
- Issuing an *employee handbook* as an ongoing source of reference about policies, procedures, rules and other relevant matters.
- Meeting with HR and/or departmental managers or mentors to plan, agree and implement initial development, including coaching, instruction and training required to commence performance.
- Involve recruits in participative exercises and interactions with other staff, both on the job ('sitting with Nellie' or shadowing, for example) and informally (encouraging social interaction).
- Briefing by the immediate manager, supervisor or mentor. Explain the nature of the job and the goals of each task, of the recruit's job and of the department as a whole. Highlight important rules and procedural requirements. Identify people to whom the recruit will report, to whom he should go with complaints or queries and so on.
- Monitor recruits' initial progress and commence an ongoing cycle of feedback, review, problem-solving and development planning.

5.5   After three months, six months or one year, the performance of a new recruit should be formally appraised and discussed. Induction should be seen as the beginning of an ongoing process, not a one-off briefing.

Chapter summary

- The aim of human resource planning is to ensure the availability of the right quantity of the right skills at the right price and at the right time.
- A systematic approach to recruitment and selection is an important part of this process.
- Tools involved in the HRP process include job analysis, job description, competence analysis, role analysis, and person specification.
- Purchasing staff require both general attributes (such as honesty and reliability) and also particular skills needed to fulfil their specialist function.
- Recruitment processes involve establishing policy and procedure, engaging the market, and screening applications.
- Selection processes may include interviews, testing, and assessment centres.
- Induction is the process whereby a person is formally introduced and integrated into an organisation or system. In larger organisations, this is typically achieved by means of a formal induction training process.

Self-test questions

Numbers in brackets refer to the paragraphs where you can check your answers.

1   Define human resource planning. (1.1)

2   Describe the stages in a systematic approach to HRP. (1.8)

3   In what circumstances may recruitment be necessary? (2.1)

4   List typical contents of a job description. (2.11)

5   What are the advantages of competence-based profiling? (2.20)

6   List the elements of (a) Rodger's Seven Point Plan and (b) J Munro Fraser's Five Point Pattern of Personality. (2.26, 2.27)

7   List general attributes required in purchasing staff. (Table 9.1)

8   What are the objectives of recruitment? (3.1)

9   What are the benefits of the internet as a means of recruitment advertising? (3.12)

10   What are the benefits of effective selection procedures? (4.1)

11   What are the advantages of interviews as a selection method? (4.9)

12   Explain the use of personality profiling in selection. (4.16)

CHAPTER 10

Training and Development

Assessment criteria and indicative content

 Prepare a plan for training and development of personnel in the procurement and supply function

- Costs and benefits of training
- Methods, delivery and evaluation of training
- Training needs analysis
- The application of personal development plans
- Performance review and appraisal

Section headings

1 Learning, training and development
2 Purposes and benefits of training
3 Training needs analysis
4 Training methods and delivery
5 Development
6 Evaluating training and development
7 Performance management

Introduction

In this chapter, we look at the crucial managerial role of supporting the development of people. First, we distinguish between some of the key terms in this area, including 'learning', training' and 'development'. Then we suggest why such processes or interventions are important for individual, team and business performance.

Over several sections, we then go on to outline a systematic approach to the planning and management of training, and trace it through its various stages, from the identification of training needs, to the delivery of training by various methods and media, and the evaluation of the process.

Finally, we look at the wider process of performance management within which learning, training and development interventions may be planned – including the process of performance appraisal. This topic is not explicitly mentioned in the syllabus, but it underpins any systematic, planned approach to training. The primary goal of training is to improve performance, and performance management both (a) ensures that training interventions are directed at identified improvement or capability needs and (b) acknowledges that training is only *one* of the possible interventions that may be required to facilitate performance improvement.

1 Learning, training and development

1.1 There are several related terms in the area of employee development, and it is helpful to start by distinguishing between them.

- **Learning** may be defined as 'relatively permanent change in behaviour that occurs as a result of practice or experience' (Bass and Vaughan).
- **Training** has been defined as 'a planned process to modify attitude, knowledge or skill behaviour through learning experiences, to achieve effective performance in any activity or range of activities'. In other words, training is learning applied to helping people to perform their current job role better.
- **Development** is the wider process of growth in people's knowledge and capabilities, with the aim of helping them to cope with change, and increasingly fulfilling their potential. Development involves various activities and relationships by which individuals: access self-managed learning opportunities; gain experience, so that they can take on more responsibility or different job roles over time; and are given guidance and support to formulate and pursue personal and career development goals.

1.2 The modern approach to human resource development can be defined as 'the process of achieving outstanding organisational performance through empowering people to achieve and give of their best'.

Organisational and individual learning and development

1.3 Training and development are directed at building and sustaining long-term competitive advantage or service improvement: they are strategic activities. There has been a misperception that training is the province of HR specialists, but it is increasingly being recognised that it must be integrated with:

- The strategic planning and direction of the enterprise, taking into account the knowledge, skills and capabilities required by its current and future activities and challenges
- The line management of staff at the departmental and team level
- Ownership of the development process by employees themselves.

1.4 Tom Boydell *(Guide to the Identification of Training Needs)* argues that learning and development may occur on four levels.

- Individual: including personal, skill and career development
- Group development: eg integrating cross-functional procurement teams through team-building activities, or informing staff about new policies and procedures
- Occupational and professional development: developing technical competencies and ethical standards relevant to specific occupational or professional groups (such as procurement and supply chain management professionals)
- Organisational development: eg planned change interventions to improve organisational performance and member wellbeing (eg the implementation of total quality management).

1.5 The pursuit of human resource development has increasingly moved from traditional systematic **training** processes (with the focus on formal teacher-directed acquisition of specifically job-relevant knowledge and skills) to a **learning** approach, which emphasises continuous, self-managed and experiential learning, aimed at the development of broader-spectrum, transferable competencies (such as interpersonal, management, teamworking and learning skills); continuous incremental improvement; and learning to learn (in order to support lifelong learning).

1.6 Self-directed and manager/coach-directed learning and development activity is often based on what we called 'opportunistic' learning: using experiential learning, coaching and problem-based learning to capitalise on learning opportunities arising naturally in the course of work.

1.7 Nevertheless, in most organisations, planned formal learning interventions are implemented with a view to meeting specific, identified performance improvement needs, or filling gaps in knowledge, aptitudes or skills. This is often associated with **systematic training**: training undertaken on a planned basis as a result of applying a logical series of steps'.

A systematic approach to training

1.8   Figure 10.1 depicts a systematic approach to planned training programmes – which we will explore in detail in the rest of this chapter.

Figure 10.1 *A systematic approach to training*

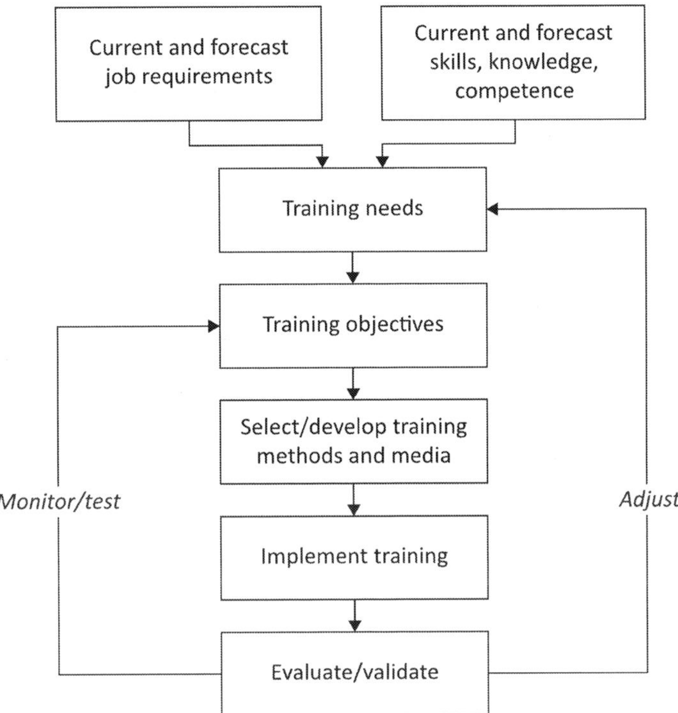

1.9   Mullins emphasises the elements involved in a planned and systematic approach to the management of training: Table 10.1.

Table 10.1 *Systematic management of training*

Commitment	Clear commitment to learning, training and development (reflected in adequate resourcing) from the top down, supported by line managers
Training needs analysis	Effective capability gap analysis at organisational, departmental and individual level (discussed in Section 3 of this chapter)
Involvement	Staff should be given a sense of ownership and partnership in training
Objectives and policy	Training programmes should define who should be trained, what they should be taught, how training should be undertaken and how outcomes will be evaluated
Training scope and pace	Training should reflect priority areas within training needs, to avoid information overload: planning manageable learning 'chunks' and time for consolidation
Training methods	Consideration must be given to appropriate delivery methods for the learning need and trainee learning styles
Access	Regard should be given to the training needs of minority and disadvantaged groups within the workforce; barriers to accessing adult learning; and appropriate methods for diversity (eg in terms of disability, age, language)
Review and evaluation	There should be ongoing monitoring of progress; a supporting performance management system (discussed in the final sections of this chapter); and the maintenance of training records. Where possible, evaluation should be related to objective, measurable factors: eg increased output, fewer accidents or customer complaints, reduced absenteeism and so on.

Training policy

1.10   The organisation (and individual functions such as purchasing and supply) will need to formulate a training and development policy which addresses issues such as the following.

- How training is envisaged as contributing to strategic objectives and the HR plan
- The desired outcomes of training (skills, knowledge, competence, awareness and attitudes, employability, ethics and so on) and how they are to be monitored and evaluated
- How training needs and objectives will be determined
- Access to training: what types and grades of staff will have access to different types and levels of training; equal opportunities commitments
- Responsibilities for initiating, planning, implementing and evaluating training
- How far the organisation is committed to investment in training and development

2   Purposes and benefits of training

2.1   Employee training and development are widely believed to be a 'good thing'. After all, it is now recognised that people (and their commitment, contributions and capabilities) are key resources of the organisation for adding value and securing competitive advantage. But why should organisations make development a priority? Don't they just recruit the skills they need – and use the ones they've got?

2.2   It isn't always easy to measure or quantify the benefits of employee development. What monetary value can you put on employee satisfaction, say, or reduced stress in the face of organisational change? Even if the performance of an individual or team measurably improves after coaching or training, how do you know it has improved because of training, given all the other variables involved?

Benefits of development to the organisation

2.3   Perhaps the most obvious benefit of training to the employing organisation is enhanced knowledge, skills, competence, awareness, ethics etc in the workforce, which should:

- Enhance the job performance of the workforce, in terms of productivity, quality, customer service and so on (potentially a key source of competitive advantage)
- Add value to the organisation's human assets (which represents shareholder value) and
- Contribute to process efficiencies (eg reduced errors and wastage) and profitability.

2.4   One of the cornerstones of modern strategic management is that successful performance and competitive advantage is not gained solely through programmes and activities, but through people: people add value to material, financial, information and other resources. This is particularly crucial in an ever-changing, networked, knowledge-based, customer-focused business environment. The modern approach to human resource development can be defined as 'the process of achieving outstanding organisational performance through empowering people to achieve and give of their best'. People are now seen as key resources and assets of a business: enabling it to deliver service, differentiate itself from its competitors, relate to its customers, and mobilise knowledge and creativity.

2.5   Development activity also demonstrates the organisation's commitment to employee involvement and empowerment, and creates opportunities for greater interest, challenge, personal development and self-confidence in the job. Most modern writers on management identify the satisfaction of these 'higher order' needs as a key source of enhanced employee satisfaction and motivation, which in turn may create positive benefits for the organisation.

- Improved commitment and contribution from employees
- Loyalty and retention, with reduced skill wastage from labour turnover
- Cost savings, from a reduction in factors such as absenteeism, disciplinary problems, conflict and poor morale

- Enhanced 'employer brand': the organisation's reputation as an employer (eg as Investors in People), which can help to attract and retain quality labour, in competition with other organisations in the labour market

2.6 Meanwhile, developing people's capabilities supports employee empowerment, which leads to greater participation in decision-making, responsibility, initiative and information-sharing between all levels of the organisation. This in turn may lead to a cluster of benefits.

- More positive employee relations (with less industrial conflict and less need for restrictive industrial relations negotiating and conflict resolution machinery)
- Contribution to innovation and problem-solving by front-line (customer or supplier-facing) and technically expert staff
- More responsive and empowered customer service, which is regarded as a key source of brand differentiation and competitive advantage
- Less need for detailed supervision, freeing management for more proactive roles (or delayering).

2.7 Responsiveness to changing customer demands, and adaptability to increasingly dynamic business environments, is also a priority for many organisations. Employee development gives crucial support to flexibility and change management.

- Enhancing workforce versatility – especially if training has the effect of multi-skilling individuals, so that they can perform a range of team roles and team leaders can allocate tasks without job or skill demarcation barriers. Functional flexibility of this kind in turn enables more efficient labour utilisation, and better ability to adapt to changing task requirements.
- Allowing the organisation to be proactive in developing skills for future strategic requirements
- Building up the human resources and core stability needed to meet any internal and external changes and challenges that arise
- Giving individuals and teams key coping skills for change (which might otherwise be a cause of stress and resistance)
- Supporting a culture of continuous learning, improvement, experimentation and information sharing. This has come to be known as a 'learning organisation' culture.

2.8 Development can also support an organisation's objectives for corporate social responsibility (CSR), where it is used:

- To enhance workers' employability, or value and mobility in the external labour market. (This is an important part of modern 'psychological contracts' between employers and employees, since job security can no longer be guaranteed.)
- To offer increasing job enrichment (added challenge, responsibility, variety and satisfaction within the job) where promotion prospects are limited eg by delayering
- To improve health and safety performance
- To ensure compliance with best practice, benchmarked standards (such as Investors in People) and government policy on developing vocational skills.

Benefits to the individual

2.9 We have already touched on some of the benefits for the people being trained and developed. Most obviously, there is the intended benefit of enhanced knowledge, skills and competencies. However, these in turn offer:

- Psychological benefits, in the form of increased self-esteem, job security, and sense of achievement
- Financial benefits, in the form of opportunities for increased performance-related rewards
- Enhanced opportunities for promotion or career development
- Opportunities for job enlargement (more varied tasks) and/or job enrichment (more responsibility, challenge and autonomy in the job)
- Greater job satisfaction and quality of working life

- Opportunities for employees to extend their own interests, skills and social contacts; to meet their own development needs; and to enhance their value and mobility in the labour market
- Spin-off benefits of training needs analysis (if problems are identified to which training is not the only answer): improved work methods, systems and so on.

2.10   We might note that benefits also accrue to wider society, in terms of learning skills for employment and economic growth; skills for life-long learning and self-development; and the underpinning of democratic processes and responsible citizenship.

Does training always offer these benefits?

2.11   Training might (and should, all other things being equal) improve performance, but just 'doing training' is not a cure-all remedy for poor performance. A contingency approach must be applied to situations where employee performance is below the desired standard. The problem may not be a skill gap which is amenable to training: it may be in systems, technology, procedures, motivation or attitude, organisation structure, leadership and so on. Counselling, disciplinary action and problem-solving may be more effective interventions – and we discuss this issue in the broader context of performance management, in the final section of this chapter.

2.12   If there is a skill gap, its precise nature and extent must be identified (through performance measurement and training needs analysis), so that training can be targeted directly at required performance improvement, and so that training resources can be justified and allocated where they will be most effective. Jones & Oliver, for example, distinguish between:

- 'Focused' training (effective), where employees are trained only in directly job-relevant skills, in which they have an identified skill or knowledge gap (as a result of systematic training needs analysis); and
- 'Unfocused' training (often ineffective), where training arises as a result of *ad hoc* requests by employees or managers, training company marketing or blanket training policies (eg to ensure that the training budget is spent).

2.13   Training must also be appropriately designed and implemented for the training need and the learning styles of trainees, in order to maximise learning and transfer of learning to the job. So, for example, classroom learning will not suit a 'hands-on' training need such as operating a particular e-purchasing system.

The costs of training

2.14   The direct costs of training will include the following.

- Training and instruction rooms and equipment
- Training materials and resources
- The salaries of in-house training staff
- The costs of outsourced training activities, consultants, third-party course providers and so on
- The time (usually with pay) of the staff attending the training courses, and the cost of any lost production due to their attendance (or the cost of temporary replacement staff or overtime working)
- The travelling and accommodation expenses of staff attending off-site training courses
- Opportunity costs of staff time, training space, equipment etc (which may otherwise be used for more directly revenue-earning activities)

2.15   There may also be indirect or consequential costs of training.

- Disruption to working patterns and output as a result of teething problems, learning curves, poor adjustment or difficulties in transfer of learning to the job
- Errors and scrap work produced in the course of 'trial and error' learning (which may have additional costs if learning is 'on the job')
- Increased staff turnover, as a result of the enhanced skill portfolio, employability and career mobility

of trained staff (although opportunities for development may also contribute to retention, as a source of job satisfaction).

3   Training needs analysis

Informal identification of training needs

3.1   Some training requirements may emerge relatively informally in the course of work.

- Changes in legislation, technology or work methods create a knowledge or skill gap which must be filled in order for the individual to maintain a competent level of performance (or to enhance his or her career potential). Examples may include the introduction of age diversity legislation, or the acquisition of new software.
- Critical incidents (problems or events which affect a key area of a team's effectiveness) may be observed or reported and then analysed. These may suggest that there is a need for training: for example, customer complaints, significant over-spend on a project, loss of a key supplier, or disciplinary problems. Critical incidents may be identified by the individual, the team leader or third-party stakeholders (such as customers or suppliers).
- Developmental discussions (such as performance appraisals, coaching or mentoring) may be used to focus on the individual's goals and aspirations and identify learning (or other interventions) needed to attain them. Managers – acting as 'coaches' – are in an ideal position to discuss these matters with team members.
- Self-assessment and personal development activities may lead individuals to identify areas in which they are not satisfied with their performance, or in which there is potential for growth. This may involve informal self-nomination for advertised training courses, say, or it may be more systematic (eg using training needs questionnaires, or 360-degree feedback appraisal reports).

3.2   Training needs may also, however, need to be more systematically assessed. A wider, more objective viewpoint will allow the leader (and the organisation as a whole) to take into account the organisation's *future* skill requirements, given its strategic and human resource plans. It will also enable greater integration of training and development, to support overall performance (rather than merely individual improvement).

3.3   The problem with self-assessed training needs, in particular, is that individuals rarely have a full or objective picture either of the skills they currently possess (since it is not always possible to know what you don't know), or of the skills that may be required as the job and team develops.

Systematic training needs analysis

3.4   Training needs analysis, very simply, involves the following processes.

- Measuring what employees need to be *able* to do in order to perform a job competently and in line with performance standards
- Measuring what employees actually *can* do
- Identifying any 'gap' between the two, as a potential need for learning, training and development

3.5   At the functional or departmental level, formal training needs analysis is most common when there is a change in the role of a department; the department is restructured; there is a change of policy (eg because of new legislation); or new systems are introduced (eg because of new technology). These scenarios present a need or opportunity to identify skill or knowledge 'gaps' (learning needs) for the whole function or department. The purchasing department takes over responsibility for transport, say, or introduces an EDI system: what does it need to be able to do now, that it did not before?

10

3.6   At the job level, formal training needs analysis is most common for groups of new staff, or following complaints or problems, or where new jobs have been created. What does a person in this job need to be able to do, that they may not be able to?

3.7   At the individual level, training needs analysis may be less formal, utilising self-appraisal, or ongoing feedback from a superior or mentor, say: what areas might benefit from improvement? Formal analysis may also be used: if a person is new in the job, say, or if a staff member is experiencing problems, or as part of ongoing appraisal and development planning for individuals. What does this individual need to be able to do in order to perform better, or be considered for promotion?

3.8   In more detail, a process for training needs analysis (TNA) may be as follows.

- Define the required level of competence for the job, agreeing key areas and benchmark standards which must be attained for competent performance (eg using job analysis and description, or competence definitions).
- Measure the present level of employees' competence, via agreed methods of assessment or testing (including self analysis, competency testing or systematic performance appraisal).
- Compare present competence with benchmark or target performance: identify knowledge or skill gaps (gap analysis).
- Design and implement interventions (including training) to remedy those gaps.
- Monitor, review and feed back on progress as appropriate.

Training objectives

3.9   Training needs should be redefined in terms of specific, measurable objectives, ideally detailing: behaviour (what the trainee should be able to do); standard (to what level of performance); and context (under what conditions, so that the level of performance is realistic).

3.10   This corresponds to the approach used in competence assessment. Competence may be defined as: 'The ability to perform activities in the jobs within an occupation to the standards expected in employment. The concept also embodies the ability to transfer skills and knowledge to new situations within the occupational area and beyond, to related occupations.'

Setting SMART training objectives

3.11   A popular framework for evaluating objectives is SMART – although we prefer an extended or SMARTER version: Table 10.2.

Table 10.2 *SMARTER objectives*

Specific	Stated in clear, detailed terms: precisely what the desired outcomes or deliverables are
Measurable	Susceptible to monitoring, review and measurement (ideally in quantitative or numerical terms) so that we know when or how far progress has been attained
Attainable	Target outcomes and standards, and the contexts and timetables within which they must be attained, must be realistically achievable, using the capacities, capabilities, readiness and resources available
Relevant	The objectives must be relevant to the strategic objectives of the unit and the business as a whole: they must lead somewhere meaningful
Time-bounded	Target timescales and deadlines for completion (or review) must be included in the objective: it is not open ended
Evaluated	The objective must have been assessed as worth pursuing, given the investment in time or effort it will require: this may involve some form of cost-benefit analysis
Responsible	The objective must take into account potential impacts on key stakeholders, in the light of the unit's (and organisation's) ethical responsibilities towards them

Training plans

3.12   A typical training plan for a business unit or function might include the following elements.

- The training objective
- The number of people requiring the training
- The timescale or schedule for training
- The method(s) chosen
- Resources (people, machines, space, materials) and support (authorisation, time off) required
- The training budget
- How learning will be measured and assessed (post-training tests, observation or sampling of work, impact on results and so on) and by whom.

3.13   Training programmes may be job based (covering the processes, equipment, relationships and workload of the job itself); skills based (aimed at acquiring or improving a specific skill such as negotiation); or academic or professional (aimed at securing academic or professional qualifications via examination or competence assessment, say).

4   Training methods and delivery

Off-the-job training

4.1   Off-the-job training may be provided by the training department of a larger organisation. In-house training may be used for training in skills relevant to the organisation's particular products and markets, as well as more generic training eg in negotiating, interviewing, teamworking and so on. Off-the-job training may also be provided by external training providers: universities and colleges; private sector training providers and consultants or brokers; and publishers of distance learning programmes.

4.2   Various methods may be used by internal or external training providers.

- **Training room instruction**: similar to on-the-job instruction training, but in a dedicated training environment, using a simulation of workplace equipment and methods.
- **Lectures or taught classes**, which may incorporate elements of instruction, case study, role play and other techniques to overcome the limitations of passive information absorption. The term **bite-sized learning** is given to the trend towards breaking training up into short, varied chunks to facilitate learning.
- The use of **case studies, role plays, in-tray exercises** and so on, to simulate work problems and interpersonal scenarios. These approaches allow trainees to experiment with relevant skills without the risk of doing so on the job.
- **Open learning** or **distance learning**. Employees access technology-assisted instruction where and when it suits them, using training manuals, workbooks, video (and video conferencing for group sessions), tapes, computer-based packages and so on. Some face-to-face tuition may be used periodically to assess or reinforce learning or to add more interactive and group work.
- **Visits and tours**. Trainees are given opportunities to observe other sites, departments, operations and so on.
- **Development centres**. Groups of trainees take part in a varied programme of simulations, role plays and other learning activities, which are facilitated, assessed and fed back by trainers.
- **Outdoor training**. Physical tasks and activities in challenging environments are designed to aid self-awareness and skill development in areas such as motivation, leadership, teamworking and problem-solving. A facilitator aids reflection and analysis of decisions and processes after the event.
- **E-learning** (which we described in an earlier chapter).

The CIPD suggests that e-learning offers benefits including: immediate availability; ease and flexibility of access; consistent message; cost reductions (reduced cost of trainers and trainee time); and easing of tracking of results and course completion. However, in some settings, there may be barriers to e-learning such as poor technology infrastructure, lack of IT skills, poor quality content and lack of employee motivation.

Group training (T-group) methods

4.3 The purposes of group learning are as follows.

- To give each individual a greater insight into his own behaviour and how he appears to other people, via feedback from other group members
- To give an understanding of intra-group processes and dynamics, including communication, influence, leadership and so on
- To develop each individual's skills in controlling and participating in intra-group processes and dynamics
- To develop appreciation and management of diversity, through raising awareness and building relationships between people whose interactions might otherwise be based on prejudices and stereotypes
- To encourage people to learn from each other, sharing knowledge and skills, to build the team and foster a continuous learning orientation

4.4 Group training (using T-groups) is based on 'encounter groups', which allow people to practise their interpersonal skills in a controlled group and receive feedback from group members, guided by a facilitator. The T-group is usually small (8-12 participants), leaderless and unstructured, with no agenda or planned activities. The facilitator draws the group's attention to its behaviour as it struggles to cope with this situation. Participants are encouraged to be more receptive to the feelings, behaviours and needs of others. The main mechanism for learning is feedback received from other members of the group on how an individual is communicating, relating and responding.

4.5 This is a popular tool of **sensitivity training**, which focuses on helping individuals to:

- Understand their own behaviour; gain insight into how others perceive them; and understand the consequences and effects of their behavioural choices
- Develop behavioural flexibility, so that they can adapt their behaviours to the requirements of a particular situation or relationship, in order to gain more effective outcomes (agreement, co-operation and so on).

4.6 One of the theoretical foundations of this approach is the **Johari window**: a framework for developing self-insight which is often used to guide analysis in a T-group process. Individual behaviours are classified according to a matrix (Figure 10.2) according to whether it is known or unknown to the individual himself and known or unknown to others.

Figure 10.2   *The Johari window*

	Known to self	*Unknown to self*
Known to others	**Public**	**Blind**
Unknown to others	**Hidden**	**Unknown**

4.7 One of the key functions of the T-group is to create an atmosphere of openness and trust, so that members can be encouraged:

- To reduce 'blind' behaviours (such as body language or unconscious patterns of relating) by becoming more aware of them through feedback from others

- To reduce 'hidden' behaviours (including feelings and thoughts concealed from others) by appropriate self-disclosure, supported by feedback from the group as to whether they customarily conceal too much or too little about themselves.

On-the-job training methods

4.8 On-the-job training in the workplace is very common, especially where the work involved is not complex. Various methods may be used.

- **Orientation or induction training**: a new person is introduced and integrated into an organisation or team. Induction training is designed: to help new recruits to find their bearings; to begin to socialise them into the culture of the team; to support initial performance; and to identify ongoing training and development needs.
- **'Sitting with Nellie'**: the trainee is placed beside an experienced worker (Nellie) and learns by observing her work and imitating her methods, under supervision, working with the actual materials and equipment involved in the job. (This is less effective if 'Nellie' passes on poor work habits…)
- **Systematic job instruction** can be added to a 'sitting with Nellie' approach, where the skill is not readily amenable to observation and requires explanation.
- **Coaching** is defined by the CIPD as: 'Developing a person's skills and knowledge so that their job performance improves, hopefully leading to the achievement of organisational objectives. It targets high performance and improvement at work, although it may also have an impact on an individual's private life. It usually lasts for a short period and focuses on specific skills and goals.'

  Coaching is a collaborative, results-oriented series of developmental discussions, during which the coach facilitates the coachee in agreeing to learning goals and exploring appropriate methods of (primarily self-directed) learning. The coach is available for teaching, guidance and feedback on progress or attainment, as required. Coaching has also been identified as a *leadership style* which focuses on developing people through a blend of directive and supportive behaviours. Team leaders have many formal and informal opportunities to guide, facilitate, challenge and give feedback on performance and progress.
- **Mentoring** is a longer-term developmental relationship, focused on broader issues of personal or career development. It is typically carried out by a more senior member of the organisation (often not the mentee's immediate manager, so that there is greater freedom to discuss concerns and issues.) A mentor may occupy a role as the individual's 'wise (or critical) friend', teacher or coach, counsellor, role model and supporter or sponsor in the organisation, as the trainee (and the relationship) develops over time. A mentor should help the trainee achieve greater self-awareness; encourage him to formulate and clarify career and personal development goals; and support him in taking responsibility for self-development.
- **Action learning** is a team learning approach, where small groups of people meet to collaboratively tackle real organisational issues or problems facing each of the members. The purpose is for group members to support and learn from one another. A facilitator helps the group to debrief and exchange feedback on the process, so that learning covers both content (the solutions to the problems) and process (how to work together in problem-solving).

4.9 **Experiential learning** (where trainees learn from practising new skills in their own role or experiencing different roles) may be accomplished by a number of methods.

- Practice, feedback, reflection and adjustment (learning by 'trial and error'), using everyday work as a learning and improvement opportunity
- Job rotation or 'work shadowing': the trainee is given different jobs in succession, in order to gain wider experience
- Temporary promotions or 'assistant to' positions: individuals experience or observe more challenging roles
- Project or committee work: trainees might be co-opted to project teams or committees to gain

experience of relevant areas of the organisation's activities, as well as multi-functional team processes and problem-solving.

Choosing the right method

4.10 The most appropriate method should be selected according to the following criteria.

- The nature of the skills, competencies or knowledge to be developed (requiring theoretical knowledge or hands-on practice, say)
- The benefits of learning outside the job context (less risk; less distraction; standardisation; suits theoretical and reflective learners) or within it (relevance to the job, team and environment; better transfer of learning; suits hands-on learners)
- The abilities and learning preferences or styles of the trainees (eg using Honey & Mumford's classification)
- The availability and cost-effectiveness of alternative methods.

4.11 A summary of training methods and their merits is given in Table 10.3.

Table 10.3 *Comparison of some major methods of training*

METHODS	ADVANTAGES	DISADVANTAGES
On-the-job methods		
Sitting with Nellie	• Learning in context • Immediate feedback and adjustment • Establishes relationships as well as skills	• Only as effective as 'Nellie' • Transfers work culture (not necessarily best practice)
Coaching	• Flexibly adjusted to trainee pace and needs • Involves trainee in problem-solving • Learning connected to job performance	• Requires coaching skills
Rotating or shadowing	• Trainees experience responsibility with controlled risk • May increase job satisfaction • Aids management succession planning	• May be perceived as not 'real' work • May be perceived as 'nuisance' by permanent workers
Action learning	• Builds relationships • Addresses real work problems • Builds learning, problem-solving and interpersonal skills	• Requires skilled facilitation
Off-the-job methods		
Training room instruction	• Learning is practical but without pressures of live work • Suits range of learning styles	• Doesn't take into account real work context
Lectures or taught classes	• Suits theorist and reflector styles and subjects based on theory or principles • Suits large numbers of trainees	• Doesn't suit active or pragmatic styles • Difficulty of absorbing large amount of information passively • Relative inflexibility to individual learning needs
Case studies, role plays, simulations	• Allows experimentation without risk • Allows active problem-solving and participation	• May not transfer to real job context • Euphoria of 'getting it right' in training may cause anti-climax at work
Open or distance learning	• Economical, especially where trainees are geographically dispersed • Flexible for learner pace, needs, circumstances	• Only as effective as design of materials and programme • May not suit active or pragmatist styles
Visits and tours	• Aids generalisation and application of learning • Raises awareness of big picture	• Limited depth of content • Limited flexibility to individual learner needs
E-learning	• Economical where hardware and software available • Flexible to trainee pace, needs • Standardised training	• Technology may alienate learners • Learners may not be expert users • May not transfer to real job context

5   Development

5.1   From an individual perspective, development may involve a number of general processes, which may be more or less supported or facilitated by the organisation.

- **Management development** is a range of planned and deliberate development processes designed to improve managerial competence, and to ensure that the organisation has effective managers in place to fulfil its current and future plans
- **Career development** is a range of planned experiences and pathways for career development (and/or advancement) within an organisation, in order to (a) enhance or refresh the intrinsic rewards of work (from the individual's point of view) and (b) identify and develop people with potential for career progression, in order to support management succession planning (from the organisation's point of view).
- **Professional development** is a range of planned development processes aimed at improving performance in an existing job role; improving skills and competencies in readiness for future work roles or organisational change; acquiring transferable skills and competencies for general 'employability' or career change; and maintaining the up-to-date knowledge and technical competence required for membership of a professional body such as CIPS (eg 'continuing professional development' or CPD).
- **Personal development** is a range of processes which support the growth and maturing of the individual towards 'self-actualisation' (the fulfilment of one's personal potential), including continuous capability improvement, learning to learn, growth in self-awareness and emotional competence, and so on. Where the individual takes primary responsibility for identifying and capitalising on opportunities for personal development, this may be referred to as 'self development'.

Management development

5.2   Theories of leadership no longer suggest, as they used to, that 'leaders are born, not made': attention has shifted to how management and leadership skills can be developed. Management development is 'an attempt to improve managerial effectiveness through a planned and deliberate learning process' (Mumford).

5.3   Increasing attention has been focused on systematic management development in recent decades, for a number of reasons.

- Management development can promote improved performance capability – both for the managers *and* for the teams and processes they manage. Managers are responsible for aspects of processes and performance which – arguably – cannot be optimised in any other way.
- Management development supports management succession: a planned pool of promotable individuals who can fill leadership gaps when people are promoted or transferred, retire or leave.
- Organisational support for career development may help the organisation to attract and retain quality managerial talent.

5.4   Management development programmes typically involve some form of formal management education and training – from short skill-based training courses (eg in time management or leadership) to ongoing competence development (eg using in-house or nationally accredited competence frameworks) to the pursuit of formal qualifications such as an MBA. In addition, there is likely to be the use of: performance management (to develop competence through ongoing goal-setting, coaching and mentoring); work experience (eg role shadowing); experiential learning; mentoring; and planned career management.

Career development

5.5   A career may be defined as the pattern of work-related experiences that span the course of a person's working life. Career development processes enable individuals to be intentional about the purpose and direction of their personal development, and their contribution to the work organisation.

5.6   Management development includes career development and succession planning by the organisation, which in turn require attention to a number of issues.

- The types of experience a potential manager will have to acquire: experience in different business functions, for example, or in general (as opposed to functional) management, or in different international divisions.
- The individual's guides and role models in the organisation. Individuals with potential should be encouraged to measure themselves against peers (assessing their own weaknesses and strengths) and emulate desirable role models. This may be formally recognised by the appointment of a mentor, for example.
- The scope and variety of opportunities and challenges offered to the developing employee. Too much responsibility too early can be damagingly stressful, but if there is insufficient challenge, the employee may never be stretched towards his full potential.
- The provision of career management programmes, such as: identification of career paths within the organisation; career planning guidance, information and advice; development programmes; formal mentoring; and help with adjustment to mid-career issues (such as career plateau) and late-career issues (such as approaching retirement).

5.7   The current trend for delayered, decentralised structures has increased the difficulty of creating career opportunities for upward progression. Alternative career moves may have to be considered. These include sideways transfers, secondments to project groups, short external attachments and so on.

Professional development

5.8   Professional and managerial techniques are continually developing, becoming more sophisticated and complex. Professional institutions such as CIPS have formally recognised this situation by providing for their members to keep up to date with developments.

5.9   **Continuing professional development** (CPD) is a self-managed process, with the individual continually reassessing his learning needs in the light of changes, and seeking to meet those needs via available avenues. Membership of a profession requires an undertaking to develop and maintain standards of competence and ethics on an ongoing basis. A team leader may act as a mentor or supervisor for team members' CPD – as well as seeking similar support, guidance and feedback for himself.

5.10   Dobler, Burt & Starling *(World Class Supply Management)* recommend that 'professional purchasing managers should ensure that their personnel receive training on current thinking and techniques in the areas of requirements development, source selection, pricing, cost analysis, negotiation and supplier management, as well as ethical and professional standards.'

5.11   Ethics training may be an important element in professional development of purchasing staff. Dobler *et al* note that 'All members of the procurement system must respect their roles as agents of their employer and must represent the best interest of their organisations.' Relevant personnel should receive periodic training or coaching with respect to the organisation's standards of ethical and professional conduct.

Personal development

5.12 Personal development, taking account of employees' wider needs and aspirations, may seem like an unnecessary luxury, but businesses are increasingly offering employees wider-ranging development opportunities, rather than focusing simply on skills required to do their current job better. The business case argument is that personal development creates more rounded, competent employees, who may contribute more innovatively and flexibly to the organisation's future needs. It may also help to foster job satisfaction, commitment and loyalty, and to create a culture in which learning and flexibility are valued: a learning culture.

5.13 Here are some tools of personal development.

- **Personal development plans** (PDPs) are action plans for people's career development which make employees responsible for seeking and organising learning and development opportunities.
- The use of a **personal development journal (PDJ)** or learning log: a structured approach to using the experiential learning cycle, by reflecting on identified problems and critical incidents (as potential learning needs) in writing. This enables the individual to capture experience; bring blind and unknown behaviours into conscious awareness; analyse the effects of behaviours; and plan to modify unsuccessful behaviours in future.
- **Self-development and support groups,** which meet to discuss personal development and work issues, give each other feedback and so on
- Seeking and using **feedback information**: self-analysis questionnaires, self-appraisal processes, personal SWOT analysis – and so on – to increase self-awareness and identify learning and development needs
- The use of **experiential learning** to turn everyday work experiences into opportunities for reflection, learning and change
- The use of **knowledge sharing** systems, such as the internet and corporate intranet; other people (especially coaches and mentors); and communities of practice.

5.14 Continuous development programmes are often based on the use of negotiated **personal development plans** (PDPs) or **learning contracts**. A PDP is generally prepared by the individual and his line manager. While they may act as a mentor or HR/training manager for guidance, line managers generally retain responsibility for monitoring the learner's progress.

5.15 The role of the mentor or HR advisor (Eric Parsloe & Monika Wray, *Coaching and Mentoring)* will be to: provide guidance on the preparation of the PDP (eg helping to identify learning needs); resourcing self-managed learning (eg offering information about learning opportunities); providing support, guidance, and feedback as required during implementation; and assisting in evaluation (usually carried out by formal evaluation with the line manager or supervisor).

5.16 The process of personal development planning may be summarised as follows.

- **Analyse your current capability profile**; eg using personal SWOT (strengths and weaknesses) analysis; competence review; or self-assessment of learning needs
- **Formulate learning and development goals**
- **Develop an action plan** including: SMART objectives; methods to be used; and timescales and methods for progress review and final evaluation.
- **Agree the action plan as a 'learning contract'** with a coach, mentor or line manager, to promote accountability, and gain assistance with resourcing, monitoring, feedback and evaluation.

6   Evaluating training and development

6.1   It is important that training activities be evaluated in order to ascertain:

- Whether specific training objectives have been met (and therefore whether the processes of planning and delivering training have been effective)
- Whether the training intervention was 'worthwhile', representing a return on the organisation's investment
- What improvements are required – or possible – for the future.

6.2   This process needs to be carried out at various stages of the training process: before training (to check that plans are feasible and cost-effective); during training (so that shortcomings in the plan or its delivery can be adjusted in 'real time' to improve the outcomes); and after training (to appraise its effectiveness and adjust future plans, where required).

The Kirkpatrick model

6.3   Training can be evaluated at different levels, using different criteria. The **Kirkpatrick model** *(Donald Kirkpatrick, Evaluating Training Programmes: the Four Levels)* proposes evaluation at four levels.

- Level 1: **trainee reactions** to the experience can be measured. Verbal feedback or feedback forms and attitude surveys can be used to ask trainees whether the training programme was relevant to their work and whether they found it useful.
- Level 2: **trainee learning** can be measured, to see how far the programme met specific learning objectives. This can be done using post-training competence assessment or testing, and discussion with trainers.
- Level 3: **changes in trainees' job behaviour** and performance can be measured, to measure how far learning has been transferred or applied to on-the-job tasks. This can be done using observation or work sampling, or performance appraisal. For more extensive training projects, a review group (by questionnaire or group discussion) may be used to get input from a sample of training stakeholders.
- Level 4: **performance** can also be monitored at a higher level to assess the impact of training on organisational results and culture. Training may change attitudes to quality, ethics and so on. It may also show a knock-on influence on labour turnover, accident rates and other HR indicators. This is usually reserved for senior management review of training in general.

Cost/benefit analysis

6.4   The costs of training should be compared to the benefits obtained, in a systematic cost/benefit analysis. We mentioned the direct costs of training earlier. However, many of the benefits of training programmes are qualitative rather than quantitative, and are therefore difficult to identify in financial terms.

- Benefits may consist of long-term paradigm shifts and cultural changes (within the workforce, management, customer base or supply chain) which take time to emerge to the point where they offer a measurable return on investment.
- Training tends to have knock-on effects on team spirit, technological change, communication, ideas generation and so on. Added value may accrue in unanticipated areas, which are not being monitored as part of the training validation system and which may be overlooked as training effects.
- Benefits accruing from soft training outcomes such as enhanced motivation, satisfaction and loyalty are difficult to predict and measure accurately.
- There are many variables in job performance and improvement. It may be difficult to attribute quantifiable post-training added value to training effects alone.

Benchmarking: Investors in People (IiP) Learn this!

6.5 The identification of knowledge and skill gaps – particularly in vocational areas – has been a priority of UK governments for some decades, in order to improve the UK's skill base in relation to global competitors. One of the roles of government (and related agencies) is to encourage and facilitate organisational training by stimulating employer demand for skills: researching and promoting the business case for learning and development, and promoting benchmark standards such as Investors in People.

6.6 The Investors in People scheme (IiP) was launched to provide a national benchmark standard for investment in employee training and development. Organisations seeking accreditation under the scheme must audit their current training practice and provision and bring them into line with published standards. The key principles of the standard are set out in Table 10.4.

Table 10.4 *The Investors in People standard*

PRINCIPLE	KEY INDICATORS (RELEVANT TO PERFORMANCE APPRAISAL)	EXAMPLE EVIDENCE REQUIREMENTS
Developing strategies to improve the performance of the organisation	A strategy for improving the performance of the organisation is clearly defined and understood.	People can explain the objectives of the team and organisation, and describe how they are expected to contribute to developing and achieving them.
	Learning and development is planned to achieve the organisation's objectives.	Managers can explain team learning and development needs, how these link to achieving specific team objectives and how the impact will be evaluated.
Taking action to improve the performance of the organisation	Managers are effective in leading, managing and developing people.	Managers can give examples of how they give people constructive feedback on their performance regularly and when appropriate.
	People's contribution to the organisation is recognised and valued.	People can describe how they contribute to the organisation and believe they make a positive difference to its performance.
	People learn and develop effectively.	People can describe how their learning and development needs have been met, what they have learnt and how they have applied this in their role.
Evaluating the impact on the performance of the organisation	Investment in people improves the performance of the organisation.	Managers can give examples of how learning and development has improved the performance of their team and the organisation.
	Improvements are continually made to the way people are managed and developed	Managers can give examples of improvements they have made to the way they manage and develop people.

6.7 Benefits claimed for IiP (or from the involvement, training and development activities arising from it) include: improved staff performance, earnings, productivity and profitability; customer satisfaction; improved staff motivation; reduced costs and wastage (as people constantly examine their work for potential improvements); enhanced quality; public recognition.

6.8 The standard offers organisations the opportunity to review current policies and practices against a recognised benchmark; a framework for planning future strategy and action; and a structured way to improve the effectiveness of training and development activities.

7   Performance management

Performance management

7.1   Performance management is the process by which shortfalls and weaknesses in individual and team performance are identified and addressed through various types of improvement or development intervention, on an ongoing basis.

7.2   Connock *(HR Vision: Building a Quality Workforce)* notes that 'In the late 1980s, the emphasis moved from performance appraisal to performance management. Whilst setting clear and measurable objectives was always a major part of earlier schemes, the emphasis was more on the appraisal of past performance. Under performance management, there is a dual emphasis: on setting key accountabilities, objectives, measures, priorities and time scales for the following review period and on appraising performance at the end of the period.'

7.3   Armstrong *(How to be an even better manager)* provides a useful overview of the performance management process.

'Performance management is a continuous and flexible process which involves managers and those whom they manage acting as partners within a framework which sets out how they can best work together to achieve the required results. It focuses on future performance planning and improvement rather than retrospective performance appraisal. It provides the basis for regular and frequent dialogues between managers and individuals or teams about performance and development needs.'

7.4   There are four key activities in performance management.

- **Preparation of performance agreements** (also known as performance contracts). These set out the individual's or team's objectives, how performance will be measured, the competencies needed to achieve the objectives and the organisation's core values.
- **Preparation of performance and development plans**. These set out identified performance and personal development needs in order for performance agreements to be met.
- **Management of performance throughout the year**. This involves the continuous process of providing feedback on performance; conducting informal progress reviews; and dealing with performance problems as necessary, using interventions such as motivation and reward, counselling, coaching, training and disciplinary action.
- **Performance review and appraisal:** taking a view of an individual's progress to date and reaching an agreement about what should be done in the future. Performance appraisals should be collaborative, problem-solving, developmental discussions – not 'interviews'. They should ideally be separated from performance evaluations for the purposes of setting rewards, in order to remove the potentially judgemental and adversarial element from the discussion, and to keep it developmentally focused. A range of developmental and improvement interventions may result from these reviews, including: counselling, training, disciplinary action, motivation (improvement goals, rewards and incentives) – or problem-solving and adjustment of the work situation, methods and technology.

Performance review and appraisal

7.5   Appraisal may be defined as: 'the regular and systematic review of performance and the assessment of potential, with the aim of producing action programmes to develop both work and individuals.' Appraisals are sometimes referred to as personal development reviews (PDRs).

7.6   In all organisations, the performance of each employee is assessed by someone. Often this is a subjective, *ad hoc* activity carried out by the individual's immediate superior in the course of day-to-day operations. Increasingly, however, organisations are choosing to formalise the assessment and feedback process and use it in a proactive attempt to improve business performance and manage the potential of employees for ongoing skill and career development.

7.7　Different organisations use performance appraisal for different purposes, but the following are some of its potential uses.

- To generate and exchange feedback on individual and team performance, as information for management and to provide feedback for the learning and motivation of the employee
- To appraise past performance in relation to relevant standards in order to determine merit pay awards, or (more generally) to set salary levels for the following period
- To identify potential in the employee for career development, and the planning of management succession in the organisation
- To identify the training and development needs of the individual or team, in order to plan and subsequently evaluate appropriate programmes
- To provide a context for counselling and problem-solving, to resolve any barriers to employee performance
- To aid continuous learning, quality and service improvement, and innovation: providing a context for open discussion of performance issues, and encouraging upward communication to harness employee 'front line' knowledge and commitment

7.8　Note that *systematic* appraisal has key advantages both for the organisation and for its management (information for performance management, development, succession planning and so on) *and* for individual employees (clarity of goals and targets, feedback for learning, reinforcement and reward for motivation, the opportunity to discuss work problems and development needs). It is, in particular, the basis of a needs- and improvements-focused approach to employee training and development, which in turn offers a wide range of performance, competitive and change management benefits to the organisation.

A systematic approach to appraisal

7.9　A typical performance appraisal system would therefore involve the following stages.

- Identification (or review) of criteria for assessment
- Preparation of an appraisal report by the appraisee's manager (and others, where appropriate eg in the case of upward, peer or 360° feedback), giving feedback on the appraisee's performance in relation to relevant assessment criteria
- An appraisal interview, allowing an exchange of views about the results of the assessment, problem solving, target-setting for improvement and so on
- Provision for review of (or appeal against) the appraisal, if required to establish the fairness of the procedure
- Preparation, agreement and implementation of action plans
- Follow-up monitoring of progress

This assessment would typically take place on an annual or six-monthly cycle.

7.10　A systematic approach to appraisal is thus a classic control system, incorporating planning, measurement of performance, comparison of performance against plan, and adjustment of performance or plan in an ongoing cycle (illustrated in Figure 10.3).

Figure 10.3 *Formal appraisal as a control cycle*

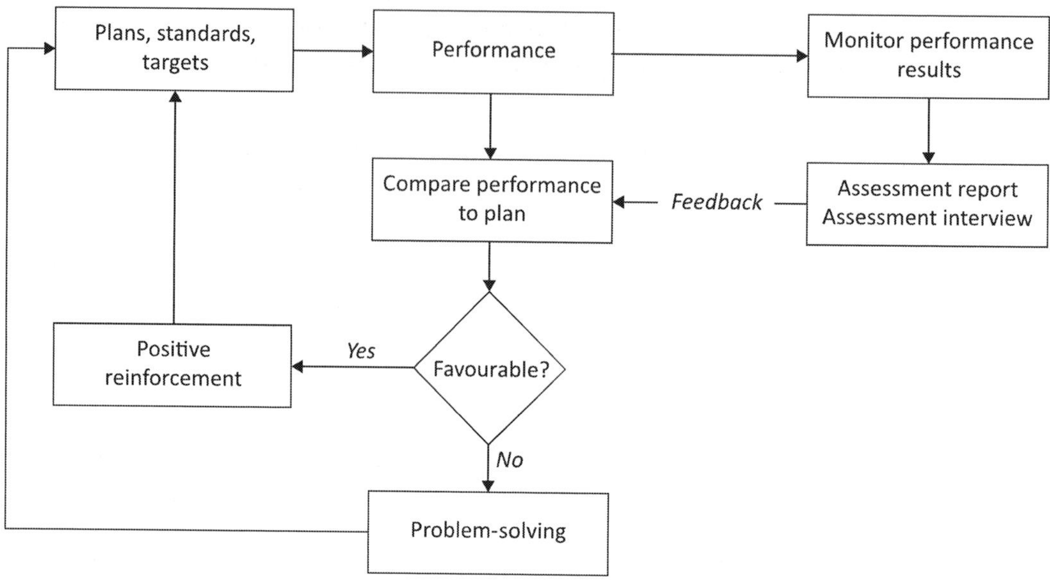

Selecting criteria for review and appraisal

7.11   Relevant criteria for performance appraisal might be based on job, role or competence descriptions; departmental or team plans, performance standards and targets; or individually negotiated goals and targets. In order to support motivation, learning and development, any performance measures should be:

- Meaningful, specific and based on critical success factors in the job
- Measurable: related to objective, observable behaviours and outcomes
- Focused on job performance and results, rather than personal qualities (such as 'reliability' or 'loyalty'): in other words, reflective of the appraisee's contribution to unit and organisational objectives
- Related to areas and outcomes which are within the appraisee's control.

Multi-source feedback on performance

7.12   The most common arrangement is appraisal by the appraisee's immediate superior. The supplier usually has the most detailed knowledge of the tasks carried out by the individual, and their work context, and is therefore in a good position to assess how well the appraisee performed and to appreciate any problems that may have affected performance. The appraisal can then be seen as part of the ongoing process of performance management. However, appraisal by a superior alone, if not well managed, may be liable to unchecked subjective judgements, and may affect (and be affected by) the working relationship between the parties concerned.

7.13   In order to get a more rounded picture of individual performance, feedback assessments may be sought from a range of key stakeholders in the employee's work.

- **Peer appraisal** is useful as an element of a more comprehensive appraisal process, particularly in regard to inter-personal criteria such as ability to work with others, communication, conflict resolution and so on, which can best be assessed by those 'on the receiving end'. This method may be awkward to implement, however, because of co-workers' reluctance to judge or 'betray' a colleague and the work group by conveying negative feedback to management. (Conversely, management may not set a lot of store by positive feedback from colleagues.)
- **Upward appraisal** (by the appraisee's line subordinates) is not widely used, but on the increase. It is

a particularly useful tool for appraising the effect of a manager's leadership style on team members. Again, however, it may be difficult to elicit feedback, because of fears of retribution.

- **Internal customer appraisal** may be relevant in purchasing and supply, to assess the quality of service and relationship management provided to other departments. Internal customer satisfaction should be a key performance measure.
- **Appraisal of buyer performance by suppliers** may be particularly useful feedback, since it may be important for the organisation to maintain 'good customer' status (and the benefits it brings) with key suppliers. Suppliers will be in a good position to provide feedback on the effectiveness and efficiency of contracting, negotiation, contract and relationship management, and so on. However, again, it may be difficult to gather meaningful feedback if suppliers are reluctant to alienate a buyer on whom they rely for business.

7.14   **Multi-source appraisal (360-degree feedback)** is based on the recognition that the employee's immediate boss is not the only (or necessarily the best) person to assess his performance. It is designed to enable a range of stakeholders in a person's performance (including the appraisee) to comment and give feedback. The information is usually collected (anonymously, where appropriate) through questionnaires.

7.15   The advantage of multi-source feedback is that it offers a rounded picture of an employee's performance. It gives a more complete and relevant assessment and reduces the risk of bias. It also increases the amount and openness of task and performance-related communication in the organisation.

The appraisal interview

7.16   In an influential analysis, NRF Maier (1958) suggested that there are three basic approaches to appraisal interviewing.

- In the **tell and sell** method, the appraiser tells the individual how his performance has been assessed, and then tries to gain acceptance of the evaluation and improvement plans. This approach requires unusual interpersonal skills on the part of the appraiser, in order to overcome judgement (by the appraiser) and passivity (by the appraisee); convey feedback in a constructive manner; and motivate forward-looking behavioural change.
- In the **tell and listen** method, the appraiser tells the individual how his performance has been assessed, and then invites comments. The appraiser no longer dominates the entire interview, and there is some opportunity for improvement counselling, rather than mere direction. The appraisee is encouraged to participate in the review and the development of improvement targets and methods. This approach recognises that the appraisee's skill or motivation may not be the sole source of performance shortfalls: the interview is an opportunity to gather helpful feedback about barriers arising from job design, methods and so on.
- In the **problem-solving** approach, the appraiser abandons the role of judge altogether, and becomes a performance coach, counsellor and learning facilitator. The interview is a two-way dialogue, focused not on assessment of past performance, but on future solutions to the individual's work issues, performance barriers and proactive suggestions for improvements. The individual is encouraged to recognise problems, think solutions through, and commit to learning and improvement. Such an approach is more forward-looking, participative, developmental and satisfying to both parties. It may also stimulate creative problem-solving.

7.17   Maier argued that many organisations waste the opportunity represented by performance management for upward communication and organisational learning and development. A development-focused organisation should harness the aspirations and abilities of its employees by taking the opportunity to ask positive and thought-provoking questions such as: Could any changes be made in your job which might result in improved performance? Do you have any skills, knowledge, or aptitudes which could be made better use of in the organisation?

Giving feedback

7.18   In addition to (and as part of) these formal performance management approaches, managers have a key role in giving performance feedback to team members. As we saw in Chapter 4, feedback may be of two broad types.

- **Motivational** feedback (praise, encouragement) is given to acknowledge, reward and encourage positive behaviour or performance by the team member. Its aim is to boost the team member's confidence.
- **Developmental** feedback (constructive criticism, coaching or counselling) is given when an area of the team member's performance requires improvement, helping the individual to identify the problem and plan for change. Its aim is to increase the team member's competence.

Chapter summary

- The main purpose of training and development is to raise competence and therefore performance standards. It is also concerned with the personal development needs of employees, facilitating and motivating them to fulfil their potential.
- Benefits of effective training and development should accrue for both employees and organisation, but depend (to an extent) on the 'focus' with which training needs are identified, enabling training resources to be justified and targeted at relevant, performance-enhancing areas.
- A systematic approach to training includes: analysing training needs; formulating training objectives; selecting, planning and implementing training methods and media which take into account the needs of the organisation, task and trainees; and monitoring and evaluating the results of training.
- Training needs may be identified as a result of change or critical incidents; set out in standards or competence frameworks; self-assessed by employees; or systematically analysed using job analysis and skill audits.
- A wide range of training methods, media and technologies is available. They may be broadly divided into on- and off-the-job approaches. On-the-job approaches have the key advantage of immediate relevance to the work context, and high transfer of learning. Off-the-job approaches have the key advantage of removing the risk, pressure and distractions of the work context from the learning process.
- Development is a process whereby employees gain experience; receive instruction and guidance from superiors; enhance their ability and potential through training and education; set career goals; and access the opportunities open to them in the organisation.
- Performance management is the process by which shortfalls and weaknesses in individual and team performance are identified and addressed through various types of improvement or development intervention, on an ongoing basis. It includes formal and informal processes of employee performance appraisal.

Self-test questions

Numbers in brackets refer to the paragraphs where you can check your answers.

1   Distinguish between learning, training and development. (1.1)

2   List stages in a systematic approach to planned training programmes. (Figure 10.1)

3   List ways in which employee development supports flexibility and change management. (2.7)

4   What are the benefits of training and development for the individual? (2.9)

5   What are the processes involved in training needs analysis? (3.4)

6   List typical elements in a training plan. (3.12)

7   What are the purposes of group learning? (4.3)

8   List on-the-job training methods. (4.8)

9 What is continuing professional development? (5.9)

10 What are the four levels of evaluation in the Kirkpatrick model? (6.3)

11 What are the four key activities in performance management? (7.4)

CHAPTER 11

The Regulatory Framework

Assessment criteria and indicative content

Develop a recruitment and selection plan to meet the skills and knowledge needs of the procurement and supply function

- The regulatory aspects of the employment of personnel in the procurement and supply function

  — Forms of discrimination and harassment
  — Legislative regulation on employment practices

Section headings

1. The legal framework on employment
2. Equal opportunity
3. Health and safety
4. Employment rights
5. Employment protection

Introduction

In this chapter we look at the various laws and regulations which affect the relationship between employers and their employees. (Of course, there are many other legal aspects to purchasing and supply management, but they are beyond the scope of this syllabus.)

There are increasing legal and political constraints on managerial decision-making in these areas, aimed at: protecting employees from bias, discrimination and exploitation in accessing and retaining employment opportunities; protecting employees from health and safety risks at work; and so on. In recent years, the social policy of the European Union has added momentum to this trend: European Directives are still being enacted into the law of member states in the areas of equal opportunities, industrial democracy and employment rights. Some issues are very current: there is brand new legislation in areas such as sex discrimination and age discrimination, for example. You will need to keep an eye out for regular updates on the CIPS student website, as the requirements change. And if you are based outside the EU, you should research your local legislation covering this area of the syllabus.

In this chapter, we consider why the legal environment is particularly important for change management. We then look at recent and forthcoming legislation in the areas specifically mentioned in the syllabus.

1 The legal framework on employment

1.1 The legal environment consists of legislation, regulations, voluntary codes of practice and other requirements formulated by governments (by enacting legislation or statutes), courts (by setting legal 'precedents' or case law) and regulatory bodies.

1.2 This is a particularly important area for environmental monitoring and change management because:

- The organisation's response is not 'optional' or left to managerial discretion: compliance is required and enforced by various sanctions and penalties
- The requirements are constantly changing, as courts and tribunals define them through their decisions, and as legislators and regulatory bodies issue new provisions and amendments.

1.3 Legal provisions affect businesses in many areas: fair trading and competition; contracts; data protection and privacy; copyright and intellectual property; incorporation and corporate governance; financial reporting; and so on. However, this syllabus focuses on recent developments in **employment law**: laws and regulations on equal pay, equal opportunities and diversity, health and safety at work, working hours and conditions, employment protection rights and so on.

EU Employment Directives

1.4 In addition to UK legislation (Acts of Parliament) and related regulation, there is a wide range of EU employment-related directives. These are still in the process of being enacted into the law of member states, including the UK – so this in an area worth continual monitoring. Some of the key directives are summarised in Table 11.1.

Table 11.1 *EU employment directives*

SUBJECT	IMPLEMENTED IN UK	RELEVANT UK LEGISLATION
Safeguarding employees' rights in transfers of undertakings and businesses	1979	Transfer of Undertakings (Protection of Employment) Regulations 1981 [TUPE]
Employer's obligation to inform employees of conditions relevant to the contract or employment relationship	1993	Employment Rights Act 1996
Organisation of working time	1996	Working Time Regulations 1998
Establishment of European Works Councils or procedures for informing and consulting employees	1999	Transnational Information and Consultation of Employees Regulations (1999)
Parental leave	1999	Maternity and Parental Leave etc Regulations 1999
Part-time work	2000	Part-time Workers (Prevention of Less Favourable Treatment) Regulations 2000
Equal treatment in employment and occupation	2006	The Equality Act 2010

Impact of employment and equal opportunities legislation

1.5 The 'positive influence' of employment and equal opportunities legislation on the management of the purchasing function can be seen from a number of points of view: that of management (how has legislation made the task easier?); the organisation (how has it improved performance?); and the employee (how has it improved the quality of working life?).

1.6 Several arguments may be cited for the positive influence of such legislation, from each of these viewpoints.

- It enhances the ability of the organisation to attract and retain quality, skilled staff, by broadening the labour pool and creating a positive employer brand and climate for a diverse workforce.

- It enhances the appeal of the organisation and its brands to an increasingly diverse consumer base, by making the organisation more representative of its market.
- It supports fairness and justice in the workplace. This is not a purely ethical issue, since enhanced rights for employees are also intended to be beneficial for management and organisations: consultation with employee representatives on issues of concern, for example, can facilitate change management and foster innovation and problem-solving.
- It provides minimum standards of protection for all parties in the workplace eg in regard to health and safety at work, and reduced compliance risk.
- It enables individuals (including managers) to develop work/life balance eg through family-friendly policies and the right to request flexible working.
- It creates transparency within organisations, in the interest of stakeholders and the general public.
- It supports managerial decision-making, policy development and compliance. Stakeholder consultation, legislative provisions and related Codes of Practice give purchasing managers clear guidelines for good practice within the employment relationship.

1.7 Having made this case, however, it is important to acknowledge the counter-arguments of: the costs and administrative burden of compliance (increased bureaucracy, legal advice); the cost of increased worker rights and entitlements; loss of managerial prerogative (managers' right to manage), particularly in crisis situations; changes to managerial and organisation culture as a result of diversity; potential for 'over-sensitive' claims and conflicts; and so on. UK business has long favoured voluntary self-regulation over legislation, but as the recent introduction of age discrimination and sexual harassment provisions show, legislation is sometimes necessary to enforce good practice…

2 Equal opportunity

2.1 'Equal opportunity' in an employment context means that everyone has a fair chance of getting a job, accessing training and benefits and competing for promotion, regardless of individual differences or minority status. It is, effectively, non- or anti-discrimination.

The previous legal framework

2.2 In the UK, the legal framework on discrimination included several core statutes in particular areas of discrimination: that is, in relation to particular 'protected characteristics'.

- The **Sex Discrimination Act 1975** (and subsequent amendments) outlawed discrimination in employment by reason of sex, marital status, and change of sex or gender reassignment.
- The **Race Relations Act** 1976 (and many subsequent amendments) covered discrimination on grounds of colour, race, nationality, and ethnic or national origin.
- The **Employment Equality (Religion and Belief) Regulations 2003** prohibited discrimination on the grounds of religion or belief. Organisations are still working out the full implications of these provisions in practice, but they may raise issues such as: handling requests for time off for religious observances and holidays; rights to wear religious head-gear and symbols (which may conflict with corporate dress codes); protection from religious harassment and vilification (including offensive jokes) and so on. Some proactive organisations have gone further: for example, setting aside space for prayer and providing kosher and halal meals in corporate canteens.
- The **Disability Discrimination Act 2005** made it unlawful for an employer (with more than 20 employees) to discriminate against a disabled person in deciding whom to interview or employ, or in the terms of the employment offer; in the terms of employment and the opportunities for promotion, transfer, training or other benefits; in decisions relating to redundancy and dismissal.
- The **Employment Equality (Age) Regulations 2006** outlaw direct discrimination (for example, not providing medical insurance to employees aged 50 or older), indirect discrimination (for example, requiring all new recruits to take a health and fitness test which older people may find more difficult to pass) and harassment on grounds of age.

The Equality Act 2010

2.3 After years of review and planning, the complex and varying protections given by all the above legislation have been harmonised and consolidated within a major new piece of legislation: the Equality Act 2010. This Act provides a cross-cutting legislative framework: 'to protect the rights of individuals and advance equality of opportunity for all; to update, simplify and strengthen the previous legislation; and to deliver a simple, modern and accessible framework of discrimination law which protects individuals from unfair treatment and promotes a fair and more equal society.'

2.4 One of the key aims of the Act is to make discrimination law easier to understand and comply with, removing unnecessary burdens on organisations in order to support economic recovery in the wake of the 2009 recession. It applies to discrimination in relation to the full range of protected characteristics: age, disability, gender reassignment, marriage and civil partnership, pregnancy and maternity, race, religion and belief, sex and sexual orientation.

Forms of discrimination and harassment

2.5 There are five basic types of unlawful discrimination under the legislation.

- **Direct discrimination**: where a job applicant, employee or former employee is treated less favourably than another because of a protected characteristic.
- **Indirect discrimination**: where an employer does something which has (or would have) a worse impact on people with a protected characteristic than on people who do not have that characteristic – *unless* they can show that what they have done, or intend to do, is *objectively justified.* (For example, an employer may offer applicants for a job one time for interview, and an observant Muslim might not be able to attend at the allocated time, for reasons of religious observance. Unless the employer can objectively justify the lack of flexibility, this may be indirect discrimination because of religion or belief. Similar examples might concern changing shift patterns to include early morning starts, which would disadvantage women responsible for child care.)
- **Victimisation**: where a person is treated badly because they have complained about discrimination, or have done anything to uphold their own or someone else's equality law rights. (For example, if an employer refuses to shortlist a qualified person for a job interview, because he had accused the employer of discriminating against him in the past.)
- **Harassment**: an employer must not harass a job applicant, employee or former employee. Harassment is defined as unwanted conduct which violates a person's dignity, or creates an intimidating, hostile, degrading, humiliating or offensive environment for a person.
- **Discrimination arising from disability**: a new definition, where an employer treats a disabled person unfavourably because of something connected to their disability, if (a) they cannot show that the treatment is objectively justified and (b) they knew or could reasonably have been expected to know that the applicant is a disabled person.

2.6 There are several legitimate **exceptions** to these provisions.

- If an employer can show that a particular protected characteristic is central to a particular job (a **genuine occupational requirement**), they can insist that only someone who has that particular protected characteristic is suitable for the job. Examples might be authenticity in dramatic performance; reasons of decency or privacy (eg same-sex counsellors or changing-room attendants); or reasons of legal or customary restrictions (eg in work outside the UK).
- An employer can take into account a protected characteristic where *not* doing so would break another law. (For example, a driving school would have to reject a 19-year-old applicant on the basis of age, because driving instructors must by law be over 21.)
- An employer can take protected characteristics into account if there is a need to safeguard national security.
- If an employer is a religion or belief organisation, it may require a job applicant to hold a particular

religion or belief, or (in the case of posts such as a minister of religion) to have or not have a particular protected characteristic, where this is necessary to avoid conflict with the strongly held religious convictions of a significant number of followers.

- Other organisations, such as educational establishments, and the civil and armed services, may be able to require particular characteristics (eg woman teachers, or people of a specific nationality).

2.7 The legislation does *not* permit **positive discrimination**: actions which give preference to people with protected characteristics, regardless of genuine suitability or qualification for the job. However:

- *Disabled people* may be treated more favourably than non-disabled people, in acknowledgement of the additional barriers to work that they face
- The act encourages **voluntary positive action**: steps taken by an employer to encourage people from groups experiencing disadvantage or low participation to take up employment opportunities, including jobs, training, promotion, transfer or other development opportunities.

Specific provisions

2.8 In regard to **recruitment and selection**, employers:

- Must avoid all forms of discrimination in all aspects of recruitment, and make reasonable adjustments for disabled people
- May take 'positive action' to encourage people from groups with a track record of disadvantage or low participation to apply for jobs
- May not ask job applicants about their health or any disability, until they have been offered the job (outright or conditionally). Questions are only permissible if they are asked to support reasonable adjustments for the recruitment process; if they relate directly to a person's ability to carry out a core function of the job; or if a specific impairment is an occupational *requirement* (eg if the employer wants to recruit a Deafblind project worker with personal experience of Deafblindness)
- May not refuse to employ a woman because she is pregnant, suffering pregnancy-related illness, or on maternity leave; and may not ask a woman whether she intends to have children, whatever her age or marital status. (This should not be taken into account in deciding suitability for the job.)

2.9 In regard to **working hours, flexible working and time off**, employment law sets out people's rights to rest breaks; annual leave; paternity, maternity, adoption and parental leave; family emergency leave; time off for public duties and trade union responsibilities; and the right to request flexible working arrangements (part-time, term-time, working from home some of the time, working flexi-hours and so on) and have those requests seriously considered. From the point of view of *equality* law, employers:

- Must avoid all forms of discrimination when making decisions about what hours an employee should work, whether to allow them to work flexibly and when to allow them time off
- Must make reasonable adjustments for disabled people
- Must objectively justify any inflexibility in regard to working hours, where requests for changes relate to religion and belief (eg breaks for prayer times)
- Must not treat people less favourably if sickness absence is related to disability or pregnancy
- Must not discriminate (eg on the grounds of sexual orientation or age) in responding to requests for maternity, paternity, adoption or parental leave.

2.10 In regard to **pay and benefits**, employers:

- Must avoid all forms of discrimination in decisions on pay and benefits
- Must apply objective criteria (such as market rate for the job, skills and qualification or performance in the job) fairly.

2.11 In regard to **career development (training, promotions, and transfers)**, employers:

- Must avoid all forms of discrimination in all aspects of career development, and make reasonable adjustments for disabled people

- Must not stop someone doing training because they are pregnant or on maternity leave, unless a specific risk to health and safety has been identified
- Must not deny someone access to promotion opportunities because they are pregnant or on maternity leave.

2.12 Further detailed provisions are made in relation to additional management issues such as:

- Access to facilities (eg prayer rooms or breast-feeding facilities)
- The non-discriminatory application of dress codes
- The non-discriminatory use of appraisal, performance management and disciplinary procedures
- The application of procedures and decisions regarding dismissal, redundancy (eg selection for redundancy) and retirement.

Remedies for discrimination

2.13 If a job applicant, employee or former employee believes they have been discriminated against, they have three potential courses of action.

- Complaining informally to the employer
- Using the formal grievance procedures of the organisation or – if the issue requires escalation
- Making a claim to the Employment Tribunal, within three months (less one day) of the alleged discrimination. The burden of proof lies first on the claimant to convince the Tribunal that discrimination has taken place. The burden then shifts to the employer, to show that they did *not* in fact discriminate.

2.14 The main remedies available to the Tribunal, where unlawful discrimination is found, are as follows.

- To make a declaration that the employer has discriminated
- To award compensation for financial loss suffered and/or injury to feelings
- To make a recommendation requiring the employer to act within a certain time to remove or reduce the bad effects on the claimant.

Equality policy

2.15 In addition to responding to legislative provisions, many employers have begun proactively to address the underlying problems of equal opportunities. The formulation and promotion of an effective equal opportunities and diversity policy requires buy-in from key stakeholders.

2.16 Implementing an effective policy may require any of the following measures.

- Analysing the business environment, to determine whether and how far the organisation reflects the population and the customer base
- Carefully defining diversity and its business benefits
- Appointing equal opportunities champions at a senior level to put issues higher on the corporate agenda, and ensuring that diversity values are included in corporate strategy
- Establishing a representative working party to formulate policies and codes of practice
- Communicating and promoting the policy, involving staff at all levels (diversity handbook, awareness training, discussion groups, mentoring schemes, training, intranet pages and so on)
- Supporting implementation of the policy through HR processes: including diversity in selection criteria, training and coaching (especially for leaders), career management and reward
- Monitoring and benchmarking progress at regular intervals (diversity score cards, employee surveys, statutory monitoring and reporting where required).

Equality in practice

2.17 **Flexible policies** on working hours and career shapes facilitate employment for women with family responsibilities. Under the Employment Act 2002, mothers and fathers of children under six years of age (or disabled children under 18) have the right to request a flexible working arrangement. Flexible hours, part-time working, term-time or annual- hours contracts (to allow for school holidays) may be used. Career-break and return-to-work schemes may be developed, including training for women-returners. The provision of workplace childcare facilities is another possibility for larger organisations.

2.18 The **accelerated development** of women and minority groups can be achieved by fast-tracking school leavers (as well as graduates) and posting managerial vacancies internally, giving more opportunities for movement up the ladder for groups currently at lower levels of the organisation. Positive action may be taken to train disadvantaged groups, or to encourage them to undertake training in which they have previously been under-represented (the one area in which positive discrimination is permissible). The Metropolitan Police, for example, piloted a scheme of pre-training training (in literacy, numeracy, current affairs, physical fitness and interpersonal skills) to prepare applicants from minority groups to compete on an equal basis for training places.

2.19 In the area of **disability**, similar positive action policies may include the provision of wheelchair access, braille or large-print versions of documentation, text-based telecommunications systems, interpreters and so on.

2.20 More generally, many organisations attempt to address underlying discriminatory attitudes and behaviours: offering awareness and/or sensitivity training to educate managers and staff on the nature and effects of discriminatory or harassing behaviour; establishing counselling and disciplinary frameworks to manage offensive behaviours; and perhaps offering assertiveness training for women and minority groups.

3   Health and safety

3.1 Wider attention has been given to health and safety issues, with consumer demand for social responsibility by organisations (underpinned by the competitive need to attract and retain quality labour) and widespread exposure of abuses through disasters such as the Bhopal chemical plant and Piper Alpha oil rig explosions. So why should organisations plan for health and safety at work?

- To protect people from pain and suffering (obviously, we hope)
- To comply with relevant legal and policy standards
- To minimise the costs of accidents and ill-health (including disruption to work, sickness benefits, repairs, replacement staff, legal claims etc)
- To enhance their ability to attract and retain quality staff
- To avoid negative PR and enhance their employer brand and reputation for corporate social responsibility.

The management of health and safety

3.2 Under the Health and Safety at Work Act 1974, every employer has a general duty to ensure the health, safety and welfare at work of all employees, so far as is reasonably practicable. Various aspects of this responsibility, included in the Act and subsequent Regulations, are set out in Table 11.2.

Table 11.2 *Employer and employee duties in managing health and safety*

EMPLOYEE'S DUTIES	EMPLOYER'S DUTIES
Health And Safety At Work Act 1974	
• To take reasonable care of himself and others affected by his acts or omissions at work • To cooperate with the employer in carrying out his duties (including enforcing safety rules) • Not to interfere intentionally or recklessly with any machinery or equipment provided in the interests of health and safety	• To provide safe systems (work practices) • To provide a safe and healthy work environment (well-lit, warm, ventilated, hygienic and so on) • To maintain all plant and equipment to a necessary standard of safety • To support safe working practices with information, instruction, training and supervision • To consult with safety representatives appointed by a recognised trade union • To appoint a safety committee to monitor safety policy if asked to do so • To communicate safety policy and measures to all staff, clearly and in writing
The Management Of Health And Safety At Work Regulations 1992	
• To inform the employer of any situation which may pose a danger	• To carry out risk assessment, generally in writing, of all work hazards, on a continuous basis • To introduce controls to reduce risks • To assess the risks to anyone else affected by their work activities • To share hazard and risk information with other employers, including those on adjoining premises, other site occupiers and all subcontractors entering the premises • To initiate or revise safety policies in the light of the above • To identify employees who are especially at risk (other legislation cites pregnant women, young workers, shift-workers and part-time workers) • To provide fresh and appropriate training in safety matters • To provide information to employees (including temporary workers) about health and safety • To employ competent safety and health advisers.
Health And Safety (Consultation With Employees) Regulations 1996	
	• To consult all employees on health and safety matters (such as the planning of health and safety training, changes in equipment or procedures which may substantially affect health and safety at work, or the health and safety consequences of introducing new technology)

4 Employment rights

Working hours, break and leave entitlements

4.1 The Working Time Regulations require that workers cannot be required to work more than 48 hours per week on average (the average being calculated over a 17-week period), unless the worker has agreed to this voluntarily, in writing.

4.2 For young workers (aged 15–18), the Regulations require that they cannot be made to work more than eight hours per day or 40 hours per week. These limits apply to every day and every week, ie they are not calculated by means of an average over a longer period. There are limited exceptions to the rules.

4.3 Adult workers are entitled to 24 hours off in each seven-day period, and at least 20 minutes uninterrupted rest break if their working day is longer than six hours. Young workers are entitled to two days off in each seven-day period, and 30 minutes rest if their working day is over four-and-a-half hours long.

4.4 All workers are entitled to paid leave (holiday), from the day they start work, at the rate of one-twelfth of their annual entitlement per month worked. From April 2009, annual paid leave entitlement is 28 days (up from the previous level of 20 days).

Maternity and paternity rights

4.5 Parenthood rights are extensive and complex, and a purchasing manager should ideally seek specialist advice.

- **Maternity rights** include the right not to be discriminated against or dismissed on grounds of pregnancy or childbirth; the right to statutory maternity leave (52 weks, up to 39 weeks of which can be paid); the right for a mother to return to work after maternity leave; the right to Statutory Maternity Pay (SMP); and time-off for ante-natal care.
- **Paternity rights** include: Statutory Paternity Leave (two weeks); and Paternity Pay
- **Statutory adoption leave** (52 weeks) is available for parents adopting a child (provided that they have worked continuously for the current employer for at least 26 weeks before being matched with a child by the adoption agency)

Flexible working arrangements

4.6 Anyone can ask their employer for flexible working arrangements, but the law (Employment Act 2002; Work & Families Act 2007) provides some employees with the statutory right to have such a request considered:

- If they have worked continuously for the employer for 26 weeks and have not made a similar request within the last 12 months *and*
- If they have, or expect to have, parental responsibility of a child under 7, or a disabled child under 18 (who is receiving a disability living allowance)
- If they are the carer for an adult spouse, partner, near relative or someone who lives at the same address.

4.7 The request must be made in writing, and may cover hours of work, times of work and place of work (eg working at home part of the time), and may include requests for different patterns of work (eg shifts).

4.8 Under the law, employers must 'seriously consider' an application, and only reject it if there are legitimate business, economic or technical reasons for doing so. (The right is to *ask* for flexible working – not to obtain it...)

Employment Act 2002 

4.9 The Employment Act 2002 (and subsequent amendments including the Dispute Resolution Regulations 2004) is a wide-ranging package, covering a number of issues which may be relevant to managers. The main provisions are listed in Table 11.3.

Table 11.3 *Employment Act 2002*

Support for working parents (and enabling businesses to retain their skills)	• Rights of working parents and carers to request flexible working arrangements, and have their request 'seriously considered' • A new right for fathers and adoptive parents to paternity and adoption leave and pay – as well as improved maternity rights and pay.
Dispute resolution in the workplace	• Encouraging internal resolution of workplace disputes, by introducing minimum internal disciplinary and grievance procedures, and encouraging employees to raise grievances with their employer before applying to an employment tribunal. • Requiring information about disciplinary and grievance procedures to be included in written particulars of employment • Altering the way unfair dismissals are judged, so that – provided the dismissal is otherwise fair – minor procedural shortcomings by the employer will not be penalised. • Providing for more efficient delivery of employment tribunal services.
Fixed-term workers (supporting flexible working)	• The right of fixed-term employees to get at least the same pay and conditions as similar permanent employees working for the same employer – unless the employer can justify different treatment. • Limits on the use of successive fixed-term contracts (ie really a permanent job)

Employment Relations Act 2004

4.10 The Employment Relations Act 2004 came into force in stages between October 2004 and 2005. It is another broad-ranging package of provisions in regard to collective labour law and trade union rights (amending the Employment Rights Act 1999: a useful reminder that legislation is constantly being reviewed and updated...), including:

- Measures to improve the statutory union recognition procedure: clarifying 'topics' for collective bargaining; providing for earlier communication between unions and workers; and protecting workers from intimidation during ballots for recognition or de-recognition
- Extending the protection against dismissal of employees taking official, lawfully organised industrial action
- Measures to improve some individual employment rights (eg clarifying the role of the 'companion' in grievance and disciplinary hearings).

5 Employment protection

Termination of employment

5.1 Termination of employment is not explicitly mentioned in the syllabus. It certainly comes under the heading of 'regulatory aspects of the employment of personnel', however, and is a major issue in human resource management, since the HR plan may require the reduction of a labour surplus as well as recruitment to meet a labour shortage.

5.2 Employees may leave an organisation voluntarily or by agreement, through resignation, the end of a fixed-term contract or retirement. However, where they are *required* to leave employment, there is a need to protect their rights and livelihoods against injustice or exploitation by employers. This is where employment protection legislation applies. The main legal provisions cover *dismissal* and *redundancy*.

5.3 **Dismissal** is the termination of an employee's contract by an employer, with or without notice, including the ending of a fixed-term contract without renewal on the same terms. If an employer terminates the contract of employment by *giving notice*, the period of notice given must not be less than the statutory minimum or the express terms of the employment contract – whichever is greater.

5.4 Rare circumstances may justify 'summary' or instant dismissal, without notice. The law protecting employees from 'unfair' dismissal requires that summary dismissal be limited to cases of serious breaches of contract, such as gross misconduct (theft, violence, open refusal to obey reasonable instructions, endangerment of other staff), or serious neglect of duties, breaches of trust or conflicts of interest affecting the organisation's business. Even then, the onus is on employers to justify fair dismissal.

5.5 A claim for **wrongful dismissal** is open to employees at common law in the UK, if they can show that they were dismissed in breach of contract (for example, with less than the required notice, or 'without just cause or excuse') and that they thereby suffered loss. Damages may be claimed to compensate for the loss: payment for the entitlement to notice, balance of wages due under a fixed-term contract and so on. In practice, such claims are less common now that *unfair* dismissals offer wider remedies.

5.6 Under the Employment Rights Act 1996 (and some provisions of the Employment Relations Act 1999) every employee who is under the normal retiring age and has been continuously employed for one year, whether full-time or part-time, has the statutory right not to be **unfairly dismissed**.

5.7 There are five basic reasons on which the employer may rely in order to justify a dismissal as *fair*.

- Lack of capability or qualifications to perform the work (provided that adequate training and warnings have been given)
- Misconduct (provided that warnings suitable to the offence have been given)
- Redundancy (provided that the selection method used was fair)
- Legal impediment: the employee could not continue to work in the position without breaking a legal duty or restriction
- Some other 'substantial' reason, such as marriage to a competitor or refusal to accept re-organisations made in the interests of the business and with the agreement of other employees.

5.8 Dismissal is automatically deemed *unfair* if the cause given for the dismissal is because of:

- Unfair selection for redundancy
- Actual or proposed membership of a trade union, or trade union activities
- Transfer of the undertaking (unless there are ETO – economic, technical or organisational – reasons for it), under the Transfer of Undertakings (Protection of Employment) or TUPE regulations
- Pregnancy, unless by reason of it the employee becomes incapable of doing her work adequately
- Actions taken to avert danger to health and safety at work, or to enforce statutory employment rights (eg equal pay)
- Industrial action during the first eight weeks of a dispute, under the Employment Rights Act 1999
- Disclosing information which the employee believed exposed malpractice, injustice or health and safety dangers at work (ie 'whistleblowing'), under the Public Interest Disclosure Act 1998

5.9 To claim unfair dismissal, the employee must show that he is a qualifying employee and that he has in fact been dismissed. The onus is then on the employer to state the principal reason for dismissal, justify its reasonableness, and show that formal warnings were issued, training given, proper investigations and record keeping carried out and fair dismissal procedures followed (with rights of appeal and so on) – although some of these procedural requirements may be relaxed under the Employment Act 2002.

5.10 The Employment Tribunal to which a complaint of unfair dismissal is made may order various remedies, including *reinstatement* (giving the employee his old job back), *re-engagement* (giving him a job comparable to his old one) and *compensation*: a basic award, calculated on the same scale as redundancy pay, a compensatory award for any additional loss (earnings, benefits), and a punitive additional award, for example if the employer has unreasonably failed to comply with a reinstatement or re-engagement order. The Employment Relations Act 1999 raised the ceiling for unfair dismissal awards – and provided that there should be *no* limit on compensation pay-outs for employees dismissed as 'whistle blowers'.

Redundancy

5.11   In the UK, redundancy is defined as dismissal:

- Where the employer has ceased to carry on the business
- Where the employer has ceased to carry on the business in the place where the employee was employed
- Where the requirements of the business for employees to carry out work of a particular kind have ceased or diminished, or are expected to
- For reasons 'not related to the individual concerned'.

5.12   Redundant employees are entitled to compensation in the form of *redundancy pay*, for loss of security – and to encourage them to accept redundancy without damage to employee relations. However, they are not entitled to compensation if they are of pension age or over, or if the employer has made a 'suitable' offer of alternative employment which they have 'unreasonably' rejected.

5.13   From a purely humane point of view, it is obviously desirable to consult with employees or their representatives and to give warning of impending redundancies. Beyond this, the employer has a statutory duty to consult with any trade union which is independent and recognised by the employer for the purposes of collective bargaining. If there is no such trade union, the employer must invite (and, where necessary, train and arrange for) elected employee representatives to receive information.

5.14   Consultation must begin 'at the earliest opportunity', defined as a minimum of 90 days before the first dismissal of 100 or more employees at any one establishment, or 30 days before the first dismissal of between ten and 99 employees. It must cover reasons for dismissals, numbers employed and numbers to be dismissed, and the period over which the dismissals will take place. It must also cover not just those who are going to be made redundant, but those affected by the dismissals – for example, those who may have to take on extra duties.

5.15   Redundant employees have further rights to 'reasonable' time off work with pay to look for another job or arrange training, to accept alternative work offered by the employer for an agreed trial period and to refuse that work (if unsuitable) at the end of the trial period without prejudice to redundancy pay.

5.16   There are various approaches to selection for redundancy, such as 'last in, first out' (newcomers are dismissed before long-serving employees, although this may discriminate against younger age groups), retention by merit (on performance or added-value criteria), enforcing early retirement, or seeking volunteers. Each method has implications for employee morale and organisational effectiveness – and whatever method is used, it should be (and be seen to be) applied with rigorous fairness.

5.17   Where possible, procedures and benefit packages should be planned well in advance (as a contingency measure) rather than as a reactive measure in the context of cost-cutting and hostility. Many large organisations provide redundancy services and benefits well in excess of the statutory minimum, with regard to consultation, notice periods, terms, counselling and aid with job search, outplacement training in job-search skills – and even counselling of 'survivors' who frequently suffer trauma as a result of downsizing.

Transfer of Undertakings (Protection of Employment) Regulations 2006

5.18   The TUPE Regulations 2006 (a revision of 1981 Regulations) came into force in April 2006. They are intended to preserve employees' rights to employment protection, terms and conditions in the following circumstances.

- When a business or undertaking, or part of one, is transferred to a new employer (as under the old Regulations) *or*

- When a 'service provision change' takes place. This is a major change from the 1981 regulations, including cases where services are outsourced, insourced or re-assigned by a client from one contractor to another.

5.19 The regulations have the effect that employees employed when the undertaking is transferred or changes hands automatically become employees of the new employer, on the same terms and conditions.

5.20 The new employers must take over the contracts of employment of all employees: they cannot pick and choose. They cannot dismiss employees because of the transfer *unless* there is a sound economic, technical or organisational (ETO) reason entailing changes in the workforce: in this case, dismissal would be defined as redundancy, and the usual rights and procedures would apply. Otherwise, the dismissal will be deemed unfair by an Employment Tribunal.

5.21 The new employers take over all rights and obligations arising from the employment contracts, except some provisions for old age and invalidity. They also take over any collective agreements made on behalf of the employees, which were in force before the transfer.

5.22 Representatives of any employees affected by the transfer (eg their recognised trade unions) have the right to be informed about the transfer, and consulted about any proposed measures concerning the employees. In addition, the revised Regulations place a duty on the old employer to provide information to the new employer about the transferring workforce: this is called 'employee liability information'.

5.23 Be aware that this is part of a much broader body of employment rights and protection law. Dismissals, redundancies and trade union consultations are complex matters – and beyond the scope of this syllabus. If in doubt, a purchasing manager should consult the HR or legal department of the organisation before taking any action.

Chapter summary

- There is a wide range of employment legislation and regulation impacting on the work of procurement and supply.
- A key area of regulation is concerned with equal opportunity. This is the concept that everyone has a fair chance of enjoying employment benefits.
- Both employers and employees have closely defined responsibilities in relation to workplace health and safety.
- Other employment rights covered by legislation and regulation include working hours, maternity and paternity rights, and flexible working arrangements.
- The right to remain in employment is covered by regulations on dismissal, redundancy and transfer of undertakings.

Self-test questions

Numbers in brackets refer to the paragraphs where you can check your answers.

1   List positive influences of legislation on employment and equal opportunities. (1.6)

2   Describe different types of discrimination that are unlawful in the UK. (2.5)

3   What general measures may be required in order to implement an equality policy? (2.16)

4   List the duties of an employee, under UK legislation, in relation to workplace health and safety. (Table 11.2)

5   What is meant by redundancy? (5.11)

Subject Index

"